"The world of higher music education is at an inflection point. The old models are no longer adequate for preparing musicians for today's rapidly changing world. The uncertainty of the path ahead is both daunting and at times paralyzing. *Redefining Music Studies in an Age of Change* is the much needed boulder plunging into the middle of our glass-flat pond. It will rock the boat, challenge the status quo, ruffle feathers, start discussions, and inspire us to look at our world through new eyes. This book is a vital catalyst and guide for the institutional change that we so desperately need. Bravo to Campbell, Sarath, and Myers for challenging all of us to fulfill the vast and beautiful potential of what higher music education can be today."

—**Brian G. Pertl, Dean, Lawrence University Conservatory of Music**

"The need for foundational change in teaching and learning of music becomes stronger as we proceed in this digital and global age. This highly important book shows us how urgent the need for change has become and how these changes can be made in music academies, conservatories, colleges and universities."

—**Wouter Turkenburg, Head of Jazz Studies at the Royal Conservatory, The Hague, The Netherlands**

"Creativity, diversity and integration are calling cards for the national dialogue exploring the very best preparation for young artists entering the ever-changing cultural landscape of the 21st century. This volume is a must-read for educators committed to imparting the diverse skill building and deep learning that will equip artists as transformational change agents, deep connectors and musical leaders in our future world. Ed Sarath, David Myers and Patricia Shehan Campbell are bellwethers for this movement, passionately heralding a brand of fluid, integrative and rigorous training that transcends strictly defined applications and invites us to mentor artists of impact, meaning, and social change."

—**Susan D. Van Vorst, Dean, Conservatory of Music, Baldwin Wallace University**

"Emerging out of Sarath's, Myers's, and Campbell's impressive range of expertise and experience, together with extensive dialogue and collaboration among them, this book opens up vital new perspectives and possibilities to challenge existing orthodoxies. Beyond critique, however, these are the lenses that will empower higher music education faculty to shift their frames of reference and evolve curricula in relevant and exciting ways. It is essential reading for anyone involved in music education."

—**Helena Gaunt, Vice Principal and Director of Academic Affairs, Guildhall School of Music & Drama, London**

"In 2014 the College Music Society Taskforce on the Undergraduate Music Major issued its bold and compelling *Manifesto* for sweeping curricular change that would better prepare students for the global, social, and economic realities of 21st-century music making and understanding. Now, three of the manifesto's authors expand on its claims with a book that will surely become foundational for all educators and administrators who seek to chart new curricular paths apt for their own institutions and visions. . . . . What makes the book particularly valuable is the way it addresses processes of change—the How—as well as the content and rationale for change—the What and the Why. For the authors are not content merely to articulate a vision. As the last chapter argues, those who recognize the need for change must now move 'from words to action.'"

—**Jeffrey Magee, Professor and Director, University of Illinois School of Music**

REDEFINING MUSIC STUDIES IN AN AGE OF CHANGE

Redefining Music Studies in an Age of Change: Creativity, Diversity, and Integration takes prevailing discourse about change in music studies to new vistas, as higher education institutions are at a critical moment of determining just what professional musicians and teachers need to survive and thrive in public life. The authors examine how music studies might be redefined through the lenses of creativity, diversity, and integration, which are the three pillars of the recent report of The College Music Society taskforce calling for reform.

Focus is on new conceptions for existent areas—such as studio lessons and ensembles, academic history and theory, theory and culture courses, and music education coursework—but also on an exploration of music and human learning, and an understanding of how organizational change happens. Examination of progressive programs will celebrate strides in the direction of the task force vision, as well as extend a critical eye distinguishing between premature proclamations of "mission accomplished" and genuine transformation. The overarching theme is that a foundational, systemic overhaul has the capacity to entirely revitalize the European classical tradition. Practical steps applicable to wide-ranging institutions are considered—from small liberal arts colleges, to conservatory programs, large research universities, and regional state universities.

Edward W. Sarath is Professor of Music at the University of Michigan, Director/Founder of the U-M Program in Creativity and Consciousness Studies, and President/Founder of the International Society for Improvised Music. Active as artist and scholar, his previous book—*Improvisation, Creativity, and Consciousness: Jazz as Integral Template for Music, Education, and Society*—is the first to appropriate to music principles of an emergent worldview called Integral Theory.

David E. Myers is Professor of Music Education and Creative Studies in the School of Music at the University of Minnesota, where he served as the school's director from 2008–2015, and an administrative consultant for music at Augsburg College. He founded the Center for Educational Partnerships in Music at Georgia State University and is the American consultant for a joint European Master of Music degree for New Audiences and Innovative Practice.

Patricia Shehan Campbell is Donald E. Peterson Professor of Music at the University of Washington, where she teaches courses at the interface of education and ethnomusicology. She is chair of the Advisory Board of Smithsonian Folkways and consultant in repatriation efforts for the recordings of Alan Lomax to communities in the American South. Author of *Teaching Music Globally, Music in Cultural Context* and *Musician and Teacher*, she is recipient of the international Taiji Award for the preservation of traditional music.

REDEFINING MUSIC STUDIES IN AN AGE OF CHANGE

Creativity, Diversity, and Integration

Edward W. Sarath, David E. Myers, and Patricia Shehan Campbell

NEW YORK AND LONDON

First published 2017
by Routledge
711 Third Avenue, New York, NY 10017

and by Routledge
2 Park Square, Milton Park, Abingdon, Oxon, OX14 4RN

Routledge is an imprint of the Taylor & Francis Group, an informa business

© 2017 Taylor & Francis

The right of Edward W. Sarath, David E. Myers, and Patricia Shehan Campbell to be identified as authors of this work has been asserted by them in accordance with sections 77 and 78 of the Copyright, Designs and Patents Act 1988.

All rights reserved. No part of this book may be reprinted or reproduced or utilised in any form or by any electronic, mechanical, or other means, now known or hereafter invented, including photocopying and recording, or in any information storage or retrieval system, without permission in writing from the publishers.

Trademark notice: Product or corporate names may be trademarks or registered trademarks, and are used only for identification and explanation without intent to infringe.

Library of Congress Cataloging-in-Publication Data
Names: Sarath, Ed, author. | Myers, David (David Eugene), 1948- author. | Campbell, Patricia Shehan, author.
Title: Redefining music studies in an age of change : creativity, diversity, and integration / by Edward W. Sarath, David Myers, and Patricia Shehan Campbell.
Description: New York, NY ; Abingdon, Oxon : Routledge, 2016. | 2016
Identifiers: LCCN 2016008813| ISBN 9781138122383 (hardback) | ISBN 9781138122390 (paperback) | ISBN 9781315649160 (ebook)
Subjects: LCSH: Music—Instruction and study. | Education, Higher—Curricula. | Curriculum change.
Classification: LCC MT1. S27 2016 | DDC 780.71—dc23
LC record available at http://lccn.loc.gov/2016008813

ISBN: 978-1-138-12238-3 (hbk)
ISBN: 978-1-138-12239-0 (pbk)
ISBN: 978-1-315-64916-0 (ebk)

Typeset in Bembo
by Apex CoVantage, LLC

CONTENTS

Preface		ix
Acknowledgments		xiv
1	The Lay of the Land *Patricia Shehan Campbell*	1
2	Diverse and Shared Practices of Music and Human Learning *Patricia Shehan Campbell*	18
3	Models of Change *David E. Myers*	34
4	Transforming Music Study From Its Foundations: A Manifesto for Progressive Change in the Undergraduate Preparation of Music Majors *Patricia Shehan Campbell, David E. Myers, and Edward W. Sarath*	45
5	Navigating the Manifesto and the Waves of Paradigmatic Change: Creativity, Diversity, and Integration Reconceived *Edward W. Sarath*	86
6	Black Music Matters: Jazz as Transcultural Gateway *Edward W. Sarath*	106

7	Wider Ramifications of the Manifesto *David E. Myers*	126
8	From Words to Action: Practical Steps Toward Realization of the Manifesto's Vision *Edward W. Sarath, David E. Myers, and Patricia Shehan Campbell*	142

Index *156*

PREFACE

Students who choose to pursue an undergraduate major in music generally do so because of a passion that asserted itself years earlier. That passion may have been nurtured through formal or informal studies and in exclusively classical realms, or perhaps in some confluence of classical, popular, jazz, "world," folk/traditional, and other sources. Whatever the impetus, music students generally follow their Muse, often recognizing that music careers, unlike those in business or other career-oriented trajectories, require large measures of individual persistence, collaborative effort, and willingness to subsist on modest incomes. Yet, the narrow musical horizons these passion-filled students face in music schools too frequently limit or stultify their passions, boxing students into course-heavy, technical, and information-based programs that are at odds not only with the realities of musical worlds beyond the academy, but even with students' own knowledge and experience of those worlds prior to pursuing higher education. This misalignment of the structure, content, and process of undergraduate music studies, both with students' interests and needs and the realities of the musical worlds in which they will live and work, calls for a radical rethinking of not only the curriculum but of the overarching aesthetic and cultural orientation of the field. This book, which has evolved from The College Music Society report, *Transforming Music Study from Its Foundations: A Manifesto for Progressive Change in the Undergraduate Preparation of Music Majors*, proposes and explicates radical rethinking of how musicians are educated in ways that we believe are essential for our art, its practitioners, and the place of music and musical artists in society.

Short of being clairvoyant, none of us can predict with precision what the future might bring to our students over the course of their careers. Nor will we know exactly how a multitude of social, political, economic, cultural, and artistic influences may affect their roles as musicians. Specific to this book and its purpose, we, as authors, make no claim to have a full and complete understanding of the musical worlds our students will confront. We do know that our students will work in a world representing far more demographic diversity—racially, culturally, ethnically, and economically—than the one for which university music major studies has typically been oriented. We maintain that students must be nurtured not only as creative musician–leaders who understand, embrace, and successfully navigate these musical complexities, but also as innovative artists whose work embodies the larger concerns of music's relevance within the dynamic sociocultural and political complexities of a global society. We have named such musicians as creative improvisers–composers–performers, emphasizing music as an active process of sound and feeling that not only expresses our shared humanity, but engages and connects people across the spectrum of social and cultural identities.

Since the founding of the National Association of Schools of Music in 1924, the basic structure of undergraduate music programs in the U.S. has not changed appreciably. Born of a desire to educate musicians who would advance classical Western European music through homegrown orchestras and opera companies, and a need to educate teachers to perpetuate the appreciation of classical music in schools, music in higher education has not kept pace with dramatic changes in society nor with the realities of music beyond the academy. This places music in stark contrast to radical changes in the higher education of students in fields of medicine, the sciences, and social sciences. Despite music's centrality to civilization, the core aspects of undergraduate music study have remained largely insulated from relevance to issues arising from a shrinking global society, technology's influence on every aspect of our lives, including the creation, performance, distribution of, and access to diverse music, and growing tensions associated with demographic and economic divides. On a more immediate level, music studies are largely disconnected from the complex realities of the ways musicians in the Western world have managed their careers throughout history, and how this longstanding career model that crosses the boundaries of performing, teaching, researching, improvising, composing, and managing is not only organic to music itself but also essential for career development. Moreover, even within the realm of their almost exclusive emphasis on classical music, music schools and departments persist with cultural and curricular assumptions that are at odds with the well-documented artistic and economic problems of the classical music enterprise.

Certainly, there have been musically, politically (through standards and accreditation), and socially induced curricular changes over the past century, but, as we contend in this volume, those changes have been mostly superficial and are seldom systematic. They have been additive to the established core of music studies rather than influential of fundamental change to its foundation.

And they have lacked the radical reimagining of both the needs of career musicians and the needs of society for the roles and contributions of career musicians. Issues of diversity and inclusion, for example, which are now urgently paramount across society and constitute a leading concern of professional music organizations and their funders, find little substantive discussion in music schools and departments. Our institutions not only lack major, targeted initiatives to attract and graduate members of underrepresented populations, but music majors' experiences with music beyond the Western classical canon are often confined to one or two required courses, with any additional experience being largely elective.

Redefining Music Studies in an Age of Change: Creativity, Diversity, and Integration finds its origins in shared concerns, such as those already listed and others, among the Task Force on the Undergraduate Music Major (TFUMM), the group of eight college and university music faculty from across the U.S. whose efforts resulted in the release of the Manifesto, as the report has come to be known. The group's exchange across dimensions of artistic practice, pedagogy, scholarship, leadership, and innovation was dynamic and productive. Over eighteen months, we gathered, argued, discussed, contemplated, critiqued, and synthesized out of our diverse perspectives on the needs of undergraduates. The resulting report was intended to be catalytic for reflecting upon and considering a paradigmatic change in music studies, consistent both with music itself and with societal needs in the 21st century. As is explicated in the chapters preceding and following Chapter 4 (the Manifesto report), the Task Force argued ultimately that the three pillars of creativity, diversity, and integration would be our recommended avenue of fulfilling the goal of creative improviser–composer–performer graduates. While we take the position that creativity must permeate the curriculum as well as the attitudes and behaviors of music majors, we also assert that multiple dimensions of diversity must be embedded into the content and process of undergraduate education. And in tandem with these aims, we argue for a program of study that features integration across coursework and learning experiences, one that rigorously adheres to the high standards of embodied learning and teaching that exercises ears, bodies, and minds while providing increased space for student choice and collaborative determination of career-oriented trajectories.

Far more quickly than we could have imagined, the report gained traction from almost every quarter of the music world, both in and beyond academe. It emerged as a central topic of conversations in professional journals, newsletters, and blogs, at national and international conferences, and in graduate seminars at major universities in North America and abroad. It continues to draw analysis and interpretation by academic and creative (and administrative) posts, and has realized the original intent of the Task Force in inspiring dialogue on undergraduate music major studies. After a presentation on the report at an international conference in London's Guildhall School of Music and Drama in March 2014, Tony

Woodcock, former CEO of the Minnesota Orchestra and president of the New England Conservatory of Music, wrote in his blog:

> Given the time and freedom to research, analyze, think, discuss, and reflect that we all need in our ever more busy lives, we could start to do things very differently. This could allow us to place music at the centre of human endeavor and innovation rather than languishing at the periphery as many see us at the moment.

Of course, not all voices saw the report as catalytic for discussion or accurate in its claims of longstanding stasis in current programs. Some worried that we had overstated the limitations of current practices in teaching music theory; others found our emphasis on creativity to supplant the need for foundations in interpretive (conventional) performance practice; still others questioned the very use of the word "Manifesto" in the report's title. And yet, the prevailing response was mostly one of thoughtful intrigue, making evident the fact that there is a growing cohort of individuals within and beyond academe who believe that the education of musicians must change in dramatic ways. Where and when, we are led to ask, will we reach the tipping point that launches the full-out national and international effort to reinvent programs and curriculums that emanate from a comprehensive understanding of the nature of music itself, the varied sonic expressions known as music, the social and cultural dimensions of music, and the need for musician–leaders who advance the richest possible experiences in music for all people? And when, we must also ask, will these essential matters become the basis of increased rigor in the education of musicians, rather than the development of technical and informational prowess that currently poses as rigor?

As we have interacted with music faculty locally, nationally, and internationally around the thrust of the report itself, we have repeatedly been asked to elaborate on the conceptualization of the curricular changes we put forward and the potential for change institutionally. Faculty express concern that they have not been educated to work in the creative contexts we advocate, nor do they have confidence that they can be instrumental in effecting change in their respective environments. For these reasons, we have incorporated into this volume suggestions for how our recommendations for a revitalized and progressive curriculum actually work in complementary ways with sophisticated approaches to change. And we have addressed the broader implications of such change for music careers and for benefits to communities and society. We have not laid out a single route to reform, and have no intention to mandate top-down, hard-and-fast, singular solutions to change. We offer no recipes, no pure and perfect blueprint. We are respectful of the local contexts of tertiary-level music studies; of the composite of current university faculty and their education, training, and expertise; and of the varied missions of music major programs in research universities, liberal arts colleges, conservatories, and two-year community colleges.

We acknowledge the importance for us as authors to consider where this book fits in the lengthy bibliography of considerations, reports, task forces, and symposia that have called for change in higher education. We are aware that there are many current calls for change, continuing efforts to implement curricular and teaching revisions, and attempts to document innovations that are occurring in institutions. And we applaud the many discussions of "21st-century curriculum" that are increasing in our field and profession.

What we have found missing in these conversations, however, are philosophical perspectives and discourse that emanate from a nexus among the nature of music itself, the fundamental nature and work of being a musician in society, and the responsibilities of musicians to contribute to the public good. Ours is an attempt to catalyze a holistic curricular view that challenges longstanding assumptions about music and musicians in the world and insists on rigorous critical reflection about the future of our art and the extent to which music in higher education bears responsibility for shaping that future. We call in this text for a deeper, richer, more meaningful level of discourse and change—one that is willing to question everything without fear that we are somehow disparaging a legacy that we acknowledge has served an important, though limited, function and purpose.

In producing this text, we have drawn on our combined backgrounds, experience, and scholarship that cross the bounds of creativity, ethnomusicology, pedagogy, jazz, classical performance, world music performance, research, consciousness studies, and policy. Our hope is that this volume will provide further impetus to the imperative for a growing movement of radical reform in music in higher education, and that this reform will be the basis of an optimistic and enlightened future for conscious engagement with the transformative value of music in human life and living.

ACKNOWLEDGMENTS

We would like to extend our appreciation to our fellow members of the CMS Task Force on the Undergraduate Music Major—Juan Chattah, Lee Higgins, Victoria Levine, Timothy Rice, David Rudge—without whose participation, insights, and input the Manifesto would never have seen the light of day. We thank the many colleagues who attended presentations on the work of the TFUMM at CMS conferences in Cambridge, Massachusetts in 2013, St. Louis in 2014, and Indianapolis in 2015. We also greatly appreciate the feedback extended to us from colleagues across a wide array of disciplines, including performance, music history, ethnomusicology, music education, and music theory, often following the national conferences of their respective fields in which the Manifesto received prominent attention. Special thanks to the National Association of Schools of Music, the accrediting body in the field, for both placing the Manifesto on their agenda and providing space for presentations on this work at their national conferences. Finally, our great appreciation to Constance Ditzel, our editor at Routledge, for not only her guidance in the publication of this book, but also her longstanding support for visionary enterprise in music studies.

1

THE LAY OF THE LAND

Patricia Shehan Campbell

This book seeks to take the prevailing discourse about change in undergraduate music studies to entirely new vistas. In response to the sheer range of music that exists and is accessible to societies across the globe, the book emphasizes the need for new strategies for navigating this expanse, and elaborates on the gulf that—even after decades of reform appeals—is still apparent between much of what happens in most music schools and the broader musical landscape beyond these schools. If the preparation of undergraduate music majors is to become relevant to the work they will be required to do in the world, not only is a wholesale shift in music studies needed, but also in the deliberations that guide the change process.

At universities, colleges, and conservatories, four-year programs of study are at a critical moment of determining just what professional musicians and teachers need to survive and thrive in public life. Following the appearance of the documentary report of the Task Force on the Undergraduate Music Major within The College Music Society in October 2014, we—as three agents of that Task Force of eight members of university faculties in music—have been heartened by the widespread response to that provocative document. We present this "Manifesto" in this volume, along with justifications for it and clarifications of what it might mean in various higher education contexts. We are acutely aware of the need to not only continue, deepen, and extend this conversation, but also to offer guidance regarding its practical manifestations. In examining the relevance of undergraduate music major studies through the lenses of creativity, diversity, and integration (the three pillars of the documentary report), not only do new conceptions for existent areas—such as studio lessons and ensembles, academic history/theory/culture courses, and music education coursework—come into view, but so also do areas off the beaten track, that is to say, the more traditional routing of higher education music studies. These areas include late-breaking attention to music technology, the mixing of media, contemplative studies, and an attendant and continuing consciousness of communities living locally and globally. The identification of new areas to be added to the existing model, however, is neither new to change conversations, nor is it—in itself—adequate to the kind of change needed. What must complement this approach is the identification of new premises that help guide individuals, institutions, and the field at large toward new ways of apprehending this broader spectrum as an integrative, self-organizing whole. In short, the time has come for the foundational rebuilding of the field from its conceptual and curricular core on up. Recognition of this has been lacking in change conversations, and is a key contribution of the Manifesto that has eluded recognition even among supporters of the report. We see the primary purpose of this volume to be the elucidation of these unique elements of the Manifesto and elaboration on how they may be operationalized.

The Lay of the Land

Context is everything, such that the circumstances for the kind of transformation of undergraduate music major studies advanced in the Manifesto can be understood through the prism of elements of reform at large and historically within the field of music. In this chapter, I reveal "the lay of the land," insights into the need for deep reform in the education of musicians in tertiary level programs. My aim is to offer perspectives on reform at large, across fields and in all levels of education, and in the roles and functions of music at various levels of formal learning. The chapter embraces the notion that innovation and change are processes of introducing improvements developed through study and experimentation and thus are both natural and intentional. Reform is natural in that it happens in agreement with the human circumstances that surround music as a creative art that is in perpetual motion, adapting and responding to societal change. Reform is intentional in that it involves dynamically thoughtful musicians of all manner and form—creative and re-creative improvisers, composers, performers, scholars, and educators—who strive to fashion the very best education and training for their students at a time when an unprecedented skill set is required that derives from a broad array of musically expressive practices from across the world.

A contextualization of higher education music reform requires a backdrop of historical and contemporary perspectives on reform beyond music—in business, the sciences, medicine, and education. A review of reform efforts in music at all levels of education, too, will offer insights on the half-century of gatherings and projects that include the development of standards to express goals and outcomes of musical education of children and adolescents that prepare them for tertiary-level music major learning (as well as to prepare music majors for their work with aspiring young musicians in schools and communities). With my adept and ardent coauthors Ed Sarath and David Myers, I wish to raise questions as to why, rather than following the call for reform, the content and method of music teaching and learning continues its conventions decades past recommendations for reform (even as I wonder whether this present call for reform will convert to action or remain rhetorical only). In my effort to contextualize the Manifesto, I follow with a chronicling of the work of The College Music Society's Task Force on the Undergraduate Music Major in 2013–2014, and briefly convey something of the early response to the Manifesto. I recall the substance of our work during the vibrant period of exchanges with five other members of the Task Force during this period, and I build further meaning into declarations of the Manifesto that have emerged since then from our three-sided contemplations, our interpretations, and our context-specific experiences in putting ideas to actions. Finally, I offer an organization chapter by chapter of the contents of this volume, and make the case for delving deeply into the content and method of contemporary practices in undergraduate music major programs and also their limitations from the standpoint of the three pillars, as construed anew in the Manifesto, of creativity, diversity, and integration.

The Nature of Reform

Inquiring into the nature of reform as it occurs internationally and across a wide span of systems and circumstances sheds important light on reform efforts in music studies. It is a human penchant to want to improve, redress, and amend elements of a system that appear unfit or unsatisfactory for the people it purports to serve. Reform results from the observation and study of components that are out of tune, out of time, and out of touch with the needs of people. For systems that have functioned well at one time but turn out of alignment with present needs, reform efforts span a spectrum of change from fine-tuning selected components to the revolutionary effort to overthrow the system in full. Contemporary efforts for change are evident in struggles with electoral reform, tax reform, and land reform. As the world turns, reform is evident in the sciences, the medical world, commerce and the corporate system, and education. People find the need for revising the vision of their work, and they are committed to finding the best practices that take their intellectual energy to develop ideas into action.

Reform is supported by notions of innovative action that seek new ways of thinking, being, and doing. Innovation appeals and is arguably intrinsic to the human psyche, and innovators in various fields enact ways of improving, modernizing, and shaking up the established pathways by advocating and advancing original and effective approaches in ways that reform the field. As a catalyst to growth, innovation requires a careful study of the field, a certain latitude to imagine and collectively brainstorm the "what if" potentials, and the courage to trial solutions that break out of conventional ways of doing things. Innovation in action requires critical interrogation that is often absent for reform circles, so that not only can ideas for change be implemented but the results of implementation can be reviewed, challenged, and refashioned again until reform is right for the field. As we glimpse the many kinds of reform occurring across disciplines, distinctions between surface modifications and deep, paradigmatic shifts, of which the Manifesto advocates for music studies, become evident.

Fields of Reform

It is difficult to imagine a domain in which the topic of reform in one form or another is not among the most central, if elusive, to be dealt with. In the corporate world, there is a complex set of policy, legal, and institutional conditions that govern activities and that require review and reform. There are institutional arrangements within businesses that influence the way key actors and authorities operate. Companies and corporations pronounce long-standing golden rules to follow and legacies of integrity to build and preserve. For the benefit of the organization and its employees, there is periodic need to seek out change in accomplishing more effective products, technologies, or services. Occasionally, that change happens through break-away developments, as in the case of the evolution of Fairchild Semiconductor. Well known in the Silicon Valley in the late 1950s as having pioneered the manufacturing of transistors and integrated circuits, the company was a development of the need for change that could be better accomplished on the outside. Fairchild Semiconductor's strength was its innovative ideas, even as many more small businesses resulted from similar break-away and start-up actions that would allow reform and innovation to be nourished. Businesses that thrive do so as they foster positive change that meet the challenges of a time, even as dissatisfied employees whose new ideas are out of sync with older conventions pack up their ideas and shift into corporate situations that will accept and foster them.

Medical advances are coming at lightning speed, which applies pressure to reforms in hospital, clinical, and out-patient care, and to the needs for transforming the medical education. A major advance soon after the millennium was the mapping of the human genome so that the complete set of human genetic information could be understood, thus bringing about the development of preventative medicine and a cut of rapidly accelerating medical costs from increasingly expensive treatments. Heart disease deaths have dropped by 40 percent in 25 years, stem cell research has given new hope for regenerative medicine, and new drug therapies have been advanced for the cure of cancer and extended lives of HIV victims (Acton, 2012). Sophisticated imaging techniques, including the fMRI process, are now in use to trace the working of neurons by tracking changes in the oxygen levels and blood flow to the brain.

Reform efforts have been stepped up in medical training so that the training of physicians, nurses, and technicians can be advanced. University students in the health sciences are receiving training in the newest technological inventions in order to administer relief to cancer patients and clients with heart disease, diabetes, HIV, and a vast span of ailments and health challenges. They are learning the uses of medication to treat disease and to promote healthy functioning. They are learning through coursework that alongside the scientific understandings and technical developments in the field, medicine remains "a calling, not a business" with the need for animating professionalism through altruism, respect, honesty, integrity, honor, and accountability. The mission of medical education is in high gear in the reform of residency training that is based on learning patient-centered, high-quality care and geared to achieving benchmarks of clinical competence overall. Indeed, many teaching hospitals and clinics associated with medical programs are undergoing substantial redesign all in an effort to meet the rapid changes in scientific research and societal needs.

Reform is apparent in education, in all fields and at every level, and reform both within and across disciplines is apparent and necessary (Klein, 2005). Clark Kerr (1991) posited three historic periods in the transformation of American higher education. The first encompasses the founding of Harvard and William and Mary with principles of autonomy, diversity, flexibility, and competitiveness present in the newly emergent American way, even while the classical curriculum was adopted from Oxford and Cambridge. A second wave of change came in the post–Civil War period, ca. 1870–1910, when the influence of the German university model brought science to the fore, and land-grant universities rose up to serve society through agriculture and industry programs. By the early 20th century, the older aims of preparing students for the fields of medicine, law, and teaching (and theology) were rapidly expanding, and universities were growing Ph.D. degree programs in the emerging research universities such as Harvard, Cornell University, Johns Hopkins University, the University of Chicago, the University of Michigan, and Stanford University. The third historic period was the period of 1960–1980, when the student population rose exponentially from 3.5 million to 12 million, public education increased to 80 percent of all colleges and universities, and comprehensive universities replaced small colleges and many professional fields from engineering to business administration met the demands of societal and student-expressed needs.

Within university colleges and departments of education, where change agents are committed to relevant teaching and learning, those of professorial rank quite naturally want to improve existing programs as well as to personalize their contributions. There are both global pressures and local realities that require the continuous attention of faculty and students, administrators, and policymakers (Cloete et al., 2006). Among the critical issues of reform are the accelerated pace of technology, the improvement of digital literacy, the blended learning that features formal and informal experiences as well as on-screen and in-person strategies, and the challenges of engaging learners of identities that vary by gender, race and ethnicity, socioeconomic circumstances, religion, lifestyle, and other cultural facets. Emerging technologies and culturally diverse populations of school-age students demand in-depth study and active reform with implications for policy, leadership, and practice. While the hub of reform activity in education typically locates itself in tertiary-level institutions, the scope encompasses primary and secondary school curricular practices.

Generic efforts to develop fresh perspectives on teacher education have come and gone over the decades. The Holmes Group, a consortium of deans in colleges of teacher education at the leading research institutions in each of the 50 states, was one such effort (Labaree, 1992). Thoughtfully committed to developing a more intellectually solid education of teachers, the report rose up and settled down in the 1980s, and is now an historical moment in the reform of the teaching profession. The pendulum swings between traditional back-to-basics education that emphasizes rote learning and teacher-directed activity and progressive education practices that attend to student needs and interests. As well, the attention to educational standards and its concomitant focus on assessment has resulted in waves of reform too. Movements such as No Child Left Behind and Race to the Top are names assigned to recent attempts at change that are intended to ensure that children test at acceptable levels of competence in scholastic areas deemed of value, especially math and language arts. Transformations across fields and disciplines happen, but the pace is slow and emergent, and changes may be subtle rather than substantive. At times, efforts at transforming institutions and programs can even recede and regress, often as conservative reactions to what may appear radical to them. To be sure, there is an ebb and flow to improve upon the past. Perseverance, creative energy with a continuing momentum, and dialogue can bring about mutations, modifications, and even a metamorphosis within a field.

Reform in Music Teaching and Learning

It goes without saying that the music curriculum in higher education will always need to change in order to keep pace with changes in society, musical practices, and local circumstances (Conway and Hodgman, 2008). Reform efforts in education and schooling at large have impacted undergraduate music major programs, too, and research on music cognition and learning offers valuable insights for program content and instructional process. Faculties of music are responsible for shaping the critical skills and understandings that allow music majors to survive and thrive in a changing world. A solid attention to societal realities and research results informs an understanding of creativity, diversity, and integration as foundational to current work, encompassing as they do all subdisciplines within music and, at the same time, music's relationships with the larger arena of knowledge and skills essential in a 21st-century global-technical society. Whether one focuses on advances in new understandings of the interior dimensions of how human learning takes place, or on the ever-widening exterior gulf between music studies and the explosively diverse musical landscape characteristic of today's global society, the need for change—and as we argue, fundamental reconceptualization—in music studies has never been more self-evident, or urgent.

Since the mid-20th century, a number of events have been organized in response to this imperative that would examine possibilities for change in the ways that music is taught and learned in formal institutional settings, at all levels.

Symposia, short- and long-term projects, and documents have arisen since the mid-20th century in music and music education circles, with particular attention to reform at the elementary and secondary school levels, with implications, if not direct ramifications, for music programs in higher education. Not surprisingly, university programs in music education have responded to calls for reform with curricular changes to pedagogical methods courses, while courses in music theory, history, and performance have remained largely steadfast in continuing long-standing canonical repertoire and instructional processes.

The Yale Seminar transpired in 1963 as a reaction to the national concern for competition with the Soviet Union in all levels of education, from the sciences to the arts. The Seminar came on the heels of the Ford Foundation's fostering in 1959 of the Young Composers Project, which placed free-agent and university-affiliated composers into school systems; this program changed names in 1962 to the Contemporary Music Project. Despite the potential for the horizontal influences of composers into academic and applied studies at the tertiary level, few accommodations were made for university students to study compositional processes (not even when their theory courses may have been taught by composers). An awareness of the need for changes in music education at all levels spurred the organization of the Yale Seminar that, chaired by musicologist Claude Palisca of Yale University, convened a group of 31 participants, including half of whom were composers, theorists, and musicologists, the other half constituting one performer, two music critics, two jazz musicians, three college-level music educators, one school administrator, five public and private school music teachers, and the educational advisor from the White House. There was an east coast/Ivy League coloring to the gathering, as only six arrived to the Seminar from elsewhere in the U.S. (Werner, 2009). Seminar recommendations were multiple, and included the following: an adherence to the development of student musicianship through K–12 curricular programs, the featuring of a repertory of contemporary compositions and historic gems of the standard Western concert literature, a guided listening to Western masterworks, school offerings in vocal and instrumental performance (aside from marching band and stage band), and the placement of professional musicians, composers, and scholars in schools. Over 20 federally funded school music projects sprang out of these recommendations, all with the intent of addressing the development of basic musical understanding and not (just) performance technique. One of these projects, the Julliard Repertory Project, was a compilation of Western and "non-Western" art and folk music that were important in expanding the K–12 school music repertory. Despite the preponderance of theorists and musicologists at the Yale Seminar, however, it was frequently university faculty in music teacher education who creatively implemented change in the music and method by which it was taught. The potential for the transformation of tertiary-level music programs through the Yale Seminar went untapped.

Just four years later, the Tanglewood Symposium was organized in 1967 by the Music Educators National Conference (MENC) to define the role of music education in a postindustrial American society. Assembled in the Berkshire Hills of western Massachusetts, music educators met with sociologists, scientists, labor leaders, scientists, corporate leaders, performers, and music academicians; their views on the values and functions of music in contemporary society were formalized in the Tanglewood Declaration. Chief concerns were that "music of all periods, styles, forms, and cultures belongs in the curriculum" (Choate, 1968); that adequate time be allotted for school music in the curriculum; that technology be applied to music study and research; that individualized student instruction be provided; that music be integrated into humanities and related arts courses; and that teachers be equipped to work with urban populations as well as exceptional children and youth. These recommendations for change were reflected in the development of The School Music Program, a precursor to the National Standards for Arts Education of 1994. The Tanglewood Symposium loomed large in arguments for diversifying the curricular content of K–12 school music programs, opening up classrooms and ensembles to music from places in Africa, Asia, and the Americas. Like Yale before it, Tanglewood's recommendations impacted university music teacher education, but were negligible in altering content or processes in others areas of the music major curriculum. Theory, history, composition, and performance programs remained largely intact and ill-attuned to the efforts of Tanglewood.

From the same era of curricular innovation and experimentation as Yale and Tanglewood, the Manhattanville Music Curriculum Program (MMCP) was established in 1966 to provide an alternative music curriculum for grades K–12 in celebration of the ideals of discovery-based learning (Thomas, 1970). There were 22 musicians and educators, working in genres ranging from electronic music to jazz, who were gathered together at the Manhattanville College of the Sacred Heart in Purchase, New York to prepare a curriculum replete with performance, composition, and improvisation as pathways to musical understanding (Moon and Humphreys, 2000). Its keystone feature, Synthesis, was structured around the developmental phases of musical exploration: free exploration, guided exploration, exploratory improvisation, planned improvisation, and refinement. The curriculum underwent extensive experimentation and piloting testing in multiple settings, and teacher education workshops in the summer of 1969 served to prepare music educators in the MMCP ideas and materials. The program was important in its interest in interactions with music and musicians, both for children and youth in schools as well as the practicing teachers who would serve them. The lack of continuing financial support to MMCP challenged the possibilities for the wide distribution of its materials and ideas, and outside of a limited group of university music education faculty, the reform movement was unknown at the tertiary level. Once again, despite the working out of MMCP tenets in a university program, little attention was paid to it by faculty in other colleges and universities or in the realms of academic, performance, or composition.

Comprehensive Musicianship was an attempt to bring a more holistic perspective to the teaching of theory and history. Linked to the earlier Young Composers

Project and Composers-in-Schools, Comprehensive Musicianship (also known as the Contemporary Music Project, or CMP) was intended to promote the integration of all aspects of musical study, including what transpires in classrooms, private lessons, and ensemble rehearsals, and was aimed at enabling students to know the relationships and the synthesis of performance and academic music studies (Willoughby, 1990). It was significant as a curricular embrace in secondary schools, colleges, and universities, if only for a limited time, developing between 1965 and 1969, and then refined and promoted through 1973. Its concepts, which were applicable at all levels, aimed to develop creative, performative, and critical listening skills; to open up to more inclusive elements found in contemporary and "non-Western" styles (utilizing a common-elements approach); and to involve students in active music making and discovery rather than lecture-style memorization and pass learning. Undergraduate CMP-influenced theory and musicianship programs are not prevalent, nor were they in the heyday of the movement, and yet something of the attitude and approach lingers on in a few select departments and schools of music. Experimental programs in the initial years attempted to integrate into a "super-course" fragments of music history, aural skills, sight singing, instrumentation, form and analysis, and conducting, with the goal of understanding music as a total experience rather than as unrelated concepts and events. The principles of Comprehensive Musicianship were not new even then, and yet they came together in the time of this movement to create a professional consciousness that could be considered together as a guide to integration and collaboration across the subfields of music. Yet while it was awaiting adaption by university faculty, the program was sideswept to schools as tertiary-level education remained fairly stuck in its conventional groove in the ways of content and process.

Other events in the last half-century have given attention to the change in the ways and means of teaching and learning music in higher education and in K–12 schools. The Wingspread Conference on Music in General Studies was organized in 1981 to evaluate and redesign approaches to introductory and appreciation courses for college majors outside of music, whether in the arts, humanities, sciences, or social sciences. This meeting advanced ideas for courses in the integrated arts, world music, local musical communities, contemporary music, and technology, many of which have been put into place as optional and elective courses, despite the lack of integration of these ideas into the studies of music majors. In 1990, the Symposium on Multicultural Approaches to Music Education drew together music educators, ethnomusicologists, and culture-bearers for pedagogical experiences and dialogue relative to teaching music of African American, Chinese, Cuban/Caribbean, Mexican, and Native American cultures. This meeting inspired the design of—textbooks, recordings, song collections, videorecording, and eventually websites, all with the aim of multiculturalizing musical study in K–12 and university programs in music teacher education. Ongoing conference sessions and professional development institutes sponsored by professional music organizations (or hosted by university music units) are venues for cross-talk by musicians, educators, and scholars across the spectrum of performance and academic studies on the potential content areas and instructional processes that are available for teaching (and learning) music in higher education contexts.

Important questions emerge amid this morass of reform activity: What lingers past the cross-talk? Following the considerable expenditures of time and energy in discussion and demonstration of reform in music teaching and learning, what dimensions are integrated within university undergraduate music majors degree programs? How fully have past music symposia, institutes, initiatives, short funded projects, and stand-alone conference sessions addressed key realms of relevant musical study? What is the nature and extent of attention to the issues of creativity, diversity, and integration within conversations intended for the reform of music programs of study? What degree of change can reasonably be claimed to have been achieved amidst these efforts? What level of critical interrogation of the change enterprise has occurred alongside the conversation? What can we do to ensure that reform principles are not only presented and discussed, but are also shaped and applied to contemporary music teaching and learning?

In response to a growing sense that change in music studies has, with the greatest respect for the many pioneering attempts, fallen considerably short of what is needed, I initiated what could be considered the defining project of my 2013–2014 College Music Society presidency. It is one that may arguably be a defining project of the organization itself.

Chronicle of the Manifesto

The events leading up to the development of the Manifesto for Progressive Change in the Undergraduate Preparation of Music Majors deserve chronicling, so that the report can be viewed not only within the context of past reform efforts but also with a sense of its unfolding through a period of dialogue and discussion to the capstone creation of the documentary report that came to be known as "the Manifesto." A group of eight members of various music faculty committed their time in 2013–2014 to a Task Force on the Undergraduate Music Major (TFUMM), all with an earnest belief in the need for change in the education and training of undergraduate music majors. This Task Force was organized under the umbrella of The College Music Society (CMS) and by late winter, I, as president, was selecting members of the working group. My initial appointment of David Myers, University of Minnesota, as chair of the Task Force, was quickly followed by my invitations to Ed Sarath, University of Michigan; Juan Chattah, University of Miami; Victoria Lindsay Levine, Colorado College; and Timothy Rice, University of California at Los Angeles; I, too, located at the University of Washington, was a working member of the group. Lee Higgins, Boston University and York St. John University, and David Rudge,

State University of New York at Fredonia, accepted their invitations to join the Task Force several months later. Task Force members were experienced tertiary level educators across an expanse of specializations that included music history, music theory, ethnomusicology, performance (solo, chamber, large ensembles), jazz studies, and music education. We represented ourselves rather than our affiliated institutions, or our particular professional organizations, or our singular subfields, and we came together on the basis of our expressed interest in the possibilities for the reform of tertiary-level music studies. We eight colleagues rolled up our sleeves to imagine change, recommend pathways for change, and work for change in our own academic and performance contexts. Together we sought a more relevant program of study for music majors "at home," in our own institutions, and at large.

The College Music Society appeared to be the appropriate platform for launching a conversation on music major reform, as it is viewed as an organization that could draw individuals from across specializations to considerations for change to undergraduate music major programs. A professional group of about 7,500 college, conservatory, university, and independent musicians and scholars across all fields and disciplines of music, CMS has since its establishment in 1958 given attention to music teaching and learning in higher education. While the thrust of the Society's national, regional, and international meetings is partly about sharing newly composed works, musicological–theoretical interests, and performances of period repertoire, the scholarship of teaching delineates it from among the various professional societies to which university faculty belong. In the Society's publications (in its online journal, *Symposium*, and in various monographs) and conference sessions, course content, sequence, and pedagogical operations are frequent topics of attention as they play out in studios, ensembles, music history/theory/culture classes, and in small music major seminars and mass classes of music in general studies. According to its declared mission, CMS is an active agent for change at the tertiary level.

Thus it was in the spirit of change yet with an honoring of tradition that I assembled the Task Force under the auspices of The College Music Society from April 2013 to November 2014 to press for answers to the question: "What does it mean to be an educated musician in the 21st century?" The group communicated electronically, and convened by phone and through a skype-like system, with increasing frequency over the period of study and development of the Manifesto. Some members were clocking in four to five hours weekly at times to exchange perspectives on curricular approaches and content, and to craft components of an ever-lengthening draft of the document. Colleagues within the CMS membership were welcomed to a hearing at the national meeting at Cambridge, Massachusetts in October 2013, where their thoughts on the undergraduate music major programs could be expressed, dialogued, and noted by the Task Force members. I was keen to ensure that Task Force updates were regularly communicated and that calls to the membership for their input into the conversation on curricular change were delivered via the monthly newsletter, and a number of short reports, anecdotal remarks, and recommendations were submitted on topics of course content, linked courses, and program overhaul in academic and performance areas. Task Force members met for a three-day meeting in March 2014 to talk in person about the place of performance, creative composition and improvisation, and scholarship in undergraduate music major programs.

Members of the Task Force on the Undergraduate Music Major program were living out their roles as "agents of change" by considering the research and scholarship of teaching, suggesting experiences we knew, applying logic and measured intelligence to ideas that emerged, and keeping in mind the many contexts in which music is taught and learned at the tertiary level. We gathered a collective understanding of the critical pillar points of creativity, diversity, and integration, and we worked to craft ways of revealing these emphases as streams and themes in a thorough-going undergraduate music major program of study. We asserted that creativity and diversity are more than "add-ons" to conventional coursework, and argued instead for foundational change that would feature deeply creative thought and experiences with the music of Bach, Brazil, and Bali from day one of freshman year. We described a four-year degree program that could not only provide music majors with occasional opportunities to coalesce and combine contemporary improvisation, composition, and performance, but could actually take the next step in reform deliberations by invoking a shift in identity to the level of a student in perpetual motion as a composing–improvising–performing musician. Ed Sarath's chapters (5 and 6) go into this identity shift in depth. We were imagining paradigms far beyond those of earlier reform projects — dramatic changes that would cut through to the core of key qualities vital to a higher order of musical thinking and doing.

We wondered and even worried about details of difference of interpretation of a one-size-fits-all set of recommendations, and we recognized that colleagues would understand that what emerged from the work of the Task Force would serve to catalyze conversation and locally crafted curricular change. From May to October 2014, five webinars were offered by Task Force members, and three Forum pieces by members appeared in *Symposium*. The Manifesto was released in late October and made available in full on the CMS website. Its contents were the focus of a four-hour preconference symposium just ahead of the 2014 CMS national meeting at St. Louis, as well as a plenary address featuring all eight members of the Task Force as well as dialogue sessions to follow. The CMS Board reviewed and discussed the Manifesto, and determined that it would stand as a report from this ad hoc committee in alignment with the organization's policy.

In my last presidential missive, I wrote of the Manifesto to the membership in the CMS monthly newsletter in December 2014, urging readers to "study it, share it with colleagues, [and] work with aspects that are truly relevant to the needs of students in the workaday world ahead of them." I continued with a request to "document responses to the Manifesto and bring it to the attention of Task Force members." Finally, I noted that

> We music professionals are in a position to cultivate and advance change in musical expression and curricular practice, and CMS has the capacity to foster change. The charge of the Task Force (April 2013–November 2014) is finished, and they have met the challenge put to them. It is now up to activist CMS members—and all of us—to determine next steps to take in raising up educated musicians for the 21st century.
>
> From the President, CMS Newsletter, *November 2014, P. 1*

Reaction to the Manifesto

Just following its release, the principles of the Manifesto were discussed at Autumn 2014 meetings of American professional societies of music, including the Society for Music Theory (SMT), the Society for Ethnomusicology (SEM), and the National Association of Schools of Music (NASM). Reception to the Manifesto was unequivocally strong and positive by SEM members and curious and cautious in NASM sessions, while the responses of some SMT members were immediately critical of the report. A flood of remarks came forward electronically to members of the Task Force from professors across specializations on faculties in the U.S. and abroad, and they were charged with enthusiasm for the attention that could be given to the pillars of creativity, diversity, and integration in curricular reform. Invitations were pouring in to Task Force members to speak to (or facilitate dialogue among) faculty on university campuses and at conferences, and to the extent that it was possible, there were dialogue sessions in many venues beginning January 2015. The report triggered the formation of working groups, publications, program agendas, panels, and dialogue sessions, including presentations at meetings such as The Reflective Conservatoire (London), Cultural Diversity in Music Education (Helsinki), the Mountain Lake Symposium (Virginia), the pedagogy group of the American Musicological Society (Cincinnati), the Society for Music Teacher Education (Greensboro, North Carolina), the Midwest Band Clinic (Chicago), and more. Responses to the Manifesto were offered in newsletters of professional organizations, and on professional and personal blogs. While arguably anecdotal rather than systematically analyzed, there was a surge of attention to the Manifesto as a means of launching study and discussion by faculty in various venues of realistic ways of reforming music major curricular programs.

To be sure, the Manifesto was provocative and for some, controversial. Some readers of the report were uncomfortable with aspects of the report's radical assertion for change; indeed, even the term "Manifesto" was viewed by a few as extremist or militant. Yet the term was retained as consistent with many calls for action, and because it was fitting of the report's intention (and the reception by most readers) to offer progressive ideals and practices for enacting change.

A few expressed concerns that the report conveyed false impressions of the core music major curriculum, that music major programs were already doing what the Manifesto recommended, and that members of the Task Force were not fully representative of all specializations on music faculties. On this last point, I had determined at the outset that the appointment of just eight members who "represented themselves" as accomplished and thoughtful members of music faculties, and who would work together in examining the status of music programs and recommending change, was far more important than commissioning a large and unwieldy group who might not commit themselves to the cause for change.

Within a year of the Manifesto's release, and as the round of Autumn-time conferences came into view, a wide array of panels and presentations on the Manifesto had been programmed at meetings of scholarly and professional societies of music in 2015, including the CMS national conference in Indianapolis. Through this period, there were some who continued to wrestle with the possibility of an edited and more restrained version, suggesting that phrases be sculpted and terms trimmed up so that the report could avoid any occasion to appear potentially disparaging to colleagues. By early 2016, The College Music Society had finalized a version that appeared to address concerns, and a revised Manifesto was produced that was abridged but close in spirit and substance to the Manifesto's original "conference copy" first circulated in October 2014.

Far beyond The College Music Society, the Manifesto has already had a considerable impact on considerations for change in tertiary-level music major programs. Vital changes are well underway in several key music major programs, while actions in other programs are yet to be revealed and put into curricular practice.

Manifesto in Motion

Significant steps need to be taken if the vision of the Manifesto is to become reality, which brings the discussion back to the purpose of this volume. Although the report presents a range of general reform principles and strategies that is unprecedented in reform literature, the initial intent was not to be overly prescriptive—instead our inclination was to invite institutions to invoke their own creativity, with their own resources in mind, in pursuing corresponding change avenues. While of course we retain this ideal, we also believe in this next phase of work: namely, that a more focused articulation of change strategies is in order, which this book provides. Central, moreover, to effective implementation is a closer reading of the report. In our extensive deliberations with readers of the document, we have noted among both enthusiastic advocates and colleagues with concerns that there are aspects of the report that have eluded recognition. A primary example, in which Ed Sarath goes into depth in his chapters, is the foundational—as opposed to additive—role of creativity and how this gives rise to new paradigms of diversity and integration. This not only sets the reform vision of the Manifesto apart from much other reform efforts, it also is key to new, practical pathways. Confusion about the foundational versus additive place of creativity is the most prominent reason behind premature claims that "we are already doing what the report advocates." This volume offers an opportunity to raise the bar in terms of critically interrogating such claims and highlighting key principles that, being new to change discourse, may easily remain hidden from view.

We also believe it is important to acknowledge areas of disagreement within the Task Force as a whole, and even—albeit in rarer instances—among the three of us as coauthors of this volume. Though these differences have spawned lively, sometimes tense, though typically collegial exchanges, we cannot emphasize enough the importance of this to the foundational change endeavor. While naturally nothing of substance would result from our efforts if we did not share significant common aspirations, we believe the forum we established within our own ranks for the coexistence of contrasting ideas that could bump up against one another, and potentially generate new insights, represents a principle that will be invaluable to both national and local conversations inspired by our work. As a preview of what will be encountered in the coming pages, here is an example: Whereas Ed Sarath places great emphasis on distinguishing between multicultural approaches to diversity and his preferred transcultural paradigm, I believe important contributions are yet to be had within concentrated studies of individual cultures (and the intercultural realm) that might be overlooked in the transcultural, even as Sarath insists that the transcultural could accomplish those within its expanded, creativity-based framework. In fact, the two of us define "transcultural" differently, but respect one another's distinctive pathways as ethnomusicologist and educator (Campbell) and jazz/improvised music artist, educator, and scholar (Sarath). The point is not that one needs to choose sides on this important topic, but that the perspectives offered are the result of a higher order of conversation—one that is informed by considerable thought, reading, reflection, and respectful, albeit often lively, conversation. This is a very different kind of conversation than has typically prevailed around the discussion of diversity and one that is needed if the field is to make progress in this all-important domain.

Another example of disagreement involves the place of African American musical practices in the change vision, a point around which significant differences were expressed among the entire Task Force team. We do not expect that all readers will embrace Sarath's prominent positioning of black music (particularly African American music) as both important unto itself and also as a powerful transcultural gateway. Nor, more provocatively, Sarath's contention that lingering ethnocentric tendencies, even among reformers who profess a commitment to diversity, impede progress on this front. However, we do share his assertion that this is a topic that has not received nearly the kind of attention it warrants, particularly given the highly charged climate of race conversations at this juncture in U.S. and global history. We view the presence of African American (and African diasporic) music in tertiary-level music major programs as a vital component of studies by music majors, and suggest that the creation, performance, and academic study of black music should quite naturally become a trademark of 21st-century music major programs in America.

In terms of areas of accord, we believe our commentary on the nature of change is among the most important contributions of the book and readers will find recurring attention on this front. In addition to the preview provided in this chapter, where music studies reform is situated within a cross-disciplinary and cross-cultural look at change, David Myers grounds the commentary in models of change in Chapter 3, with strong correlations emerging between his appropriation of Agyris's and Shon's "double-loop" critical inquiry and Sarath's notion of "higher order" change discourse and its related critical inquiry parameters. My own investigations in the realm *ngoma*, which underscores the inextricable link between music, movement, drama, and ritual in cultures across the world, not only poses important ramifications for music studies but represents yet another lens in this book on the change phenomenon. We hope readers appreciate the juxtaposition and points of synthesis in these perspectives as much as we do.

The chapters ahead will divulge more on these and many other issues in detailing a plan for the reform of music teaching and learning in higher education. Chapter 2, *Diverse and Shared Practices of Music and Human Learning*, will reveal music as sound, behavior, and values that are both pan-human and culture-specific, with attention to the ways in which humans are wired to receive, learn, create, and advance musical practices. *Models of Change* are featured in Chapter 3, which examines various orders of change that are possible in individuals, organizations, and communities through the lens of Schon's and Argyris's double-loop model. This chapter sets the stage for the foundational change advocated in the CMS Task Force Manifesto. The full and final edition of the Manifesto is found in Chapter 4, which is intentionally located in a central position between chapters leading to and from the report of recommendations for change. Chapter 5, *Navigating the Manifesto and the Waves of Change: Creativity, Diversity, and Integration Reconceived*, distinguishes between lower-order and higher-order conceptions of the three pillars of the Manifesto. Whereas creativity, diversity, and integration are not new in reform discourse, they have been approached not as foundational pillars but items to be added to the current model. *Black Music Matters: Jazz as Transcultural Gateway*, Chapter 6, elaborates on the importance of black music in any emergent music studies program and issues a critique and analysis of patterns—including ethnocentric tendencies and hegemonic language—that have contributed to the marginalization of this musical realm. Chapter 7, *Ramifications for Education and Society at Large*, goes beyond the music-specific recommendations of the Manifesto and considers ramifications for society at large. *From Words to Action: Practical Steps Toward Realization of the Manifesto's Vision*, is the focus of Chapter 8, which emphasizes the need to differentiate between superficial reform and the foundational transformation delineated in the Manifesto, and suggests specific strategies contained in the Manifesto for music faculty convinced of the need to reform current curricular practice. In this final chapter, both small steps and all-embracing strategies are posited, including the creation of a pilot program is recommended as a particularly promising approach.

This book will enable us to center important questions that can be grappled with productively once the deeper principles of the Manifesto are highlighted.

How, given the emphasis on creativity, does the report address the critical area of craft development? Are schools to encourage creative exploration at the expense of rigorous skill evolution? Or might creativity and craft be seen as coevolutionary? If so, what principles underpin this dynamic relationship? With the report's emphasis on cultural diversity, how will students and faculty navigate the sheer breadth of traditions that might be covered? Which musical practices, of which cultural communities locally and in the world, should be critical components of music major study? Should study embrace analytical listening, performance-based participatory experience, and engagement with visiting artists and locally living musicians? What is the place of the music of one's own culture within the overall global imperative? How is creativity and diversity integrated within the curriculum rather than offered as an "elective, a single course stuffed into the time of one academic term, an addition to a 19th-century-fashioned core curriculum for the music major? We are deeply grateful for the opportunity to examine these and many other key questions in hopes of helping our field advance to an entirely new era of meaning, relevance, and traditional and contemporary excellence.

References

Acton, Ashton. 2012. *Heart Diseases: Advances in Research and Treatment.* Atlanta, GA: Scholarly Editions.

Banks, James A., 2016. *Multicultural Education: Issues and Perspectives*, 8th edition. New York: Wiley & Sons.

Choate, Robert. 1968. *Documentary Report of the Tanglewood Symposium.* Washington, DC: Music Educators National Conference.

Cloete, N., Maassen, P., Fehnel, R., Moja, T., Gibbon, R., and Perold, H. 2006. *Transformation in Higher Education.* Amsterdam: Springer.

Conway, Colleen M., and Thomas M. Hodgman. 2008. *Teaching Music in Higher Education.* New York: Oxford University Press.

Deardoff, Darla K., 2009. *The Sage Handbook of Intercultural Competence.* Thousand Oaks, CA: Sage Publications, Inc.

Gay, Geneva, 2010, 2nd edition. *Culturally Responsive Teaching: Theory, Research and Practice.* New York: Teachers College, Columbia University.

Kerr, Clark. 1991. *The Great Transformation in Higher Education 1960–1980.* Albany: State University of New York Press.

Klein, Julie Thompson. 2005. *Humanities, Culture, and Interdisciplinarity.* Albany: State University of New York Press.

Labaree, David F. 1992. Power, Knowledge, and the Rationalization of Teaching: A Geneaology of the Movement to Professionalize Teaching. *Harvard Educational Review* 62:2 (July), 123–155.

Moon, Kyung-Suk, and Jere T. Humphreys. 2000. The Manhattanville Music Curriculum Program: 1966–1970. *Journal of Historical Research in Music Education* 31:2, 77–96.

Thomas, Ronald B. 1970. *MMCP Synthesis: A Structure for Music Education.* Bardonia, NY: Media Materials, Inc.

Werner, Robert. 2009. A Review of the 1963 Yale Seminar. College Music Symposium 49.

Willoughby, David. 1990. Comprehensive Musicianship. *The Quarterly* 1:3 (Autumn), 39–44.

2
DIVERSE AND SHARED PRACTICES OF MUSIC AND HUMAN LEARNING

Patricia Shehan Campbell

In considering the transformation of the undergraduate music major, the study of music as a world phenomenon is inarguably a central feature to be worked into the curricular weave. In the spirit of diversity and equal access by all to understandings and skills that are what William P. Malm refers to as "different but equally logical," new foundational thinking can bring about a rebuilding of the music curricular core that performs an inclusionary approach befitting the demographic realities of our times. Music majors in preparation for an array of professional activities ahead benefit greatly from embracing diversity as it relates to knowing the structures, functions, and meanings of music as a global phenomenon. Not only do students gain tools that directly inform the evolution of their creative voices as improvisers, composers, and performers, but they also—as thinkers and well-attuned analytical listeners—expand their awareness of the scope of music's sonic and structural possibilities, as well as grow in an understanding of music's powerful role across a wide spectrum of human life. The Manifesto calls for musical engagement across as wide a cultural expanse as is possible, and sounds the alarm for "culturally narrow horizons of music study" that are "nothing short of a social justice crisis" (p. 60). Coincident with the convictions of my coauthors Ed Sarath and David Myers, and in full alignment with the Manifesto, I approach diversity as key to understanding music and human learning locally and across the world.[1]

Here it is essential to reiterate the Manifesto's stance: The identity of the improvising–composing–performing student, who will position him/herself as relevant to the world beyond campus life, will grow the capacities and qualities befitting a musical thinker, humanist, social visionary, and sensitive world citizen. From their first freshman course all the way to their capstone projects, music majors reap rich rewards for pressing towards an understanding of music in the West and the world. Through a carefully planned program of study, they can tune to a global span of musical expressions that stretch their musical sensibilities beyond the more parochial musical frameworks they bring with them from their secondary school programs. Their new music major identities as university students can open them to study and experience with the complexities of the musical world, and they can experience music in myriad ways that carry them beyond the familiar high school bandstands and choral risers as they grow in knowledge of music from many times and places in fully embodied ways. As John Blacking so famously posited, by delving into studies of distant cultures there is the benefit for students of understanding their own "first" culture more thoroughly than if they had never looked and listened beyond it (1973).

Through active and analytical listening, participatory experiences, full-fledged performances of music in the world's cultures, personal encounters with musicians steeped in traditions, and synthesis of diverse influences encountered in their creative work, music majors can be drawn into thoughtful consideration of these compelling questions:

- Is music a pan-human experience? What are the illustrations that provide evidence of music as a truly cross-cultural phenomenon? Is making music in beautifully artistic and social ways a natural part of who we humanly are, in every place and time?
- As a language, is music universally understood by both cultural insiders and outsiders? Are humans wired to make sense of music both near and far from their first and familiar experiences? Do we understand different musical styles differently, depending upon our cultural perspective?
- Are musical sounds, behaviors, and values specific to each culture or are they shared across the world's cultures? What functions does music fill here and there in the world? As behavior, what transmission and teaching ways are there for communicating musical knowledge and skills from expert to novice musicians?

In a conscious reckoning with diversity as it intersects with the social justice principles of "same rights" for multiple music cultures, students do well in a contemporary program of study to engage with the world's musical cultures and communities. Their deep study of a single musical culture—beyond the culture of familiar Western European classical music they have learned in secondary school on their instrument through private lessons, in school music programs, and in youth orchestras (and choirs)—can take their minds and ears to another place where music is alive and well but decidedly distinguished from the familiar experiences students know as pianists, violinists, clarinetists, trumpeters, or choristers. Their comparative study of several musical cultures advance them to an understanding of elemental musical features of familiar and less familiar music expressions and their particular treatments by musicians living in other places (and times). Deep study of a second musical culture—be it Brazilian *samba*, Balinese *gamelan* or Bulgarian vocal–choral style, and comparative musical study (for example, of African diasporic styles in Jamaica and the Georgia Sea Islands) brings opportunities to know music as a central human need, as a set of learned sonic dialects, and as a wide spectrum of expressive possibilities to be examined, performed, and played with experimentally for what may emerge. When they study with artist musicians and culture-bearers, students acquire cultural understandings, too, that emerge from the interpersonal exchange of a studio lesson or the social collective of an ensemble. The search and discovery system by students for music's sonorities and meanings add credence to the notion of music as a many-splendored thing. Their deep and comparative study of musical expressions is a launch to their working those features in innovative ways into their own personal musical voices.

I intend to argue here the social responsibility of faculty to proactively address in a full-fledged, four-year program of study the presence of music in the world as a pan-human phenomenon, with both shared and distinctive features across geographic regions and cultural groups. References to diverse musical practices will exemplify an array of sonic and cultural components, and will illustrate diverse human behaviors and values as well as "universal" or at least cross-cultural principles in operation; they will illustrate and fill out constructs of diversity briefly noted in the Manifesto. Pertinent to the work of tertiary-level teaching faculty, attention will be paid to transmission and learning as key behaviors in preserving and sustaining (and also stimulating invention within) culturally valued musical genres and styles. My aim is to encourage thought that paves the way for the making of a broad-minded program of study that will fully envelop students in meaningful musical experiences and exchanges. Such a culturally inclusive program can lead students through their evolution as world-conscious citizens in and through music for the common good of a more socially responsible society.

Music in Global Array

If viewed through the lens of anthropologist John Blacking as "humanly organized sound" (1973), then music is known everywhere in the world that humans live. In every culture and community, people think and act musically; they sing, play, dance to music, and consume music as listeners. They identify personally and collectively with particular musical instruments, styles, and forms. Some people may not have a word for music (as in the case of many First Nations groups in Canada), or they may have separate words for vocal music and instrumental music (as in certain Slavic cultures), or they may use a word for music that embraces both dance and music (as in parts of sub-Saharan Africa or in India). Still, music resounds and reverberates from young and old, in urban and rural surroundings, and across communities defined by race, class, and gender. Music is live and mediated, vocal and instrumental, sacred and secular, and it is passed on orally and in written form even as it is received aurally and by decoding notation. It is meant by some people to be "fixed" in its performance in the very same way every time, while it is intended by others to be open, flexible, and freely improvised. Music is present across the globe, and its varied practices are worth knowing.

It is astonishing, then, that with a recognition of music's universality, that in these intercultural times in which people from different cultures recognize and respectfully accept different worldviews, that programs of music in higher education should be so reluctant to open up to, and offer students, education and training in forms outside and beyond the Western European classical repertory. More than a semester's superficial survey of all the world's musical cultures (although that is often the initial entry point), university programs can offer further specialized academic courses and performance experiences that transport students beyond a mere single sampling of "exotic other cultures" to embracing music as a polyglot of many cultural expressions, behaviors, and values. As well, core courses in music history and theory, and applied (and ensemble) music can feature both parallel strands of "court music"—in historic Paris, Tokyo, and Bangkok, for examples—and polyphonic forms, cadential structures, and music for worship (or work) that press the point of music as culturally distinctive yet humanly linked.

Depending upon who they are and where they live, people value different musical timbres and tunings, as well as approaches to time, pitch, form, and other musical features (Campbell, 2004; Wade, 2013). While a solo piano sonata or string quartet may be viewed as first-rank music among some citizens of Berlin or Boston, residents of Baghdad or Bangkok may be drawn to the sounds of expressive artists of various plucked lutes or flutes. (And in an era of globalization, piano blues or an ensemble of Irish fiddle, flute, and concertina may be the preferred music of some citizens of these very same cities.) What is out of tune for some listeners may be precisely on the mark for others, as in the case of the shimmering sounds of the xylophones and gongs of a gamelan that are so widely embraced by the Balinese but which do not match the tunings of a Western orchestra so familiar and favored by Western players and concert-goers. Where a pure tone is valued by Western listeners on Western-styled instruments, many Chinese prefer that their *dizi* flutes "buzz" with the addition of a membrane over the mouth hole, and villagers in northern Ghana enjoy the rattle of bottle caps that are attached to their *gyil* xylophones. In the Zimbabwean capitol city of Harare, it is a gold standard for bands of African lamellophone (or "thumb piano") players to attach beads and shells to the iron tongues of their instruments so as to ensure rich and rattling sounds that are widely embraced by avid listeners and dancers. Meanwhile, in Kinshasa, the capitol of the Democratic People's Republic of the Congo, the musical distortions of guitars and keyboards through inexpensive and poorly made amplification systems render a gritty sound, one that might be judged by Western ears as "noise" but which is in fact has emerged as the desired Congolese popular music sound. Purification is the goal of Western music throughout its history, with the intent of distinguishing musical sound from noise and removing all the "bad" sounds from the pure and civilized musical matter (Ochoa Gautier, 2006), but it is clearly not the ideal aesthetic for all the world's expressive practices.

In studying time in cross-cultural perspective, the music of some communities is characteristically pulsive and with a regularly recurring beat, while other communities value nonmetrical and pulseless free-flowing sound (consider, for example, the opening exploratory sections of a Hindustani vocal form called *dhrupad*). Yet another element of time is found in the Japanese *gagaku* ensemble of well over a thousand years of practice, in which time is a feeling, a deeply felt life-breath, and a collective time is kept through a coordinated breathing rhythm of all the musicians. People of diverse musical practices may organize time in groups of two, three, or four beats, or they may enjoy instead the feel of additive meters that perform music in multiples of two or three (such as in 5, 7, or 11 beats) that cycle continuously (as they certainly do in Bulgaria and Turkey, for example). All instruments or voices may sound a single rhythm in musical styles, while many African ensembles of instruments are typically constructed of multiple rhythmic patterns performed simultaneously, or polyrhythms. Musical rhythm comes in many speeds and cycles, from North Indian *tala* to Korean *changdan*, and an understanding of these qualities and characteristics brings an appreciation of music in some of its conceptually genius manifestations. With initial listening can come an awareness of some of these time treatments, while greater understanding of these elements can be known through frequent and recurring analytical listening. Through engaged and enactive opportunities to sing, dance, and play music of one or more of these exemplars of time traits can arise a deeper sense of the musical complexities by students, and quite possibly the development of "the chops" to be able to transfer these traits to invented music of their own.

A similar spread of the treatments of pitch can be found in a journey across musical cultures. Many instruments offer multiple pitches (principally five, six, or seven pitches, but also more or less) that relate to one another horizontally, lower and higher, with standard intervals sounding among them. Those intervals are sometimes "whole" and "half" tones, as in the case of a diatonic scale, while other times there are microtonal quarter (or less than quarter) tones between them, as in the case of Arab music's half-flat seconds that are heard across the Arabian peninsula, through Egypt to Morocco, and over to Turkey. Musicians may express pitch vertically, for example, in octaves, fifths, fourths, thirds, seconds, chords, or tone clusters. They may join their voices and instruments together harmonically, or in unison, or in independent lines all at once, that is, polyphonically. Some musicians, particularly in Arab-influenced cultures, enjoy performing melodies heterophonically such that, for example, a fiddle and flute in Turkey might play the same melody at the same time but with different idiomatic nuances that render the sound as somewhat but not completely the same. The potential for students to feature, in their own composed and improvised music, an assortment of pitch schemes that sound in succession or simultaneously will widen through concentrated efforts by students to discern the pitch content of music in Iran, Indonesia, or India. Their efforts are steered by teaching faculty across specializations to include analytical listening to live and mediated music, guided experiences in the performance of the music—whether on culturally authentic instruments or students' own familiar instruments, and opportunities to engage with musicians about the music they make, of what pitches (and rhythms and forms) it consists, and how particular sound qualities may be achieved.

A glance at forms leads us across a vast and gloried sweep of possibilities for humanly organized sound. Some musicians prefer to introduce the musical ideas that will be further attended to later, as in the case of the North Indian classical *alap*, where vocalists and players of sitar, sarod, and sarangi choose to establish the mood through the introduction of the melodic mode, or raga. In European classical music, there is great value placed upon the sonata form in which a melodic theme is introduced, then is later modulated and, at the close of the movement is returned to itself and in the original key. Musicians may prefer a formal finishing to a piece through a cadence that signals closure by way a harmonic progression, as is the case of those who perform European sonatas or in symphonic works of the 18th and 19th centuries. Other musicians, such as those who engage in North Indian improvisational practice, delight in the cadential practice of a rhythmic pattern, or *tihai*, that is performed three times by the sitar and tabla, ending together on the count of "one." A world of musical forms exist that are open or closed, fixed or flexible (or even mixed with set sections interspersed with improvisatory passages), and with more or less repetition and contrast built into the melodic, rhythmic, textural, and timbral contact. Students can lend their ears to carefully gauging the varied ways that musician put sounds together with coherence and logic so to express the good, the bad, the ugly, the beautiful, and the sublime.

On concert stages, in clubs, and in neighborhoods, music is presented in performance by studied musicians who identify as musicians, and is also offered for participation by all those who choose to listen—or who are invited to play it, sing it, or dance it. As Walt Whitman expressed so eloquently, "I hear America singing, the varied carols I hear." In departments and schools of music in North America and elsewhere, there is the largely unrealized potential for music majors to know deep experiences in the music of an intercultural America and of selected cultural communities from across the globe. Some music major programs may require student enrollment in "African drumming," bluegrass, gamelan, gospel choir, steel band, or other "non-traditional" ensembles beyond the standard Western classical music performance groups. Such requirements advance students to musical territories beyond their comfort zones, and these initial performance experiences are valuable to their development personally, socially, and musically. Yet a one-term drum-dance course (whether the tradition is Akan, Ewe, Yoruban, or Afro-Cuban) amid years of an intensive training in Western classical repertory should not suggest a sense of "mission accomplished" in terms of the diversity pillar of the Manifesto. We need only to recognize how minimal the experiences students have with 10- to 15-week classes of introductory piano, or violin, or French horn, or voice lessons, to understand the importance of giving more than a glance in study of a selected musical practice beyond the Western classical music, be it African American gospel, Afro-Brazilian samba, Chopi xylophones of the southern African country of Mozambique, or any other unfamiliar music. This is not to discourage efforts to organize the study of local and global musical expressions but rather to beg the question of whether more extensive training in a style can be built into a program, and whether a second (or third) musical expression, system, and culture can be integrated within a four-year program of study. It is a tall order, to be sure, to live out diversity principles and work towards inclusionary practices.

Courses in study of the music in the Americas, the Caribbean, Southeast Asia, Southern Africa, the Near East, the Pacific Islands, and European folk traditions are just some of what ethnomusicologists contribute to the making of globally-conscious musicians, particularly when these courses feature visiting artists, musical and cultural analyses of locally valued practices, and opportunities to sing, play, and dance the music. This panorama of musical experiences is best fulfilled through the hiring of an ethnomusicologist (or two) who covers the world, while also hiring on an artist musician of a particular instrument or style—be it a *kora* (harp) player from Mali or a blues guitarist from Mississippi—to bring up-close-and-personal attention to knowing a given musical practice beyond an elementary, first-glimpse exposure. Foundational strides need to be made in terms of expanding the resources that currently exist in departments, schools, and colleges of music, implementing curricular changes that allow students to access these resources, and enacting a shift in culture whereby diversity efforts shift from an additive phenomenon to a core aspect of student (and faculty) identity. The weave of diverse musical expressions into first- and second-year theory, musicianship, and history courses by faculty of various academic and performance specializations is a noble yet realistic goal that will transform that way students think and do music. It is entirely within reach (although not without challenge) for faculty to integrate their courses so thoroughly that the one-sided "West is best" approach moves through its lopsided arrangement to curricular content that genuinely reflects the ideals of cultural, educational, and musical equity. A closer look at the relationship between music and behavior, and particularly at music as behavior, sheds light on the principles that need to be placed front and center for these strides to be made.

Music as Behavior

Turning attention to pedagogical practice, I consider again Christopher Small's argument for music as an activity and not a thing (1998). He coined the term "musicking" to describe music as behavior: what people do at a musical event, whether they perform, listen, rehearse or practice, improvise, compose, or dance (p. 9). All these musicking acts are exemplary of participatory musical behaviors, some more active than passive, a few more personal than social, and others more intentional than incidental. Musicking is behavioral action rather than an auditory abstraction, and music's value is based on the meaning of the musicking action to the individual and the group. The benefits of group musicking—such as playing in bands; singing in choirs; dancing in lines, couples, and squares; and going to concerts—include an improved sense of well-being, mood, and social connectedness. Much of the musicking involves behaviors that are social in nature, too, so that the associated social interactions lead to the development of meaningful human relationships (Keil and Feld, 1994, Turino, 2008). The pedagogical ramifications of musicking are considerable, especially as pertinent to music or music learning experiences that lend themselves to participatory rather than perfection-level presentational performances; see the *Ngoma* section.

The musical experience is replete with social behaviors that emanate from performers, even in their solo ventures. There are the behaviors that produce the fine sounds of a well-prepared recital, as there are also the behaviors of concert routines and protocols that have been established over time. Pianists, for example, produce sounds from the well-tutored gestures they have honed. They have learned the behaviors for positioning themselves in alignment with the instrument, how to hold their hands and angle their wrists, how to offer an even weighting of each finger they press to a key. They also know the acceptable manner for entering and exiting the stage of a recital hall, how to respond to audience appreciation and acclaim, how long to wait between movements of a piece. Members of their audience learn when to sit silently and when to applaud; they also know how to dress for the occasion of a concert (sometimes depending upon the nature of the repertoire and venue of the performance). In the concert hall, performers and audiences work in tandem for the cocreation of the musical event, performing particular behaviors that respect and continue aspects of audience agency and the social infrastructure of musical practices.

The behaviors of musicians vary from one musical culture to the next, and their social values are expressed in the music they make. In the case of gamelan music at the court of Jogjakarta in Central Java, the practice is entirely communal so that no individual musician stands out as soloist or director (albeit the drummer sets the tempo and volume of the group). The aim is for a homogenous sound so that instruments play together and in support of one another, so much so that despite the idiosyncratic nature of a bronze xylophone, a spike fiddle, and a set of tuned gongs, players are producing in heterophonic texture their simultaneous variations on the melody. They are performing together, expressing community. In a very different musical sound style, jazz—whether in Chicago or Amsterdam, in Buenos Aires or Tokyo, offers opportunities for creativity to shine out from individual players (and singers) in smaller and larger groups. The sense of community is continued by members of the jazz ensemble as they provide rhythm and texture to the soloists. Meanwhile, the soloists may reflect, in the intensity of their improvised and interpretive performance, some of the struggles of African American identity and the history of hardship that shaped this style in its origin and development.

Music is behavior, and musical performance is replete with behaviors pertinent to not only the production of sound as it was learned (which is another set of behaviors) or spontaneously felt, and in the socially interactive behaviors of musicians in groups, but also in the behaviors that surround the circumstances of performance, including its embedded routines and rituals. An awareness of musical behaviors by students can lead them to an understanding of how socially constructed music truly is, and how deeply human, too. These thoughts of music as behavior can give way to realizing that engagement in a musical culture (or style, or individual piece) through direct musical experience is the pathway to fully making sense of it. Not only does this engagement open windows to an understanding of culturally valued rituals but also to an awareness of the commonalities of music across many practices. Teaching faculty in four-year music major programs are ultimately responsible for facilitating active musicking opportunities that bring students experience in the study of music as sound, behavior, and values, and which is helped through the presence of a faculty of ethnomusicologists and expert artist-musicians of multiple expressions, traditions, and practices.

Learning Music

With the assertion of music as a pan-human phenomenon comes the understanding that music's teaching and learning processes (exemplar and relevant musical behaviors) will likewise show certain universal principles—or minimally, cross-cultural similarities. An understanding of cross-cultural processes by which music is received and retained is critical to the transmission of core knowledge, skills, and values in the undergraduate music major curriculum. Because of an extensive research literature developing in recent decades, there is now solid scientific data that clarifies the cognitive, cultural, and somatic and embodied dimensions of the music-learning process. While some revered pedagogical processes of conservatory-based music teaching and learning stand up to rigorous tests of effective educational practice, a broad cultural span of perspectives on music learning is reason for considering critically the processes that undergird and support effective means of developing thoughtful singers, players, composers, and improvisers, as well as prospective teachers, through classroom study, performance studios, and ensemble experiences. Not every teaching act yields learning, and not every learner is automatically served by the techniques of a particular teacher. A view of pedagogical practices that are widely used to good effect follows, along with an understanding that learning music of any historical period or place in the world could be enhanced through attention and application of these practices (Campbell, 1991; McLucas, 2011).

There is considerable evidence of the cross-cultural use of orality (and aurality) in the transmission and learning of music. Oral transmission is the teacher's active role in transmitting the music on the instrument, or vocally, while aural transmission is the student's hearing and receiving of the music. Both of these actions are in play in many cultures, and even in studios where European classical music is studied via the teacher's modeling of a technique or passage. I propose that we provide increased occasions for aural skill development, offering ways for students to stretch their ears, to be challenged to listen and learn not only passages but full pieces. Many of the high cultures of Asia have perpetuated their music practices through a combination of oral–aural transmission. In Thailand, for example, performers learn the music of *pi phat* and *mahori* ensembles so thoroughly by ear, through intensive practice sessions, that it is retained and continued by the musicians for the rest of their lives. *Gagaku* music of Japan is learned without notation (although notation is available to scholars), and a revered 8th-century repertoire is performed today as it was performed over 13 centuries ago as a result of an oral–aural transmission. Written notation in various standardized systems, be it Western staff notation, or cipher notation developed in the periods of Western colonization of Indonesia and India, or tablature for guitars and other lutes in the western and eastern ends of the Mediterranean region, or the vertically placed notation systems for the Chinese *qin* and Japanese *koto*, for examples, are never enough information, so much so that the teacher's musical model is essential for transmitting the music in all of its nuances. Where notation exists, it can (and often is) in use, but the potential for at least occasional experiences in learning music through the oral–aural transmission process should not be underestimated for the musicianship that it can develop.

Vocalization is a commonly found component of instrumental study in many musical practices. In North India, where the vocal art of *dhrupad* and *khyal* singing is highly regarded, and where vocal music at large is considered the bedrock of all Hindustani music, students are directed to the vocalization of ragas before instrumental studies commence, and micromelodies are sung by teachers and then imitated by students to develop their language of pitch possibilities and a treasury of melodic phrases that may later rise up in improvisatory work. There are culturally specific solmization systems in practice in India, as in Japan, China, and Indonesia, and they are present in private and group lessons on various instruments. Vocalized drum syllabuses are common in many drumming cultures across sub-Saharan Africa, for example, Akan, Ewe, Wagogo, and Wolof musicians, and are in use by master musicians working with those who aspire to learn the repertoire and techniques. "Drum language" operates in lessons on Hindustani *tabla*, Karnatic *mridangam*, Javanese *kendhang*, Japanese drums of the *kabuki* theatre, and instruments of the Chinese *luogu* percussion ensemble, where not only the durations and timbres but also the performance techniques are embedded with the mnemonic syllables. The close, vocal art of singing and rhythmic chanting can help the learning process, and may aid in advancing the long-term retention of phrases and full pieces for performance.

A measure of eurhythmic movement is evident in the making of much of the world's music, be it in the ways that the body tilts and turns in "operating" an instrument or in the natural gestures that emanate while playing or singing. The movement that is attuned to the intricacies of a musical practice is evident in the gestures of conductors whose arms, wrists, hands, and fingers communicate musical expression to performers; even the position of their bodies, the slight leans and subtle forward and back maneuvers, are "read" by singers and players.

In those traditions where music and dance are perceived as a single unit, as in much sub-Saharan African music, the voice and the body (and associated musical instruments) synchronize in the musical act. In many African diasporic settings where groups gather to make music, the human penchant for keeping together in time is evident in the joyful rhythmic maneuverings of arms, legs, and torsos (McNeill, 1995). In some dance traditions such as the Indian classical dance form of Kathak, every foot stamp and step may be intricately connected to individual durations (and drum syllables, called *bols*). In learning the dance, the drummer plays or vocalizes the complicated rhythms of the drum that the dancer then beats out with his or her feet, and the goal is that the drummer and dancer perform together these rich rhythms. In traditions like Kathak where the music is danced, the eurhythmic movement is precise, but in many more musical practices in the world—especially as they are learned, the goal of movement is for a more wholesale embodiment of the elemental features of music. Opposite the Cartesian view of the dominance of the mind over the body, a distributed cognition that allows for an embodied view of learning guarantees the development of long-lasting skills and understandings through experiences that balance the activities of the mind and the body (Borgo, 2007).

Learning music transpires in many ways, and a teacher's respect for varied ways of learning, and of preferred student modalities, can accelerate and ensure that learning and not just teaching happens. Knowledge of transmission practices, and of the extent to which musical cultures utilize oral, visual, and kinesthetic means to ensure that music is transmitted, received, and preserved, can be an end in itself: Music learned, lesson over. Or, the repertoire in all of its sonorities and structures, and the techniques for performing it, can become the base of new musical expressions. Orality and aurality, vocalization, and movement are common practices in many musical cultures, as there is also a respect for the role of creative expression in developing personal and collective ownership of long-standing genres as well as newly invented works that rise from the experiences of learning more of the world's musical cultures.

Ngoma: A Special Case of Learning

Holistic and fully embodied musical practice, referred to as *ngoma* by pro-Bantu linguistic-cultural groups, deserves the attention of those musician–teachers dedicated to their students' comprehensive and fully embodied understanding of music. On my frequent visits to East Africa, to the republic of Tanzania, and to the villages of Wagogo people that are spread across the central region of the country, I am privileged through my collaborative association with Kedmon Mapana, Wagogo artist–musician, scholar, and lecturer in music at the University of Dar es Salaam, to not only be witnessing a stunning, even staggering, set of sophisticated musical genres but also to be recognizing an important and effective way of learning and teaching that is age-old and continuing—and utterly effective. While it may seem a reach to imagine *ngoma* in operation in a university music major program, I envision this fully embodied way of learning and living music as quite suitably able to be embedded within the pedagogical ways of our core courses.

Ngoma is a particular process of participatory musicking that invites all to join in a thorough-going expression of the human spirit. In Kiswahili, the lingua franca of Tanzania, Kenya, Uganda, Rwanda, Burundi, and parts of neighboring countries, *ngoma* literally means "drum, dance, and music" (Janzten, 1992; Mapana, 2007). Like the Greek *mousike*, the Blackfoot *saapup*, and the Wagnerian *gesampkuntswerke*, *ngoma* encompasses more than music alone. It is an enveloping experience that features three or more of these facets: drumming, singing, dancing, dramatic-interactive play, poetry, costuming, and pageantry. *Ngoma* is the syncretic blend of performative matter, and functions in villages at public ceremonies, in private rituals, in celebrations, on religious and seasonal holidays, and even in competitive village festivities. It does not so much signify a particular genre as it refers to a perspective on expression that honors multimodal, integrative, holistic, and communal characteristics (Keil and Campbell, 2016).

While *ngoma* processes are found throughout much of the eastern, central, and southern African continent, it is within Wagogo culture that "the perfect *ngoma*" lives. As farmers and herders, the Wagogo are over a million in population; they are attentive to feeding their families, raising their children, and carrying on their heritage while also finding their way through the remnants of earlier colonial domination by Germany and Britain, modernization efforts (with more than a little help and influence from the U.S., South Africa, and recently the Chinese), and the Swahili-ization of their nation (which requires their shift from the Cigogo mother-tongue to the all-Tanzania Swahili language). Moreover, the Wagogo are singers, dancers, and players of a beautiful music that compels me to return again and again to Tanzania to hear it live, to dance it, and to sing it. Wagogo *ngoma* joins together song, dance, and musical instruments such as flute, a two-stringed bowed lute, a thumb piano of about 15 metal prongs called *ilimba*, and single-headed drums held between the knees and played while dancing. Sometimes dramatic episodes are enacted, and also sung, played, and danced. Song texts consist of poetic statements relevant to the health of villagers, the prevention of disease, the education of children, the perpetuation of Wagogo traditions, and various other contemporary topics of social significance.

The Wagogo value the integration of all the arts that seems to happen naturally in the act of *ngoma*'s expressive practice, and that embraces the participation of many rather than to single out and raise to star status only the select and talented few. As the basis of a paradigm for encouraging all to know their fuller musical and artistic-expressive selves, *ngoma* is social music and a collective musical experience. It is rich in polyrhythms and polyphonic voices, even as it allows individuals to shine solo in a dance maneuver or elaborate vocalized "call" before receding back into the community of musicians. It is variously entertaining, therapeutic, and powerful enough to validate the importance of individuals to the social fabric of a community. *Ngoma* invites and envelops all, and while not everyone will sing, dance, and play every time, the Wagogo way is that the invitation is a standing one, open and accepting of individuals at any time into the musicking experience.

An experience in the Wagogo way of *ngoma* is reminiscent to me of a time in childhood when we sang, danced, and played. Daily. We did so because we could, and it was wholesome, healthy, and healing to participate in such a comprehensive expressive process. Music was threaded into our very being while we played individually and collectively. There was music as we joined in regular family activity around the dinner table, and as we weathered long car rides, bounced into bedtime, and of course gathered for holidays and other festive occasions. In studies of children's musical cultures (Campbell and Wiggins, 2013), this penchant for integrative-artistic expression appears to rise out of children's playful interactions and exchanges today, and in many circumstances and settings. Today's Wagogo children, and adults as well, embrace the music they themselves make live, sitting around after a meal, singing, picking up sticks to click, gourds to shake, an occasional *ilimba* (thumb piano) or drums to play. Churches are alive with singing and dancing, as are the occasional café (in the larger villages where cafés are available), and there are hotspots of singing and "rhythmicking" (vocalized rhythms replete with dance movements) quite regularly just about anywhere in the village.

How might we embrace the concept of *ngoma* in the work we do today in our tertiary-level teaching? Could we imagine the occasional moments of *ngoma*—of singing, dancing, and playing—seeping into our lessons, lectures, rehearsals? Could we recognize just how multisensory and communally connected all music-making actually could be, if we would foster it? Could we teach/learn by ear at times, leading students to listen in order to grasp melodies, rhythms, and full-out musical form—not leaving literacy behind, of course, but offering orality as a counterbalance to score-reading? Could we require instrumental students to sing more and vocal students to study an instrument for a term or two? Could we decide to season our academic courses with opportunities to sing, play, and dance the music of study? Could we feature eurhythmics, movement, and dance in order to underscore the meaning of an embodied understanding of a musical concept? As there are on some campuses "music for dancers" courses and "dance for athletes," could there also be "dance for musicians" courses in our programs? Could we open our students to opportunities for improvisation in studios, ensembles, musicianship, theory, history/culture, and education methods courses? Could we consider performances in which some music has been learned entirely by ear, perhaps co-invented by players and singers, possibly performed "in motion" away from music stands and choral risers with distributions of performers across the stage in preconceived patterns and choreographed episodes—or moving spontaneously? Might, as Ed Sarath argues forcefully in Chapter 5, the idea of *ngoma* be more fully realized in conjunction with the shift to creative foundations as compared to interpretive performance foundations? Could an honest recognition of the widespread incidence of creative improvisation and composition be woven into musically active experiences with diverse musical cultures?

Regardless of one's responses to these questions, I think that were we to embrace *ngoma*, emanating from far-away sub-Saharan Africa, we surely would be refreshed by the blended-arts experience, as we would also confirm the holistic human essence of the music we study in higher education. I would urge our consideration of *ngoma*, and of other ways of transmission and learning beyond standard Western pedagogical practice, for how it can enrich the pursuit by our students of musical knowledge and skills.

Weaving the World of Understandings

An examination of progressive higher education programs in music calls to mind the extent to which musical diversity is made manifest across four years of study. While premature proclamations of "mission accomplished" should be resisted, these programs suggest that genuine transformation may be underway in mostly isolated settings here and there that include small liberal arts colleges, conservatory programs, large research universities, and regional state universities. There are programs where students may "opt" for participation in a gospel ensemble or a mariachi, often on their own time and without credit, where such ensembles may function on campuses as student social clubs more than as musical opportunities fully sanctioned by music departments. Rare among music major programs are meaningful efforts to celebrate local communities, where genuine community musicians are hired to the music faculty to offer regular private and group instruction over years rather than single semesters in bluegrass banjo or *conjunto* accordion. It is more likely that programs will provide minimal support to occasional (often seasonal) cameo appearances of "exotic" players, such as Irish *bodhran*, Korean *kayagum*, Afro-Peruvian *cajon*, and Arab *'ud*. While sometimes these guest artists can pique interest and prompt further learning by motivated students, these minimal experiences are at risk of essentializing cultural practices, of reducing a rich-lived experience in music to a 50-minute exposure of a limited set of characteristics. Importantly, as David Myers reminds us in Chapter 3, we can wisely apply the double-loop approach in responding to calls for diversity by thoughtfully enacting suggested changes and then reflecting upon their outcomes and implications. When necessary, we can adjust to suit the needs of our students (and present faculty).

The Manifesto argues for fully embedded diversity in the study of music as a global phenomenon, a pan-human need, a universally vital component of cultural identity as it is artistically expressed. Calls for social justice in higher education have been variously met by pronouncements from presidents and provosts, and by innovative redesigns of programs in departments of the humanities, the arts, the sciences, and the social sciences. Music faculties in North America are found dragging their feet, doing much less in the way of diversifying studies, mainly concerning themselves with conserving and preserving Western European classical music. Adding a dash of this and a dose of that are superficial excursions to the music of "other lands," which preserve and thus privilege 19th-century European works and pedagogical processes. Additive measures to accomplish diversity goals are no longer enough, and they frequently backfire through their ghettoizing of "other," "non-Western" glimpses of music beyond the well-conserved European classical tradition. An education in music at the tertiary level demands attention to engagements through the duration of an undergraduate program in listening, participating, performing music of a wide expanse of heritages, and allowing students to develop relationships with musicians who know their traditions well. While mastery of many musical instruments, traditions, and practices is not likely to occur within the scope of four years of study, the integration of diverse music and musical experiences can work in advancing the creative voice of students in their own compositions and improvisations. Co-creativity can be facilitated in a spectrum of academic and applied courses in ways that open students to "an ethic of deep empathy toward alternative voices" so that they may be empowered with a greater sociocritical awareness of marginalized communities that are far from the mainstream and dominant culture (Heble and Laver, 2016, p. 2).

An equally important outcome of studying the world's music in a continuing and integrated fashion is the development by students of a perspective on the world that respects equity while also questioning hierarchy. The Zulu phrase, "Ubuntu: I am because you are," may be within grasp by students who think and do music from diverse cultures, who recognize the importance of the sociomusical matter of a musical practice, who learn (and may perform) in comprehensive cross-modal fashion, and who evolve their creative musical potential even as they learn to honor the practices of the greater musical world.

Note

1 Due to the nuanced meanings of "multicultural", "intercultural", and "transcultural", terms that run rampant in the literature of the social sciences, the arts and the humanities as well as in common parlance (but which vary from one school of thought to the next), I have refrained from using them in this chapter. Still, it will become clear that my views are rooted in a number of works, including Banks (2016), Nettl (2015), Schippers (2010), Solis (2004), and even Campbell (2004).

References

Banks, James A., 2016. *Multicultural Education: Issues and Perspectives*, 8th edition. New York: Wiley & Sons.
Blacking, John. 1973. *How Musical Is Man?* Seattle: University of Washington Press.
Borgo, David. 2007. Free Jazz in the Classroom: An Ecological Approach to Music Education. *Jazz Perspectives* 1: 61–88.
Campbell, Patricia Shehan. 2004. *Teaching Music Globally*. New York: Oxford University Press.
——— 1991. *Lessons from the World*. New York: Schirmer Books.

Campbell, Patricia Shehan, and Trevor Wiggins. 2013. *The Oxford Handbook of Children's Musical Cultures*. New York: Oxford University Press.
Heble, Ajay, and Mark Laver. 2016. *Improvisation and Music Education*. New York: Routledge.
Janzten, John M. 1992. *Discourses of Healing in Central and Southern Africa*. Berkeley: University of California Press.
Keil, Charles and Steven Feld, 1994. *Music Grooves: Essays and Dialogues*. Chicago: University of Chicago Press.
Keil, Charles, and Patricia Shehan Campbell. 2016. *Born to Groove*. Retrieved from www.borntogroove.org
Mapana, Kedmon. 2007. Changes in Performance Style: A Case Study of "Muheme," a Musical Tradition of the Wagogo of Dodoma, Tanzania. *Journal of African Cultural Studies* 19:1, Performing (In) Everyday Life (June), 81–93.
McLucas, Anne. 2011. *The Musical Ear: Oral Tradition in the USA*. Burlington, VT: Ashgate Publishing Company.
McNeill, William H. 1995. *Keeping Together in Time: Dance and Drill in Human History*. Cambridge, MA: Harvard University Press.
Nettl, Bruno, 2015. *The Study of Ethnomusicology: Thirty-one Issues and Concepts*. Champaign, IL: University of Illinois Press.
Ochoa Gautier, Ana María. 2006. Sonic Transculturation: Epistemologies of Purification and the Aural Public Sphere in Latin America. *Social Identities* 12:6, 803–825.
Schippers, Huib, 2010. *Facing the Music: Shaping Music Education from a Global Perspective*. New York: Oxford University Press.
Small, Christopher. 1998. *Musicking*. Hanover, NH: Wesleyan University Press.
Solis, Ted, 2004. *Performing Ethnomusicology: Teaching and Representation in World Music Ensembles*. Berkeley CA: University of California Press.
Turino, Thomas. 2008. *Music as Social Life*. Chicago: University of Chicago Press.
Wade, Bonnie C. 2013. *Thinking Musically* (3rd ed.). New York: Oxford University Press.

3
MODELS OF CHANGE

David E. Myers

In our opening chapter we situated the topic of music studies reform within a broader cross-disciplinary and global context. In this chapter, I refine this trajectory by examining various theories of change and their ramifications for our field. This provides an important backdrop for a closer reading of the Manifesto, which appears in the next chapter, and also Ed Sarath's further explorations into change in Chapters 5 and 6.

Substantive curricular change has been particularly elusive in higher education, with many aphorisms directed toward the challenges of curricular reform. One commonly hears allusions to the "glacial pace" of change, presumably due to a complex of factors such as entrenched bureaucracy, political agendas, extended committee processes, and criteria for promotion and tenure. Associated tensions that may arise, both productive and unproductive, often involve questions such as these: Why is change needed, if at all? Should the curriculum lead to profession-wide change and prepare students as change agents, or should it teach marketable skills and knowledge for current employment? Should the arts and humanities be concerned with the employment of graduates, or primarily with long-touted generic outcomes such as critical thinking and communication skills? What responsibilities, if any, does the curriculum have relative to the greater good of society? These are complicated issues, and it is often the case that surmounting such complexities at a department or school level can be a tedious process of compromise that yields only limited return for the time and energy invested.

The report of the Task Force on the Undergraduate Music Major (TFUMM), published in full in Chapter 4, has recognized these complexities, acknowledging that change may occur in a variety of ways and at a variety of levels within higher education, i.e., the classroom, syllabi, degree programs, academic units, and colleges and schools of music. However, the thrust of the report, now widely known as the Manifesto, is toward broad-scale change in the undergraduate music curriculum, encouraging professors, administrators, and practicing professionals to consider historical, contemporary, and (potential) future realities that urge transformative change in the ways we educate 21st-century musicians.

Decades ago, social psychologist Kurt Lewin (1947) posited a three-part change theory that continues to influence organizational development today, and that applies to the Manifesto's call for curricular transformation. At the risk of oversimplification, Lewin's first step ("unfreeze") is to identify reasons for change that are regarded as compelling and that motivate people to undertake change. The second step is implementation ("transition"), and the third is to embed changes operationally ("freeze") to assure improvement of practice. Importantly, the third step does not represent a new level of entrenched thinking; the entire process is dynamic and ongoing.

The Manifesto sets forth compelling reasons for curricular change using strong underlying arguments rooted in the nature and practice of music historically, evolutionally, and across cultures; it offers suggestions as to what change might look like in a variety of contexts; and it recommends avenues for effecting change. The challenge is for institutions to consider these arguments and recommendations in light of their own missions, resources, and goals, and to determine how they might effect change in their own contexts. The manifestations of this process could vary in exciting ways across institutional cultures, but the inherently foundational unities would derive from those pillars and related principles the Task Force has identified as core: creativity, diversity, and integration.

A question that often arises regarding proposals for change is whether they are simply for the sake of modifying something, or whether there are, as Lewin suggests, worthy and compelling reasons. Clearly, change can involve risks, and progress is not necessarily guaranteed, particularly if change has been implemented without a thorough analysis of the need. Legendary UCLA basketball coach John Wooden reportedly once said, "Failure is not fatal, but failure to change might be" (ESPN.com staff, 2010). Progress, or improvement, seems to be implicit in Coach Wooden's statement, and his teams' successes would tend to validate that assumption. However, philosopher and mathematician Alfred North Whitehead spoke more explicitly to the relationship between change and progress: "The art of progress is to preserve order amid change and to preserve change amid order" (Morris, 1991, p. 177).

Today, change is discussed and proposed ubiquitously in higher education, often in relation to the latest curricular, instructional, or administrative fad. What the Manifesto maintains, however, is that substantive change must grow out of substantive and reasoned thought, and that, for the purposes of higher music education, the worthiness of the curriculum must be interrogated in light of the structure, the practice, and the learning and teaching of music across cultures and historical eras. In other words, the Manifesto calls for a radical rethinking of the curriculum in terms of MUSIC writ large, rather than perseveration of a status quo model that is increasingly out of alignment with the realities of music practice across cultures and societies. Today's curriculum must advance understanding of the sociocultural contexts of music expression, reflect research-based knowledge about music, and nurture students with core competencies *in* music that will, in turn, equip them to be artists, scholars, teachers, and leaders *for* music and for the greater good of society *through* music. At the heart of these professional roles are the ability to create music, the ability to value and understand diverse musical cultures of diverse peoples, and the ability to compare and integrate a broad range of knowledge and practice to inform continued learning and rigorous professional growth beyond the academy.

Harvard professor Michael Porter and Mark Kramer, managing director of FSG Social Impact Advisors, wrote in 2006:

> When a well-run business applies its vast resources, expertise and management talent to problems that it understands and in which it has a stake, it can have a greater impact on social good than any other institution or philanthropic organization.
>
> *(pp. 14–15)*

This gets to the heart of what the TFUMM report asserts about undergraduate music programs: If the intellectual, artistic, and material resources of music units (departments, schools, and colleges) are expertly applied to problems that faculty understand in relation to the stake they have in the success of graduates in a global society, and the stake that graduates have in realizing careers that vivify their passions, and if students' knowledge and capacities are developed in relation to the ways music and musicians can serve society's best interests, then music units are likely to achieve a proportional increase in perceived relevance, influence, and value both within and beyond the academy.

The problem, however, is that the current model of higher music education, derived in another era and educating musicians primarily for worlds of Western classical music that today are facing enormous economic, social, and artistic challenges, is not a viable model for the well-being of graduates or the society in which they will live and work. In 2008, Joel Podolny, former dean of the Yale School of Management, was among a group of business deans asked by the *Harvard Business Review* whether business schools bore any responsibility for the financial collapse. Podolny stood largely alone among his colleagues in asserting that yes, the schools did bear responsibility, noting that the teaching of technical skills was rarely accompanied by any understanding of the social contexts in which those skills would be applied (https://hbr.org/2009/03/are-business-schools-to-blame.html).

Higher Education in the Ecosystem of Institutionalized Music

Robert Freeman, who served as Dean of the Eastman School of Music for 24 years, reveals in his recent book, *The Crisis of Classical Music in America* (2014) that he lost his job as President of the New England Conservatory (NEC) after only two years under the accusation that he was attempting to turn the conservatory into a liberal arts college. Freeman had successfully led the Eastman School of Music in the direction of its now widely recognized leadership programs that connect conservatory education with real-world problems and demands. Yet, when Freeman posed to NEC students and faculty the question of how performance graduates expected to make their ways in the world given the disproportionate ratio of outstanding performance graduates to available earning opportunities, he was accused of compromising artistic training. Inasmuch as the Manifesto calls for change that moves well beyond the Eastman initiative, and even Freeman's compelling analysis, my primary point here is to underscore the kind of entrenchment that is not uncommon in music studies. As has been said in many contexts, what is often characterized as dumbing down may, in some instances, actually represent wising up.

Freeman points us in the right direction. His assessment of the crisis of classical music is that what he calls the music ecosystem is out of alignment. The ecosystem encompasses all of those arenas in which classical music, particularly, is performed, studied, and produced. Within that ecosystem, the role of music in higher education relative to the challenges of classical music and musicians in society is an essential question. Today, every classical music organization is being pressured by funders and the public to address issues of diversity and inclusion, meaningful engagement with communities, and integration of its work with other music and arts entities in the interest of societal well-being. And yet, only a few schools and departments of music have instituted programs, courses, and experiences that address these burgeoning needs and expectations.

In reading the Manifesto, however, what should be clear is that it embraces a much broader notion of the music ecosystem than Freeman's, as well as much other writing on the topic. In addition to broader conceptions of creativity, diversity, and integration, the Manifesto advocates the incorporation of concepts such as the African-based *ngoma* practice in curriculum reform. As explained by Patricia Campbell in Chapter 2, *ngoma* brings together music, movement, drama, and ritual in a unified performance. The TFUMM's perspective is that foundational change in the curriculum must reconsider the assumptions and purposes of higher music education in light of what we know today about the world's music. Embracing the mutually informing content and process that build understanding of both music's technical facets and its sociocultural dimensions not only broadens the education of musicians in a global society, but encourages high levels of attainment and rigor, and equips them for artistic leadership and scholarship in a wide range of professional contexts.

Addressing Resistance to Change

As noted earlier in the chapter, inimical aspects of faculty governance and bureaucratic overlays can make curricular change attempts tiresome and frustrating. Since first release of the Manifesto in October 2014, many of the recurrent questions have had to do not only with resistance to change that is seemingly inherent in the structure and systems of the academy, but also with resistance that derives from personal and professional agendas, or merely from the belief that there is no reason to undertake change, particularly the kind of broad-scale change TFUMM advocates.

Organizational psychologists often note that resistance may be a function of a lack of agreement that change is needed, of inertia resulting from change that was ineffective or a failure of leadership to model and motivate useful change, or from fear that one's job may be negatively impacted. When applying these ideas to the academy, the first need pointed out is for leaders who not only promote change, but also recognize and work with those who tend to resist change. Though music units typically have a lead administrator, much of the curricular work occurs within subunits (often organized as theory, musicology, performance, or composition) and is processed through committees charged with curricular oversight. Sometimes there is an administrator specifically charged with curriculum responsibilities; in smaller departments this role may be relegated to chairs of divisions, areas, or programs.

Regardless of the specific organizational structure, the point is that the work done in these organizational entities may be characterized as curricular but is in reality often little more than reviewing requirements, considering petitions for deviations from stated requirements, or debating and implementing largely superficial changes in titles, credit hours, or content alignment with other courses. Focusing on these matters may at times be necessary, but these emphases do not engage faculty in rich conversations and efforts around *curricular change*. Without specific intent for curricular change and the leadership to effect it, the workaday demands of academic life are likely to impede progress.

Several years ago at the University of Minnesota, the School of Music, under my leadership, undertook an organizational process specifically designed to generate cross-divisional dialogue about curricular issues. The broad goals were to encourage substantive discussions of what music graduates should know and be able to do, to foster student choice within rigorous standards, to enhance curricular flexibility and credit allotments, and to respond to change occurring in music outside the academy. In a retreat, faculty had expressed strong desire to transcend the silos of their divisions to discuss schoolwide curricular matters; and so the Executive Committee of the faculty organized flexible faculty-cluster discussions around six topics: individual and collaborative performance; historic, stylistic, theoretical, and cultural understanding; pedagogy and human learning and development; creative studies and collaborative arts; leadership, engagement, and entrepreneurship; and health and human potential. Three clusters met at a time, and faculty could choose which clusters among the six they wished to attend. Executive Committee members led the discussions, recorders took notes, and Executive Committee then reviewed the ideas and suggestions emanating from cluster discussions. These discussions became the basis for a strategic planning process in which the faculty identified major goals and actions for the school's programs.

This first attempt at enlarging curricular dialogue and engaging faculty across specializations met with the usual pros and cons of any effort to inspire creative thinking. However, the leadership provided from within the school's Executive

Committee is an example of how faculty members can become catalysts for discussions about curricular change, track the conversations that emerge, and help to fashion recommendations for curricular change.

Another way of motivating change is through funding incentives that encourage faculty to develop creative curricular approaches. If funding is disbursed for collaborative projects across specializations, then the opportunity for broad-scale curricular change becomes greater. Referencing the University of Minnesota School of Music once more, when funding from its parent unit, the College of Liberal Arts, became competitive among department proposals that showed initiatives for curricular advancement, the School of Music proposed a program entitled Creative Instructional Residency Initiatives (CIRIs). The purpose of CIRIs was to instigate curricular innovation through visiting residencies that would cover or enhance content that could not be covered by resident faculty. The goal was to develop pilot projects that could lay a foundation for sustainability through later full-time programs and positions. Among several worthy ventures, the most successful in terms of sustainability was a collaboration with the Minnesota Opera that has resulted in ongoing and significant artistic development opportunities for voice majors.

If the full transformative impact of the Manifesto is to be realized, however, important dimensions of the change enterprise need to be placed front and center in reform conversations. Research-based theories and principles from the broader literature on change and organizational dynamics must be employed as rigorously in music as they are in contexts where successful change processes have resulted in significant progress.

Assumptions Testing and Substantive Change

The literature on change offers many models for how to approach identifying needs, implementing strategies, and assessing results. Commonly, organizations looking to improve are advised to establish intended outcomes or objectives, implement change strategies, and assess the results or manifestations of change against the stated objectives. Depending on how well the strategies seem to have worked, changes may be adopted permanently (frozen, in Lewin's terms), objectives may be adjusted to accommodate for previously unforeseen conditions or impediments, or the proposed outcomes may be eliminated as viable options. Similarly, strategies themselves may be analyzed for effectiveness and altered in the interest of having another go at desired outcomes. Sometimes, curricular consultants may recommend a preliminary needs assessment to ascertain how faculty and students perceive needs for change and to establish priority goals out of the findings.

Chris Argyris and Donald Schön (1978, 1996; Anderson, 1992) defined this approach to organizational learning and change as "single-loop learning," which they contrast with double-loop learning as part of a broader and more comprehensive change framework. Single-loop learning is behavior-based and is, perhaps, the most commonly assumed method of effecting change. It cycles through goals, objectives, strategies, and assessment on the theory that altering objectives and/or strategies as a result of assessments will lead to changes in individual and organizational behavior that are (in the case of higher education) consistent with elements such as resources, faculty interests, student learning needs, and national standards of achievement.

The difficulty with single-loop learning in terms of substantive change is that it tends to take for granted generalized agreement about present circumstances and outcomes, focusing on technical issues rather than interrogating values, assumptions, and influential variables. Many have referred to such change as curricular "tinkering," which the Manifesto asserts has been the typical result of reform efforts over several decades. Assuming universal agreement on a classical music core and the technical dimensions of classical performance, a single-loop approach might expand diversity content merely by adding courses and credits, might "rethink" performance by changing rehearsal schedules and recital requirements, or might integrate a few improvising or composing exercises, or a few examples of popular or non-Western music into conventional theory classes. This is the kind of lower-level change discourse Ed Sarath addresses in greater detail in Chapter 5.

As an alternative to the single-loop approach, Argyris's and Schön's double-loop learning model takes an important further step. In a double-loop approach, change initiatives begin with a reflective process that involves testing the underlying assumptions on which goals, objectives, and strategies are based. Whereas a single-loop approach focused on lower-level change presents fewer perceived risks for individuals and an organization at large, double-loop learning requires creative and reflexive thinking and involves considerations of greater good. The greater the perceived stakes—as in the radical change proposed by the Manifesto—the more difficult it is for individuals in organizations, i.e., faculty, to engage in double-loop learning and to reflect on the implications of data, theories, values, and assumptions that challenge the status quo. In a single-loop context, decisions are often arrived at by accepting unfounded assertions as fact, by polarizing arguments around a need to "win," and by "defending" practice because it is assumed to be commonly valued. The result is likely to be one of moving *away* from something rather than *toward* something, thus limiting learning and progress (Anderson, 1992). Resonant with Whitehead's assertion about change and order relative to progress, double-loop learning entails a level of reflective scrutiny that is essential to the foundational change the Manifesto advocates. Sarath, in framing his idea of a higher order change discourse in Chapter 5, provides specific examples of single-loop and double-loop change visioning in music studies. Among the many attributes of double-loop inquiry is that it can help alleviate the typical single-loop polarizations that arise when considering convention versus change.

Toward Double-loop Learning as a Change Strategy

Increasing the capacity for double-loop learning among individuals, and thus organizations, must involve careful consideration of the sense of risk and resistance behavior that may arise when long-held assumptions are challenged. Therefore, it is important that change leaders raise substantive issues and questions to invite, rather than stifle, open-ended discussion. They must also develop keen facilitating strategies that encourage the kind of creative and reflexive thinking and respectful sharing necessary in a double-loop approach—and, I would argue, for achieving the kinds of change our students need and deserve.

For example, when faculty leaders seek to engage colleagues in considerations for change, a series of questions might frame discussion of assumptions and values underlying current curricular content. Rather than questions designed to show that change is essential, faculty (and perhaps students) may be more comfortable with low-risk, open-ended questions framed in ways such as the following: How are the musical worlds our graduates will traverse similar to and different from those of 100, 75, 50, and 25 years ago? How likely is it that our graduates will earn at least a portion of their incomes by teaching? In what ways might our graduates find themselves engaged in cross-cultural experiences where knowledge of diverse musics could play a role? What emerging examples exist of ways in which musicians are innovating career opportunities? How are those careers different from those of 100, 50, 25 years ago? How are they similar? What do today's musicians have in common with musicians of the 1600s, 1700s, 1800s, and 1900s? In what ways are they different?

As dialogues develop out of questions such as these, the focus logically moves more directly toward curricular matters. For example, given the multifaceted skills of musicians such as Bach and Mozart, how do composition, improvisation, performance, and scholarship manifest themselves in our students and graduates? Does the time-sequential approach to theoretical understanding based on the common practice period reflect the realities of contemporary music in a global society? Given the varied pathways today's career musicians pursue, is there room for more flexibility and choice in the curriculum? How are the expectations of professional musicians changing, and are our students prepared to be competitive in these regards with graduates of other schools? What might it mean to have musics of diverse cultural and sonic systems embedded into our curriculum in equity with music of the classical Western tradition? How might the "academic" study of music and "performance" studies be integrated in ways that economize curricular time, provide opportunities for a richer palette of music and extramusical studies, particularly in other art forms, and reflect more accurately the process and practice of music in real-world contexts?

Such discussions can be nonthreatening and useful in moving faculty toward thinking about the historic and current assumptions that underlie the curriculum that has characterized higher music education since the evolution of discrete music major programs, as well as the changing assumptions and variables associated with musical and societal evolution, not to mention a fuller understanding of music across cultural and stylistic boundaries. As assumptions about a 21st-century curriculum are derived and clarified, goals for programs, objectives for student learning, strategies to implement change, and assessment of resulting change can move forward.

At this juncture, music faculty can collaboratively make decisions about how much change to tackle at one time. Here is where a strategic plan can be useful in laying out priorities and the sequence in which change might be tested. For example, a group of faculty may be interested in developing an improvisatory sequence that accompanies structured theory classes and integrates the creative, aural, and analytic dimensions of theoretical understanding. Another group may be interested in exploring how musics of multiple traditions may be incorporated into this same set of classes. Or, faculty members might decide to officially structure a division, and/or degree program, around new ideas as a pilot project. This was the thinking behind the Creative Studies and Media Division at the University of Minnesota, which grew out of efforts to integrate improvisation, composition, technology, and cross-arts (i.e., visual arts, dance, theatre) within one interdisciplinary faculty group that represented formerly distinct disciplines, i.e., creativity studies, composition, improvisation, guitar, jazz, and ethnomusicology, but who were interested in holistic program development unified by a common commitment to the study and practice of creativity in multiple dimensions. In a similar vein, the University of Washington's Center for Digital Arts and Experimental Media (DXARTS) was designed to foster the invention of new forms of digital and experimental arts across music and the graphic arts, and involving not only performance but also sound engineering and information technologies. Students of the program go on to work as music and media artists specializing in interactive sonic works, music and virtual/mixed realities, and hybrid pieces that involve video, spatial sound, installation, and performance.

It is important to understand, as the Manifesto makes clear, that there is no one "right" approach to curricular change based on the pillars of creativity, diversity, and integration. Institutions and faculty must find their own right balances consistent with the corpus of faculty interested in change, possible institution-wide initiatives with which the music unit might align (and perhaps from which it can procure funding), and other contextual factors that may influence change efforts. There must be both top-down and bottom-up investment if change is to be impactful across the unit and not just in the classes of one or two professors here and there, valuable as that might be. It must be organic and often requires time for conversations to percolate and spill over into broader discussions of why and how change might benefit not only graduates but the art of music and society as well. And it must be consistent with the missions and goals of institutions in which music units reside; otherwise, change may not receive the backing of important administrators or funding for continuation. But underlying all these conditions is the need for robust and ongoing double-loop inquiry into core assumptions if the resultant change is to move beyond modifications of convention and exemplify the wholesale rebuilding, or at least something clearly in that direction, that the Manifesto advocates.

From a strategic perspective, it will be the job of the unit leader (dean, director, chair) not only to establish conditions for this new kind of conversation but also advance and advocate for the music unit's changes and any associated developments, such as new or revised degrees, agreements with other units relative to interdisciplinary initiatives, or faculty lines to secure lasting change. Tying budget proposals and management to strategic change initiatives is often core to assuring that change can be implemented; and in today's era of fiscal uncertainty, the wise administrator will demonstrate how creative reallocation of resources can contribute to the department's quality and reputation through curriculum change, a strategy that can often lay the foundation for seizing opportunities for new faculty lines when the results become apparent.

Tracking and Evaluating the Impact of Change

Clearly, it behooves a music unit to track carefully the implementation of change, to assure that sufficient support structures are in place, and to document and analyze observable impact. Importantly, change that may alter standard programmatic conventions can be disconcerting to students who are accustomed to lockstep and prescriptive programs. If change incorporates wider student choice in program planning, then advisors must be diligent in working with students to assure cohesive and rigorous programs, even within a culture of flexibility.

In today's higher education climate, assessment of student learning and program evaluations are increasingly important to upper administrators. Unfortunately, many of the standard models for assessment and evaluation do not fit music well, if at all, which means that music faculty and their leaders must develop authentic procedures and instruments that will hopefully fulfill the broader aims of institution-wide assessment and evaluation. A detailed discussion of assessment and evaluation is beyond the scope of this chapter, but clearly there need to be protocols established to assess progress relative to established standards, and to assure the readiness of graduates to fulfill the implicit and explicit promises made to them by their institutions.

In evaluating change, standard metrics such as course enrollments, grades, and targeted assessments like projects, performances, and real-world applications may be useful. In the spirit of the Manifesto, however, is the hope that students would be given increasing opportunities to design creative evidence of learning outcomes in concert with careful advisement by faculty. Students might be encouraged, for example, to think of recitals as culminating capstone projects incorporating creativity, diversity, and integration in novel ways. More attention might be given to portfolio assessment, looking at the ways students' knowledge and skill have evolved over time, and incorporating reflective analyses that give evidence of the extent to which programmatic change has achieved its aims. And of course institutions should endeavor to track graduates to the extent possible, assessing longitudinally how they apply their learning in real-world situations and contexts. Because conventional assessment approaches may be rooted in assumptions that differ from those that underlie new initiatives, the importance of double-loop critical inquiry—on the part of both change agents and colleagues who interpret the results—cannot be overstated.

Conclusion

Curricular change in higher education, particularly at the department or school level, is neither easy nor always comfortable. However, using principles of change outlined in this chapter as well as the Manifesto, and chapters that follow, the fear of change that is endemic among faculty and their leaders can be transformed into genuine excitement for new possibilities. Indeed, the opportunity to fashion curriculums that continue to send generations of students forth to effect meaning and value to society through their art should be one that every institution embraces with vigor.

While the Manifesto urges radical rethinking of the assumptions and practices that evolved in an era of growing professionalization of music and musicians in America and that focused on Western classical music as a societal value, the report also issues a powerful argument for the capacity of this rethinking to revitalize the classical tradition. Ed Sarath sheds further light on this in upcoming chapters. Only through a new conversation, however, that is predicated on identifying key underlying assumptions and principles as described by Argyris and Schön will this expanded yet inclusive vision come to fruition. The bottom line is that today's and tomorrow's graduates will face a very different society, as well as a very different, often highly sophisticated, awareness in that society. This is a society where music is a global phenomenon, rich with both singular and intersecting sonic traditions and expressions that captivate the public's ears and interests. These graduates deserve curriculums and degree programs that assure their readiness to be music leaders in that society.

References

Anderson, L. 1992. *Espoused Theories and Theories-in-Use: Bridging the Gap (Breaking Through Defensive Routines with Organization Development Consultants)*. Unpublished Master's Thesis. University of Queensland, Brisbane.

Argyris, C., and D. Schön. 1978. *Organizational Learning: A Theory of Action Perspective*. Reading, MA: Addison Wesley.

Argyris, C., and D. Schön. 1996. *Organizational Learning II: Theory, Method and Practice*. Reading, MA: Addison Wesley.

ESPN.com staff. 2010, June 4. The Wizard's Wisdom: "Woodenisms." Retrieved from http://espn.go.com/mens-college-basketball/news/story?id=5249709

Freeman, R. 2014. *The Crisis of Classical Music in America: Lessons from a Life in the Education of Musicians*. Lanham, MD: Rowman and Littlefield.

Lewin, K. 1947. Frontiers of Group Dynamics: Concept, Method and Reality in Social Science, Social Equilibria, and Social Change. *Human Relations* 1, 5–41. doi:10.1177/001872674700100103.

Morris, R. 1991. *Process Philosophy and Political Ideology: The Social and Political Thought of Alfred North Whitehead and Charles Hartshorne*. Albany: State University of New York Press.

Porter, M.E., and M.R. Kramer. 2006. Strategy and Society: The Link between Competitive Advantage and Corporate Social Responsibility (December, 2006). [Reprint R0612D]. *Harvard Business Review, HBR Spotlight*.

4

TRANSFORMING MUSIC STUDY FROM ITS FOUNDATIONS

A Manifesto for Progressive Change in the Undergraduate Preparation of Music Majors

Report of the Task Force on the
Undergraduate Music Major

Original Report: November 2014

Copy Edited Version: January 2016

Patricia Shehan Campbell
> University of Washington
> Task Force Convener & President of The College Music Society

David E. Myers
> University of Minnesota, Task Force Chair

Edward W. Sarath
> University of Michigan, Lead Author

Additional Task Force Members:

> Juan Chattah, University of Miami
>
> Lee Higgins, Boston University/York St. John University
>
> Victoria Lindsay Levine, Colorado College
>
> Timothy Rice, University of California, Los Angeles
>
> David Rudge, State University of New York at Fredonia

© 2016 Task Force on the Undergraduate Music Major

Transforming Music Study from Its Foundations:
A Manifesto for Progressive Change in the
Undergraduate Preparation of Music Majors

Report of the Task Force on the Undergraduate Music Major
November 2014

Photo credits:

Page 63 (gongs)—User:FA2010, Wikimedia Commons

Page 66 (guitar)—Tomgally, Wikimedia Commons

Page 68 (violins)—Pf1988, Wikimedia Commons

Page 72 (piano)—Wills16, Wikimedia Commons

EXECUTIVE SUMMARY

In 2013, Patricia Shehan Campbell, President of The College Music Society, appointed a national task force to consider what it means to be an educated musician in the twenty-first century and to make recommendations for progressive change in the undergraduate music major curriculum. Over eighteen months, the task force met to craft a rationale and recommendations for advancing undergraduate preparation of music majors. The Task Force on the Undergraduate Music Major (TFUMM) considered graduates' potential for successful participation and leadership in contemporary and evolving musical cultures. Moreover, given the many challenges and opportunities facing professional musicians today, particularly in the classical music realm, TFUMM considered musicians' roles in public life and how the curriculum might better reflect relevant needs, qualities, knowledge, and skills.

The creative and expressive dimensions of music have been progressing rapidly over the past several decades. Factors include an expanding, interconnected global society with cross-cultural influences and crossover stylistic expressions; performance and production happening in electronic as well as acoustic modes; advances in technology; access to and transmission of music through the internet and digital media; and growing creative impulses for many musicians in the form of improvisatory and compositional endeavors. The task force sees these evolutionary changes in two ways: 1) as untold opportunities for musicians to embrace the ubiquity of music fascination across populations and society; and 2) as a return to fundamentals of musical understanding, craft, and artistic expression that have been largely absent from longstanding models of university music curriculum.

There have been repeated calls for change to ensure that musical curricular content and skill development remain relevant to music outside the academy. The academy, however, has been resistant, remaining isolated and, too frequently, regressive rather than progressive in its approach to undergraduate education. While *surface change* has occurred to some extent through additive means (that is, simply providing more courses, more requirements, and more elective opportunities), *fundamental change* (that is, in priorities, values, perspectives, and implementation) has not occurred. TFUMM has concluded that without fundamental change, traditional music departments, schools, and conservatories could face declining enrollments if sophisticated high school students were to seek music career development outside the often-rarefied environment and curricula characteristic of America's colleges and universities.

Considering observations (by TFUMM and others) regarding dichotomies between "music in the real world" and "music in the academy," TFUMM has fashioned its recommendations on three key pillars necessary to ensure the relevance and rigor of the undergraduate music curriculum. These three pillars are *creativity*, *diversity*, and *integration*.

First, TFUMM takes the position that creativity (defined for purposes of this report as rooted in the ability to improvise and compose) provides a stronger basis for educating musicians than does interpretation (the prevailing model of training performers in the interpretation of existing works). This position does not suggest there is no longer a place for interpretive performance in the emergent vision; but suggests that when this important practice is reintegrated into a foundation of systematic improvisation and composition, new levels of vitality and excellence are possible in the interpretive performance domain. Such an integrated approach will inevitably engage students more fully with the world in which they live and will work.

Second, this integrated approach will fulfill the aims of the second pillar of our recommended curriculum: diversity. Students need to engage with music of diverse cultures and to engage with the ways that creative expression (including movement) underlies music across the globe. TFUMM takes the position that in a global society, students must experience music of diverse cultures, generations, and social contexts through study *and* direct participation. TFUMM believes that to cultivate a genuine, cross-cultural musical and social awareness the music curriculum must be infused with diverse influences, and that the primary locus for cultivation of this awareness is the infusion of diverse influences in the creative artistic voice.

Third, TFUMM asserts that the content of the undergraduate music curriculum must be integrated at deep levels and in ways that advance understanding, interpretive performance, and creativity as a holistic foundation of growth. Thus, integration is the third pillar of our reformed undergraduate curriculum.

In addition to changes within music, teaching and learning are also evolving. Recent research about perception, cognition, and motivation to learn is at odds with much traditional music instruction. TFUMM thus urges that students be more engaged with curricular planning, and that their preparation should fit logically with the likelihood of opportunities for employment. Such professionally focused content might include learning to talk about music as well as to perform it, to share research in understandable ways, to value and engage with diverse constituencies, to develop new models of concert performance that bridge performer–audience barriers, or to lead arts organizations seeking to diversify their audiences.

In line with the three pillars for curriculum change and considerations about teaching and learning, TFUMM offers a series of recommendations for change that encompass every facet of the undergraduate curriculum—from private lessons to large ensembles; from foundational theory and history in the academy to creative, diverse, and integrative applications in career contexts. This report invites those who are committed to enlivening undergraduate music curriculum for the twenty-first century to join with the task force in proposing and implementing change that serves the needs of today's and tomorrow's music majors. Most importantly, TFUMM believes that these changes will serve the greater goals of widespread valuing of and commitment to the role music plays in making us both human and humane.

READING THE REPORT IN CONTEXT

Given the precedents that have guided higher music education in the United States over the past century, TFUMM recognizes that some of the perspectives and recommendations in this report could rouse argument about fundamentals in the education of twenty-first-century musicians. Respectful argument over these issues is a potential means of progress. The task force urges readers to keep in mind the report's goal of engendering important, perhaps crucial, dialogue. The following points can help contextualize the report for local dialogues and actions:

- The report urges curricular considerations founded on the three pillars of creativity, diversity, and integration. Thoroughly defining these concepts would take three documents just as long as this one; therefore, in the interest of brevity, the task force trusts that the definitions emerge clearly from the text. Fleshing out these definitions might, in the future, be essential to implementing TFUMM's proposals.
- Some readers might question whether the report's suggestions on musicianship constitute an attack on the way music theory is currently taught in schools of music. This is not TFUMM's intent. Rather, the task force posits that the teaching of theory, as an integral component of a cohesive undergraduate curriculum, could benefit from continuing dialogue about the change proposed.
- Some readers might feel the report substitutes a current form of hegemony (that of the interpretive performer) with another (the improviser–composer–performer), still leaving other music disciplines (music education and scholarship, for example) on the margins of the undergraduate program. TFUMM, in fact, argues that focusing on creativity, diversity, and integration will bring too-frequently marginalized disciplines into the mainstream curriculum in an organic and necessary way. This is analogous to TFUMM's argument that the proposed model will lead organically to essential encounters with the diverse musics of the world and toward seeking ways to integrate the curriculum around the foundational skills that a musician in the twenty-first

century will need. These skills include the ability to improvise; to compose music relevant to the times; to perform well; to teach effectively; and to think critically about the role of music, realizing all of its contemporary and historical diversity.

- This document argues that African-derived musics, including jazz, offer unparalleled opportunities to fashion the identity of the improviser–composer–performer. TFUMM acknowledges, however, that this potential also exists in European classical music and many folk, popular, and classical traditions from other parts of the world.
- Some might read this document as advocating for a reduction in the number of hours allocated to large ensemble instruction in the curriculum. TFUMM acknowledges that if the underlying principles of this report are adopted, questions of time and credits will inevitably arise—not only for large ensembles, but for all elements of the curriculum. TFUMM is emphatically *not* advocating a one-size-fits-all solution to these sorts of issues. Time and credit issues must be debated and resolved locally.

TFUMM submits this report to The College Music Society and to the profession of higher music education as a whole, in hopes of catalyzing robust conversations, encouraging curricular innovations, and undertaking the difficult but rewarding work of programmatic change. We believe the time has come to ensure the ongoing well-being of our students, our institutions, and the art of music that we all love.

PREAMBLE

This report of The College Music Society Task Force on the Undergraduate Music Major (TFUMM) represents a strong consensus among the members of the task force on the need for fundamental change in the undergraduate music curriculum, on some basic principles for a new approach to music curricula in the twenty-first century, and on pathways for implementing these recommendations in the future.

TFUMM expresses gratitude to Ed Sarath for taking on the burden of being the primary writer of this document, with content and editorial input from the TFUMM members.

CONTENTS

EXECUTIVE SUMMARY 49
    Reading the Report in Context 51
PREAMBLE 52
WHAT DOES IT MEAN TO BE AN EDUCATED
    MUSICIAN IN THE 21ST CENTURY? 54
I. WHY THE CMS TASK FORCE? 57
    Problems and Solutions: Three Core Pillars for Reform 58
    Creativity 58
    Diversity 60
    Integration 61
II. WIDE-RANGING PRACTICAL STRATEGIES 63
    Pathways to Change I: Institutional Level 64
        Strategy 1: New Conversations 65
        Strategy 2: Self-Organizing (Bottom-Up) Mechanisms 67
        Strategy 3: Institution-Driven (Top-Down) Approaches 69
        Summary of Institutional-level Initiatives 81
    Pathways to Change II: National/International 81
        Change Consortium 82
        Change Conferences 82
        New Accreditation Protocols: NASM 82
III. CONCLUSION: A CALL FOR LEADERSHIP 83
SUMMARY OF RECOMMENDATIONS FOR CHANGE 84

WHAT DOES IT MEAN TO BE AN EDUCATED MUSICIAN IN THE 21ST CENTURY?

What are the central issues related to being a musician in the 21st century? How might they compare with issues raised a generation or even a century ago? How might one assess the litany of appeals for reform of music in higher education that have arisen over the past 50 years? Have these appeals generated substantive strides forward or merely rearranged the curricular surface? What contributions can music study make to broader educational and societal issues, including cultural diversity, multidisciplinary understanding, transdisciplinary understanding, and ecological and cultural sustainability and social justice?

In 2013, College Music Society President Patricia Shehan Campbell charged the Task Force on the Undergraduate Music Major (TFUMM) with critical examination of these and related questions about the state of college- and university-level music study. It was her belief (as well as others') that the world into which today's students will graduate is vastly different from the world around which the field has typically been conceived. Contemporary musical practices beyond the academy are often centered on creative, cross-cultural engagement and synthesis emblematic of the societies in which those practices flourish; yet contemporary, tertiary-level music study (with interpretive performance and analysis of European classical repertory at its center) remains lodged in a cultural, aesthetic, and pedagogical paradigm that is notably out of step with this broader reality.

Following a year and a half of consultation, TFUMM has concluded that fundamental overhaul of university-level music study is necessary to bridge the divide between academic music study and the musical world into which our students and students of future years will graduate. TFUMM views the following themes as central when considering this fundamental overhaul: 1) the essential purpose of music study, 2) the nature of foundational musical experiences and understandings, and 3) the content and delivery of a relevant yet rigorous curriculum that prepares students for musical engagement and leadership in an age of unprecedented excitement and avenues for growth. TFUMM believes that nothing short of rebuilding the conventional music education model from its foundations will suffice for preparation of 21st-century musicians.

Significant change is essential if we are to bridge the divide between academic music study and the musical world into which our students and the students of future years will graduate.

Understandably, a call for paradigmatic change might evoke concern about compromised integrity or achievement in conventional areas, or about the potential devaluing of the European tradition. TFUMM takes the opposite position: The creative, diverse, and integrated model it recommends will yield new levels of rigor, excellence, meaning, and transformative vitality in both conventional and newer areas of music study. Rather than subordinating the European tradition, TFUMM advocates a close critical reading of this tradition. A close reading will reveal that the European tradition is grounded in an integrated and creative process that includes, among its most revered practitioners, the skills of improvisation, composition, and performance, and in some cases theorizing and pedagogy. This collection of skills is precisely what is needed to navigate and flourish professionally in today's infinite array of culturally diverse music. If Bach, Beethoven, Mozart, Schumann, and Liszt were alive today, their musical lives would more likely resemble today's creative jazz artists (and other improvisers–composers–performers) than the interpretive performance specialists whose repertory was created in and for another time and place. From this standpoint, the longstanding conventional model of music study in vogue throughout tertiary programs actually represents a departure from the European classical tradition. TFUMM proposes a return to the authentic roots of this heritage in a way that is relevant for current musical lives. The kind of contemporary, creative exploration and synthesis that TFUMM proposes is not antithetical to traditional grounding or deep musical understanding. Rather it enhances and reinforces artistic rigor, authenticity, and relevance. For these reasons, TFUMM is committed to new, more inclusive, critical levels of change discourse.[1]

This document summarizes the key issues reviewed by TFUMM and invites further dialogue and action in response to its recommendations. Part I provides a rationale for the TFUMM project, articulates the basic tenets of the TFUMM vision, and situates it within the long legacy of appeals for change in the field, elaborating how its wide-ranging and provocative scope differs from prior reform initiatives.

Part II recommends practical strategies to be implemented by those committed to charting new terrain and assuming leadership in the broad transformation of the field that is envisioned. Both local/institutional and national/international strategies are addressed. Although TFUMM advocates systemic change, we also recognize challenges inherent in this project; thus, we delineate a range of strategies that could drive both

---

[1] Argyris's and Schön's notion of "double-loop learning"—where institutional change efforts penetrate to the very assumptions on which goals, objectives, and strategies are based—is instructive. Double-loop learning embodies elevated critical scrutiny and the potential to circumvent typical polarizations between convention and change, even when foundational transformation of the type TFUMM recommends is at play. (Argyris, C., and Schön, D. 1978. *Organizational Learning: A Theory of Action Perspective*. Reading MA: Addison Wesley.)

incremental and larger scale changes within this vision.

> ... the longstanding conventional model of music study in vogue throughout tertiary programs actually represents a radical departure from the European classical tradition. TFUMM proposes a return to the authentic roots of this heritage...

Part III concludes the document with an emphasis on the extraordinary opportunity that awaits those individuals and institutions that are driven by a love for all music, a pioneering spirit, and the courage to forge new vistas in music study that are appropriate to the present moment in musical practice and society.

TFUMM hopes that readers of this report will share the optimism and excitement about the possibilities inherent in its recommendations. It is time for academic music study to take its next evolutionary strides and to produce a new generation of artist-visionaries who will contribute a transformative worldview for 21st-century life.

I. WHY THE CMS TASK FORCE?

Over the past half century, thoughtful musicians and educators have examined the state of music in a wide array of educational contexts and discussed instructional experiences of greatest value for developing musicians—musicians who perform, invent, analyze, interpret, and facilitate music in the lives of others. These discussions led to proposed reforms of musical study. Some of the key "moments" in this ongoing discussion include The Young Composers Project (1959–1962), The Yale Seminar (1962), the Contemporary Music Project (1963–1973), the Comprehensive Musicianship Project (1965–1971), the Manhattanville Music Curriculum Project (1966–1970), the Tanglewood Symposium (1967), the Music in General Studies—A Wingspread Conference (1981), the Multicultural Music Education Symposium (1990), the National Standards for the Arts–Music (1994), and the National Core Music Standards (2014). Various documents from these gatherings have declared pathways to improve ways of teaching and learning music. The National Association of Schools of Music 2010 report, "Creative Approaches to the Undergraduate Curriculum," raises some useful questions for thinking about curriculum leadership and potential change.[2] K–12 school music transformation is the target of many of these efforts, but they also resonate at the tertiary level where preparing music majors for careers that include teaching is a significant thrust of activity.

In light of this long line of reform efforts, why the need for yet another initiative? The answer is simple: despite these past efforts, change has been confined largely to surface adjustments—what might be best characterized as "curricular tinkering"—at the expense of the systemic, foundational overhaul that is necessary. This is not to deny the emergence of coursework and programs that appear to bridge the gulf between academic and real world musical engagement—programs in jazz, ethnomusicology, world music performance, music technology, popular music, community music, music business, entrepreneurship, and other areas. Nor is it to ignore the inventories that identify courses that need to be added to an already full curriculum. Rather, it is to acknowledge that these and other additive attempts at change have left the conventional curricular and cultural core largely intact, and left newer areas on the periphery.

> New offerings atop an unchanging foundation has not only placed additional stress on the conventional curricular foundations, but has reified the divide between music study and real-world musical practice.

---

[2] For an excellent survey of various reform initiatives, see Mark, M. and C. Gary (2007). *A History of American Music Education*. Lanham, MD: Rowman & Littlefield.

Bruno Nettl observed that while musical academe has expanded the range of music studied within its borders, it has not significantly enabled the majority of students to access that range.[3] Nor has the academy taken to heart the multidisciplinary nature of the musical experience that embraces artistic expression, behaviors, and values that manifest themselves with dance and dramatic expression in cultures across the globe.

The recognition of the need for greater breadth in music training is not new, but effective ways to achieve that breadth have been elusive. Indeed, it might be argued that the scattering of new offerings atop an unchanging foundation (which was never designed to support engagement beyond the European tradition) has not only placed additional stress on the conventional curricular foundations, but has also reified the divide between music study and real-world music practice. TFUMM brings to the change endeavor not only great appreciation for prior efforts but also a keen critical analysis of their shortcomings, new principles upon which a new model can be built, and an unprecedented range of practical strategies (both institutional and national/international in scope) through which the new vision might become a reality.

PROBLEMS AND SOLUTIONS: THREE CORE PILLARS FOR REFORM

TFUMM identifies three core deficiencies in the conventional model of music study, and in response, three core pillars emerge for an entirely new framework. The first core deficiency is sub–ordination of the creation of new work to the interpretive performance of older work; the second is ethnocentrism; and the third is fragmentation of subjects and skills. When these tendencies are reversed, the three core pillars of a transformed model come into view: creativity, diversity, and integration.

CREATIVITY

One of the most startling shortcomings in all of arts education is that too many music students graduate with little to no experience or significant grounding in the essential creative processes of improvisation and composition. In contrast, students majoring in the visual arts could not gain a degree without producing a portfolio of original creative work. Yet for music graduates, a lack of skill or even cursory experience in composition and improvisation is the norm rather than the exception.[4] Ironically, although

---

[3] Nettl, B. (1995). *Heartland Excursions: Ethnomusicological Reflections on Schools of Music.* Urbana: University of Illinois Press.

[4] This analogy is not made oblivious to the absence of a parallel in the visual arts to interpretive performance in music, which in itself represents a subset of the broader and more foundational creative spectrum that TFUMM values. Nevertheless, it is also important to note the conspicuous absence of primary creative engagement, which improvising and composing embody.

appeals for inclusion of the arts in education are often grounded in the need to cultivate creativity in all students, music study has long been predicated on the subordination of creativity to technical proficiency and interpretive performance.

Over the past decade and a half, faculty, institutions, and organizations concerned with higher music education have made important efforts to incorporate more creative experience and diverse musical styles into the curriculum. Faculty advocating change have represented every field of music, including theory, musicology/ethnomusicology, performance, and music education. Most agree, however, that resulting advances have not permeated the overall curriculum as widely as might be hoped, and that continuing work is essential.

Improvising and composing are common in many change appeals, particularly at the pre-collegiate level, but recommendations are usually framed through an additive lens. The existing foundation remains largely inflexible, and provision for core creative experiences is limited to remaining space. TFUMM takes the critical step of advocating that the entire music study enterprise should be rebuilt around systematic approaches to these creative processes.[5]

> *One of the most startling shortcomings in all of arts education is that too many music students graduate with little to no experience in the essential creative processes of improvisation and composition.*

A systematic program of improvisation study may unite multiple improvisatory languages, including style-specific (for example, jazz, Hindustani, or European classical) and stylistically open approaches. Such study would provide for creative exploration and analysis and reflection on a wide range of modal-tonal-post-tonal pitch systems[6] and rhythmic practices. At the same time, studies could embrace training in aural performance, movement processes, history, culture, aesthetics, cognition, and mind-body integration. The development of technical skill and knowledge required for expert improvisatory development has ramifications for both conventional interpretive performance and contemporary musical explorations. Systematic composition studies that intertwine European-tradition concert music practices with songwriting approaches from popu-

---

[5] For more on systematic approaches to improvisation and composition, see Sarath, E. (2013). *Improvisation, Creativity, and Consciousness: Jazz as Integral Template for Music, Education, and Society.* Albany, NY: SUNY.

[6] Here and throughout the document, the modal-tonal-post-tonal spectrum aims toward the wide-ranging pitch systems that derive from European classical, jazz, popular, and other genres. Though the post-tonal portion of this spectrum might most immediately elicit associations with twelve-tone and other atonal strategies that evolved in 20th century European-inspired composition, of equal if not greater importance are the use of octatonic, whole-tone, bitonal, and other practices that do not fall readily into modal or tonal categories.

lar music and small and large ensemble jazz composition strategies expand the creative process spectrum in ways that are relevant to both traditional and contemporary music.

> . . .improvisation and composition uniquely promote assimilation of influences from the musical landscape into the emergent artistic voice, thereby enabling levels of intimacy, meaning, and understanding that are not possible when interpretive performance alone is the prescribed mode of engagement. . .

Therefore, TFUMM seeks to restore improvisation and composition to their rightful, foundational status, not by subordinating performance and analysis, but by rendering the entire scope of music study as a creative and highly-skilled endeavor. Some readers might misinterpret our position as the replacing of one form of hegemony, that of the interpretive performer, with another, that of the improviser–composer–performer, still leaving the study of music education and music scholarship on the margins. In fact, the task force holds that pursuing a curriculum that encourages improvising, composing, and performing will bring now-marginalized disciplines into the mainstream of music study in an organic and necessary way. The proposed approach has the capacity to promote new levels of vitality and excellence in interpretive performance. It also yields a framework conducive to a range of areas currently underrepresented in the curriculum. One example might be the embodied nature of musical engagement. Embodied engagement has roots in the inextricable link between music, dance, ritual, and dramatic expression that is central to cultures across the globe, and we are seeing a revival in mind-body interest in contemporary society. TFUMM believes that cultivation of the experience of music as a whole-body phenomenon is essential to a broader conception of musical knowing and expression.

DIVERSITY

The second deficiency is the ethnocentric orientation of music studies, which carries enormous societal ramifications. Once rectified, the resulting change opens important avenues of learning. Similar to the gap noted in creativity, large numbers of music majors graduate with little or no hands-on engagement with music beyond European classical repertory, let alone the cultivation of a genuine global artistic identity, which TFUMM believes is central to musical life and responsible citizenship. The extent of the problem is underscored by the fact that music majors commonly spend many years on campus without even a nod to the multicultural communities surrounding them, and that practitioners from these communities are rarely invited to engage with university students of music. Moreover, this ethnocentric lapse occurs on campuses where commitment to diversity and equality are regularly articulated by the administration, and where robust diversity discourse pervades the humanities and social sciences. The dichotomy between administrative rhetoric and curricular reality underscores the as institutional nature of the problem. TFUMM views the culturally narrow horizons of music study as nothing short of a social justice crisis.

So, complementary to the call for a creativity-based curriculum, TFUMM urges that engagement occur within a cultural expanse that is as broad as possible. Within this expanded context, it will be important to distinguish between contact with the global nature of the musical world through an identity as an interpretive performance specialist and contact through the identity of a contemporary improviser–composer–performer. The latter identity incorporates capacities for assimilation and synthesis of diverse influences that nurture intimate connections, rather than a distanced fascination, with the rich diversity of the musical world.

Analyses of the creative process illuminate how improvisation and composition uniquely promote assimilation of influences from the musical landscape into the emergent artistic voice. Thereby levels of intimacy, meaning, and understanding are enabled that are not possible when interpretive performance is the lone mode of engagement.

TFUMM's point is *not* to cast improvisation and composition over music performance (or analysis), nor to deny that creativity is possible in all forms of musical engagement and inquiry. TFUMM's purpose is to achieve a framework in which optimal levels of creativity and excellence are reached in all areas. TFUMM believes that a creativity-based foundation rooted in improvisation and composition study is particularly conducive to this optimal balance.

A creativity-based foundation is key to moving beyond the challenges and allure of what has sometimes been called the "multicultural marketplace," which is characterized by superficial contact with a "bit of this and a bit of that," and achieving an authentic transcultural understanding that is the basis for an entirely new diversity paradigm. When contact with diverse cultures informs and is informed by the emergent creative voice, it can open students to deep celebration and embrace.

INTEGRATION

The third primary deficiency of both the present curricular framework and prior reform attempts is pervasive fragmentation within the curriculum and organization of music schools. As an antidote, TFUMM endorses an expanded model of integration.

In the conventional curricular model, performance studies are separated from theoretical studies, both of which are taught separately from historical and cultural inquiry. A fractured conception of music is thus promoted, as a collection of discrete "silos" or compartments. Proposed solutions have typically been piecemeal, as for example in exhortations that music performed in ensembles should be studied in theory and history classes. TFUMM believes these partial strategies might actually perpetuate the problem of fragmentation by reinforcing a limited terrain within which integration is sought. The fact that past attempts have rarely yielded significant gains underscores the limitations inherent in a piecemeal strategy.

Previous efforts to unite theory, history, and performance have thus recognized only a limited slice of the 21st-century musical skill and aptitude set. When creativity is recognized as *core* to the overall spectrum of music study, the model is considerably expanded and gains a basis for unprecedented unification across every facet of musical study. Improvisation and composition contain aspects of performance, theory, aural skills, rhythm, embodied engagement, and historical, cultural, and aesthetic inquiry. The synergistic interplay can be harnessed in new curricular models and integrated in ways that give rise to a host of other important outcomes and areas of study. These outcomes might include heightened capacities for critical thinking, self-sufficiency, community music linkages, entrepreneurship, and an understanding of the relationship of music to broader issues.

If genuine integration has been elusive within the narrow horizons of conventional models, the vastly expanded set of culturally-diverse and cross-disciplinary skills and understandings called for in our time renders this essential educational component all the more challenging.

Genuine integration has been elusive within the narrow horizons of conventional models. This essential educational component is rendered even more challenging in the face of the vastly expanded set of skills and understandings called for in the 21st century. In advancing a creativity-based paradigm, as opposed to additive strategies that might incorporate creativity, TFUMM sets its proposal apart from prior reform appeals and resolves the paradox between diversity and integration.

II. WIDE-RANGING PRACTICAL STRATEGIES

TFUMM recognizes the challenges associated with implementing practical solutions to problems in the current undergraduate curriculum and so offers a range of change strategies unprecedented in previous calls for change.

One challenge involves engagement with broad constituencies in and beyond the field of music study. Curricular overhaul cannot occur in isolation; it must involve the many populations that influence and are influenced by it. In music this includes K–12 teachers, principals, and superintendents, all of whom potentially play key roles in shaping how musical artists and artist-teachers are educated at the tertiary level. In the realm of higher education leadership, deans (beyond music), provosts, presidents, chancellors, and regents represent another constituency typically not included in the dialogue that could significantly impact change in music study. Music students, practicing professional artists, and arts organizations are additional constituencies to be included in the multi-tiered dialogue advanced by TFUMM.

It is important to recognize that turbulence is inherent to change.

To be sure, the TFUMM vision and this report do, at times, assume an activist tone that might feel unfamiliar or disquieting to some readers. Though the report is not intended to elicit these reactions, it is important to recognize that turbulence—as Thomas Kuhn has elaborated in his study of paradigmatic change in the sciences[7]—is inherent to the change process. TFUMM thus reaches out to those who sense a need for change, who believe that change is possible, and who desire to find a way forward through the dynamic, sometimes even tumultuous, interplay between creative exploration and rigorous grounding in musical knowledge and skill. Inasmuch as music is ubiquitous across the globe and that few, if any, cultures are not enriched by the creative syncretism that increasingly defines the planetary musical landscape, TFUMM believes that music study informed by a commitment to creativity, diversity, and integration has the capacity to transform the world. We believe in the important role music making plays in addressing social, cultural, political,

---
[7] Kuhn, T. (1962). *The Structure of Scientific Revolutions*. Chicago: University of Chicago Press.

economic, and ecological issues facing the world today.

Following are strategies rooted in this vision. Pathways to Change I conveys strategies that might be pursued at the local institutional level. Pathways to Change II presents strategies to be implemented on broader, national or international scales.

PATHWAYS TO CHANGE I: INSTITUTIONAL LEVEL

To overcome the inertia of established programs and cultures dominated by interpretive performance and study of European classical music, a new integrated program—replete with creativity and diversity and still including the treasures of European heritage—will require not only curricular overhaul but new ways of thinking, conversing, and forging strategic initiatives.

TFUMM recommends three kinds of change activities at the institutional level: initiate ongoing conversations, establish self-organizing mechanisms, and deploy designs for new courses.

- Initiate an ongoing conversation committed to critical scrutiny of both conventional and alternative models of music study. If needed reform is to come to fruition, it is important that such conversations take place within traditionally organized governance mechanisms (such as curriculum committees) and in a range of other formats. Other formats could include faculty-student reflective groups, cluster discussions, task forces, or forums all charged with study, serious reflection, and critical thinking regarding curricular and instructional issues.
- Establish self-organizing mechanisms whereby dynamic and critical approaches to conservation and change become intrinsic to institutional discourse and behavior. The option-rich curriculum is a key example of such a mechanism; in it students—and by extension, faculty—are given latitude and responsibility for charting their own pathways. If an institution faces resistance to opening student options, enhanced options might initially be established within an existing program frame, much like charter schools operate within the K-12 system. TFUMM views provisions for options as "bottom-up" strategies, in that the changes are generated from the student level.
- Deploy carefully considered, "top down" (institution driven) designs for new courses and curriculums.

TFUMM advocates that institutions explore bottom-up and top-down approaches in tandem, so the transformative impact of each informs the other. In the following sections we provide some examples of applications. In doing so, TFUMM does not presume to prescribe particular manifestations to be followed in every detail. Rather, TFUMM views its primary contribution to be the articulation of core principles; applications are identified to illustrate the principles, not to prescribe a universal pathway. In keeping with its advocacy for creativity in student learning, TFUMM urges institutions to be creative in their adoption of the principles, particularly relative to each institution's distinctive identity. The interplay of top-down and bottom-up approaches is therefore advanced as a principle under which any number of applications may be possible.

TFUMM is advocating wide-scale reform, but recognizes that change typically happens incrementally. Institutions are encouraged to take what steps they can. However, TFUMM also challenges institutions to think carefully about differences between small steps that merely add to the prevailing model and incur arguments that the curriculum is already too full, and small steps that are taken with an entirely new paradigm in sight. By keeping in mind the far-reaching vision TFUMM has set forth, even the smallest steps forward will be imbued with meaning, purpose, and direction.

Strategy 1: New Conversations

Change in practice requires change in thinking. Essential to this change is a sustained level of critical discourse that penetrates to the foundational premises of TFUMM's recommendations. Discussions should probe how TFUMM's premises might inform the conventional model and alternative approaches. The following guiding questions may help elevate the level of critical discourse and set the stage for corresponding change.

- What does it mean to be an educated individual in the 21st century?
- What does it mean to be an educated, reflective musician in the 21st century?
- What are the justifications for placing creativity and creative development front and center in programs?
- In this global age and society, what justifications exist for infusing global practices and inquiry in music curricula?
- How can programs thrive in contexts that proffer impassioned pronouncements of diversity and social justice if they fail to embrace the diversity of the broader musical world, especially nearby music communities?
- How might some longstanding musical worldviews constrain thinking about change and approaches to change?
- What worldviews, both existing and evolving, might enlarge and enrich visions for music study?
- Why, after over 50 years of appeals for reform, have we not witnessed more substantive curricular change in music?
- Why did the improviser–composer–performer identity that prevailed earlier in the European tradition give way to the interpretive performance specialist identity? What would a curriculum look like that was built around the return of the first profile? How might that curriculum enhance excellence and vitality in conventional approaches to music making? In what ways might it be essential to the future of European classical music?
- What impact might Cartesian mind-body dualism have on the

fragmentation of mind and body, as well as on the curriculum, in conventional music study? How might this fragmentation be replaced by a holistic approach to musical experience with multiple modalities for physical engagement and disciplinary synthesis? How might the African concept of *ngoma* (in which the links between musical sound, dance, dramatic expression, and ritual are inextricable) inform a new model of music study?

- What would it look like to organize a music school or department around comprehensive creative, diverse, and integrated values (including interpretive performance) as opposed to the current scheme centralized on interpretive performance and the analysis and sociocultural understanding of interpretive performance?

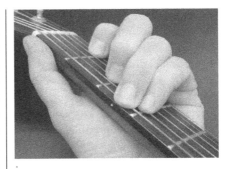

These questions will elicit reflection, insights, and potential receptivity to substantive change. Those responses will be enhanced when discourse is grounded in related literature. Although relevant research on music learning and cognition may not be a typical part of curriculum committee deliberations or faculty conversations about music learning, a wide range of resources is available and could elevate the critical integrity of these deliberations. The literature includes qualitative and quantitative studies on learning and music learning, neurocognitive research that supports hands-on and integrative approaches to learning, a growing body of diversity literature, and history of reform movements in music study and education at large. Critical examination of conventional and alternative models of music learning through many lenses—scope, integration, diversity, self-sufficiency, embodied musicianship, use of terminology and language—can also elevate the level and integrity of change discourse.

Close attention to various approaches to paradigmatic change is also in order. The following questions can further that discussion.

- How will the kind of transformation called for in this report manifest itself?
- Will change entail wholesale redesign of every course, or might it involve a redistribution of subject matter already in place, with perhaps some bottom-up new design?
- Will change require the immediate transformation of an entire school or department, or might it begin with the establishment of pilot tracks that embody new principles?
- Will emphasis be given to content and process in large-scale programmatic transformation as well as in individual classes, rehearsals, and studio sessions?

- What are the benefits and drawbacks to top-down (institution driven) strategies and bottom-up (student driven) strategies?
- What are the benefits and drawbacks of allowing faculty from diverse areas to offer coursework that fulfills core requirements typically taught by specialists in those areas?

Strategy 2: Self-Organizing (Bottom-Up) Mechanisms

Provisions for students to navigate their own curricular pathways have taken hold in many areas of the academy, but are still foreign to conventional music study. Such provisions have also eluded significant attention in music reform discourse. TFUMM, however, views curricular strategies incorporating options as a powerful means for enhancing musical and personal growth, particularly when situated within the proposed three-pronged change protocol. The bottom-up reform endorsed here should not be an isolated strategy; it should be implemented in conjunction with top-down, institution-driven approaches that involve new course and curriculum design and, potentially, new school-wide requirements.

In a musical world bustling with change, we must question curricular frameworks that limit students' responsibility for their own development and for their exploration of music in real-world contexts. When students are given options, they think more critically about who they are as individuals, as aspiring artists, and as learners. Moreover, when institutions allow students more options, conditions are created that enliven faculty creativity as faculty design new classes to meet new student interests. This may in turn enliven important self-monitoring capacities within the institution. Option-deficient curricular models guarantee full enrollments regardless of the relevance or vitality of the classes that are offered; however, option-rich frameworks usher in new parameters of accountability as students choose to enroll in more relevant and vital classes. These approaches can also help decentralize curricular authority by blurring boundaries between disciplinary areas when newly formed student/faculty constituencies engage in creative problem solving related to class offerings.

It is important to emphasize that students and faculty inclined toward conventional pathways will retain the capacity to pursue those pathways. "Options" does not mean obliteration of what is currently in place; it simply addresses the need for diversification and enhances students' ownership around whatever pathways they choose. Provision for options enhances student ownership and sense-of-being around whatever pathways they may choose, as opposed to having limiting pathways imposed upon their learning. Empowering students to discover their own learning styles and artistic aims and to chart their developmental pathways accordingly must be considered among today's most important educational goals, regardless of discipline. When students are empowered, powerful interior connections with knowledge areas can be enlivened; and, again, knowledge areas may include

conventional and unconventional realms. The result will be levels of meaning and rigor that exceed the current institution-driven format. TFUMM identifies three option-rich strategies for bottom-up curricular change.

Streamlining

One involves reducing the number of core requirements and allowing students greater latitude in the space that is opened up. TFUMM prefers the term *streamlining* to *reducing*, because reducing suggests students might be gaining less grounding than needed when, in fact, the proposed framework may result in equal or even greater grounding. For example, if the typical two to three years of core theory and music history coursework are streamlined into a one-year core in each area, students could then use the remaining credits to pursue further studies. Students might choose the same previously required coursework in theory and history, but they would now select it from an expanded slate of options. Their chosen curriculum might include coursework that covers important theoretical and historical terrain offered by faculty or areas not typically associated with these areas, for example opera faculty teaching theoretical content based on operatic examples or an ethnomusicologist teaching temporally parallel developments in Western European and Indian music. Carefully designed proficiency protocols for core musicianship areas (delineated with contemporary creative and diverse aims in mind) would help to render approaches that balance choice with developing high degrees of rigor and skill.

Similar flexibility can be implemented in private lessons and ensembles. The systematic and systemic change endorsed by TFUMM calls for critical examination of every facet of the curriculum as a potential gateway to broader, more creative, diverse, and integrated artistry. Guidelines for appropriate distributions of requirements might remain the same within an area, but students would enjoy an enhanced array of opportunities for fulfilling requirements. Students' opportunities would, of course, be somewhat dependent on faculty expertise and willingness to forge new territory with students.

Departmental Determination of Requirements

A second, closely related option-rich strategy involves individual departments or faculty areas being able to determine their own curricular requirements. For example, music education faculty, who best know the needs of music education majors, would be able to determine the curriculum for their students from the core level on up. An important byproduct of this plan would involve provisions for faculty to design the coursework they feel is needed for their students.

Student Proposed Pathways

The third strategy is perhaps the most radical approach within the option-rich protocol. It is intended as a complement to the top-down department- or division-driven approaches. This approach involves allowing students to deviate even from departmental/divisional constraints by assembling a committee of three faculty members to consult, review, and approve a student's proposed pathway. This approach represents a second-tier decentralization that further empowers students to critically examine their needs, and it impels faculty to critically examine their curricular predilections. When implemented in conjunction with expanded provisions for fulfilling and assessing newly conceived core requirements, this provision could be highly fruitful for a given student's artistic evolution.

ॐ

To be sure, the proposed approach is not without potential limitations, and thus TFUMM advocates it as one among a battery of approaches that also includes top-down, institution-driven modalities. For synergistic interplay between these approaches to be productive, difficult questions must be placed front and center in discussions. For example, in musicianship studies that are predicated on sequential skill development typically approached in four (or more) semester sequences, the idea of allowing students to pursue alternative pathways might appear particularly problematic. However, the following questions should be kept in mind: How effective is the present musicianship coursework in terms of enduring, meaningful assimilation of conventional content? How well does it prepare students with the broader slate of creative and culturally diverse abilities called for in today's world?

TFUMM's position is that the numbers of students and faculty expressing concerns about core musicianship suggests that allowing students greater capacity to chart their own pathways might be an essential part of the broader slate of change strategies.[8]

Strategy 3: Institution-Driven (Top-Down) Approaches

Bottom-up, student-driven reform should be complemented by institution-mediated strategies. The design of new courses and curricular pathways are central to top-down strategies. A newly conceived musicianship core, new degree programs, and new courses need to embody the creativity-based, diverse, and integrative nature of contemporary musical practice, which is captured in the TFUMM platform.

---

[8] These concerns around conventional musicianship models may pertain to the absence of effective pedagogy and relevant materials; the focus on harmonic practices of distant eras at the exclusion of melody, rhythm, and harmony in contemporary contexts; the lack of thoughtful mind-body integration; or to aural training that is non-sequential yet locked into mundane and non-musical exercises or disconnected from meaningful experiences in music.

New Core Skills and Understandings

A contemporary vision of musicianship requires a new foundation. Delineating what this vision might look like requires, first, a brief overview of the conventional core curriculum for music majors. The conventional core typically includes the following elements.

- 2–3 years of music theory coursework that focuses on harmony, counterpoint, and form in European common practice repertory
- 2 or more years of music history coursework that is similarly oriented toward European heritage
- Private instruction during each term in residence that focuses on developing interpretive performance skills in European or European-derived repertory
- Ensembles, with emphasis on large, conducted groups, that prepare a European-derived repertory for public performance (generally required during each term in residence)
- Piano classes that provide students with rudimentary facility at the keyboard (TFUMM views this as important, even while encouraging critical consideration of the practical functionality of the skills learned in these classes.)

Integrative approaches that might include eurhythmic movement and dance need to be regularly featured as potential pedagogical pathways to the holistic understanding of music.

While all of the listed experiences may be of value, it is important to recognize the large array of experiences and developments often not represented in the core that are equally valuable, and that are, in some instances, more foundational for 21st-century musicianship. Improvisation, composition, hands-on contact with music of diverse traditions, embodied musical practices, and contemporary rhythmic studies are a few key areas, and all need to be approached in integrative ways. These experiences can provide the basis of a case for the new curricular foundation that is as strong as arguments in support of the conventional model. TFUMM does not view this as an either-or scenario, however. It is an opportunity to arrive at a new foundation that fulfills conventional and emergent needs. Key to that opportunity is identification of principles that underlie a new core curriculum and infiltrate all coursework:

- Creative, hands-on, integrative, and culturally diverse engagement with contemporary music of many kinds,
- inquiry into the past through the lens of the present,
- balance between creative exploration and rigorous development of craft,
- mind-body integration,
- rhythmic studies informed by contemporary, globally-informed practice,
- community engagement, and
- technological applications.

Close linkages between aural, rhythmic, and embodied modalities (situated within broader integrative models that unite creative, performative, theoretical, historical, and cultural engagement) must be emphasized for their potential in constructing a new musicianship core. In this new approach, aural musicianship needs to be emphasized as much as visual literacy. Integrative approaches that might include eurhythmic movement and dance need to be regularly featured as potential pedagogical pathways to the holistic understanding of music, such that music may be deeply known through physical encounters that achieve the integration of ear, body, and brain.

Careful rethinking of coursework that is typically presumed to provide the basic aural and analytic tools required by all musicians (regardless of career aspiration) may be a fertile gateway that opens up to the proposed vision. Writing Bach-style, four-part compositions has long been presumed to be the primary source for skills in tonal harmonic practice. The effectiveness of this approach and its narrow horizons need to be carefully reassessed from a contemporary, creative vantage point. Despite changes advanced in some theory texts and in pedagogical classroom applications, theory and aural skills are still often perceived as divorced from one another, from performance, and from music history, thus providing impetus for rethinking these facets. The impetus for rethinking takes on a new urgency when the goal is expanded from a specialized interpretive performance within a monocultural repertory to globally informed, improvisation, composition, performance. The point is not to suggest that a conventional approach to music theory should bear the brunt of reform criticism, but to emphasize that if music study is to align itself with the diverse horizons of the musical world, all areas of the curriculum will need to be examined. And basic musicianship—by its very foundational nature—may well require considerable attention. TFUMM is optimistic that powerful new models of musicianship can emerge from this reexamination process, models that are consistent with TFUMM's overarching commitment to the integration of conventional areas within an expanded scope.

Though delineating specific course content in response to these points is beyond TFUMM's scope, we encourage thoughtful consideration about potential openings to a broader foundation in musicianship. For example, a particularly fertile opening could be the prominence of black music in American culture and in global musical practices. Christopher Small's work has been especially influential in ethnomusicology and music education; he emphasizes African and African American models of "musicking"[9]—with their limitless diasporic expressions,

---

[9] Small, C. (1987). *Music of the Common Tongue*. London: Calder Riverrun. (Patricia Shehan Campbell conveys from a personal conversation with Small toward the end of his life that of his three books, this one uniquely captures the heart of his thought on the importance of African-derived forms, even though this point has eluded recognition even among many of his followers.)

such as Afro-Cuban, Afro-Columbian, Afro-Brazilian, Afro-Bolivian, and Afro-Mexican styles—as key to a viable model of musicianship in a global musical landscape. Jazz and much popular music are prominent within these traditions, and when approached as self-transcending gateways that connect with the broader musical landscape, they can bring powerful tools to 21st century musical foundations.

Jazz in particular provides a rich spectrum of diatonic and non-diatonic studies that includes applied chords, modal mixtures, altered harmonies, and chord extensions. These intersect with key European common practice structures yet also encompass a modal-tonal-posttonal spectrum that connects with today's musical world. Adding jazz's improvisatory and compositional creative scope to the mix unites important content areas with the process foundations advocated by TFUMM. Music theory becomes an applied endeavor integrated directly into students' musical expression and understanding.

The case for black music as a core resource (not as a replacement for, but as a means for connecting with European and other sources) is further strengthened when contemporary rhythmic practices are considered. Here Jeff Pressing's study of the germinal importance of "Black Atlantic Rhythm"[10] in global musical practice aligns with Small's vision and adds weight to the argument. George Lewis's inclusive differentiation of Afrological and Eurological streams in contemporary musical practice might also be noted in support of this thinking.[11]

Again, TFUMM emphasizes that the point is not in any way to endorse the *replacement* of the current Eurocentric aesthetic-pedagogical model with one that is Afrocentric; rather the point is to underscore the importance of stepping back from conventional, conditioned perspectives of musical genres and perceiving those genres as waves in the 21st-century musical ocean. Improvisatory-compositional grounding is significant to the jazz portion of the Afrological wave, arguably linking it more closely to past eras of European practice than to the conventional interpretive performance

---

[10] Pressing, J. (2002). "Black Atlantic Rhythm: Its Computational and Transcultural Foundations," *Music Perception 19*, 3: 285–310.

[11] Lewis, G. (2008). *A Power Stronger Than Itself: The AACM and American Experimental Music.* Chicago: University of Chicago Press.

specialist framework. This link serves as a primary example of the important, if provocative, insights that are unearthed in TFUMM's expanded, critically robust perspective.

This reemergent, creativity-based paradigm has the capacity to transcend its own boundaries and enhance a much broader synthesis—where Afrological, Eurological, and multitudes of other waves unite. TFUMM sees the necessity for this synthesis to assume center stage in reform discourse. Therefore, TFUMM acknowledges that African-derived musics (including jazz) offer unparalleled and mostly missed opportunities to fashion the identity of the globally-oriented, contemporary, improviser–composer–performer. Our overarching aim is to not privilege any given area but to illuminate inherent capacities in all genres—including European classical music and folk, popular, and classical traditions from other parts of the world. All genres can serve as gateways to the broader musical landscape.

Although TFUMM has directed much of its critique implicitly and explicitly toward the European-based emphasis in academic music studies, we believe mainstream jazz education will also benefit by embracing and incorporating broader connections. Indeed, the veering of jazz education from the creative foundations of the jazz tradition parallels, and is arguably inherited from, the veering of European classical music studies from the creative foundations of the European tradition.[12]

TFUMM also recognizes concerns regarding teaching qualifications that arise from the kind of change proposed in core musicianship and music history studies. A commitment to such reformed approaches will likely entail professional development for faculty, perhaps through enhanced interactions with faculty not usually assigned core musicianship studies or through master classes and workshops related to creativity, diversity, and integration (which TFUMM argues should permeate the curriculum). A philosophical commitment and a desire to incorporate new processes and content into conventional programs will be necessary. Often, deeply inspired teaching comes from those who are themselves avid learners, willing to enhance their own knowledge and skill to increase their relevance and service to students who will perform, teach, and research in the years to come.

Three Approaches for Top-Down Reform of Core Musicianship

TFUMM envisions three possible approaches to institution-driven reform of core musicianship. These can be pursued independently or in conjunction with bottom-up, option-rich approaches.

---

[12] See Sarath, *ibid*, for more on this discussion, and particularly on the importance of understanding jazz as "writ large," as a self-transcending gateway to global practice.

The first approach involves a theory and aural skills class based on TFUMM's recommended principles, where jazz, popular, global, and classical European practices and materials are integrated with studies of improvisation, composition, rhythm, and skill development. This recommendation should not be conflated with add-on provisions, such as allowing students to take an upper-level theory elective in jazz or other related area or expanding aural skills coursework to include broader areas while still retaining the conventional theoretical component, which typically carries more hours and course credit. Instead, TFUMM urges that the theory and aural skills sequence be redesigned with the new principles and values at its center.

If theory and music history were conceptualized in an integrated fashion using perspectives advanced by TFUMM, opportunities would arise for richer, deeper, more rigorous understanding.

A second approach entails a more provocative move, integrating written and aural theory into a broader scope of study and practice. If theory and music history were conceptualized in an integrated fashion using perspectives advanced by TFUMM, opportunities could arise for deeper, more rigorous understanding. This understanding would merge analytical content with historical-cultural content and move from a technical-informational base to an inquiry base so students could discover the structural, textural, design, and aesthetic dimensions of the sonic experience defined as music. An inquiry-based structure puts more responsibility for factual-informational-technical learning into the hands of students, permitting class time to be used to focus on higher-order analysis and study (somewhat in the mode of the currently popular concept of a "flipped classroom"). Such an approach can provide students with a "need to know" and can make music study more challenging and satisfying. It could also permit integration of creativity, embodied musicianship, critical thinking, community music, reflection, entrepreneurship, technology, aesthetics, and cognition.

A reconceived model of music history studies, for example, might begin with cultural inquiry into the creative process itself. Students could reflect on the creative process—its personal meaning and its relationship to today's musical world and to the social, cultural, political, and economic conditions beyond music. Students could investigate aesthetic and cognitive concerns, as well as personal, interpersonal, and transcendent dimensions of the creative process. From this point of departure, past practices, conventional musicology, and ethnomusicology could be fathomed in newly relevant ways. This new approach would be in contrast to chronological and geographic organization of music history. Inquiry would be based on the experience of creating music in the 21st-century global landscape and concepts related to that experience. Concepts that might underpin a new model of musicology could include transformations in consciousness during the creative process (or what has been popularized as "flow"), the evolution of a personalized creative voice, or the challenges of authentic synthesis as opposed to superficial skimming in the multicultural marketplace. TFUMM construes this approach as encompassing more than what is typically included under "music history," and thus TFUMM suggests the initial focus be not on distant eras, but on the day-to-day ordeals and celebrations of creative artists working locally or across the globe.

This approach provides a basis for inquiry into the nature of music, its origins, evolution, and multiple expressions: Why does music sound as it does in particular times and places? Why does music have the influence that it does? Why does music continue to be a primary aspect of human interest and behavior? An entirely new foundation emerges for conventional, past-based inquiry that enables new levels of appreciation and understanding of the treasures of the past. This new approach embodies a rethinking of the typical division of musicology into historical and ethnomusicological compartments. The productivity and relevance of that division for the 21st century has so far eluded critical inquiry.

A third suggested approach for top-down core curriculum reform is a core proficiency assessment protocol. It could be administered at the end of the second year of college study. Students would need to demonstrate knowledge and skills in a variety of areas corresponding to the reformed framework. Areas could include improvisation, composition, aural skills, modal-tonal pitch languages, rhythmic languages (construed broadly), music technology, and movement. Musical inquiry aptitudes (such as history, cultural understanding, aesthetics, and cognition) could be measured by reflective writing or other protocols. Students could fulfill proficiency requirements independently, place out of core coursework and instead select upper-level course options.

Private Lessons

Private instruction is an important area of music study, and TFUMM sees potential for a broad spectrum of pedagogical practices that could sustain high levels of technique (instrumental or vocal) while contributing to the broader skill set called for by TFUMM. Various approaches to improvisation, aural musicianship, composition, world music performance techniques, and theory could be integrated within the private studio lesson, lessons with multiple students in attendance, or master classes alongside conventional technical and repertory studies. Another possibility is a more fluid private instruction format—not uncommon in jazz, in which students are given the opportunity, most likely in later years of their programs, to study privately with faculty from instrumental categories other than their own principal or primary instrument.

Inquiry would be based on the experience of creating music in the twentieth-first-century global landscape.

Ensembles

Given that much music is performed in ensembles, ensemble experience is important for students. TFUMM recognizes the complex network of considerations related to large ensembles in most music schools and departments. Ensembles are deeply embedded in the cultural history of music schools and public school music programs. While the viability of large classical and jazz ensembles is under threat in professional circumstances, it is clear that school orchestras, choirs, and jazz and wind bands provide excellent performance experiences. Large ensembles also remain an important as community orchestras, bands, and choruses continue to flourish.

It is essential to identify a continuum of ensemble formats and correlate these with real-world experience. For example, small groups in which members improvise and compose are arguably some of the most prevalent ensemble types in the United States and across the globe. In educational settings, small ensembles of improvising musicians in all styles could complement the standard classical chamber music model, or could provide the basis for a new model that achieves new kinds of synthesis.

Recognizing and respecting the highly complicated and highly charged nature of this topic, TFUMM believes that new curricular initiatives rooted in an improviser–composer–performer identity are key to a viable 21st-century ensemble framework.

Two points bear emphasis. A large ensemble—orchestra, choir, or wind band—consisting largely of aspiring contemporary improvisers–composers–performers will be capable 1) of playing a wider range of repertory, some of its own making, than an ensemble consisting largely of interpretive performance specialists, and 2) of bringing in unprecedented levels of passion, vitality, appreciation, understanding, and excellence to the performance of the works of Beethoven, Brahms, Debussy, and others, as well as to new repertory.

Contemporary improvisers–composers–performers (whose roots can be traced in part to the European classical tradition) will be able to view the European classical tradition and its treasures through a wide-angled, globally oriented, and creativity-based lens and to situate this lineage in a world music context and invoke deep levels of engagement with their audiences. TFUMM strongly endorses approaches to large ensemble teaching that incorporate standard and new works, improvisation and other modes of musical engagement and inquiry, and enhanced student participation in decisions related to rehearsal and performance goals. These ensemble approaches are recommended as complementary to, not in place of, systematic improvisation and composition studies elsewhere in the curriculum.

Contemporary improvisers-composers-performers will be able to view the European classical tradition and its treasures through a wide-angle, globally oriented and creativity-based lens and to situate this lineage in a contemporary world music context and invoke deeper levels of engagement with their audiences.

This ensemble strategy exhibits strong viability and sheds light on the seemingly conflicting need for curricular space for aspiring artists who will populate these ensembles to devote time to an expanded and integrative skill set. Increased ensemble rehearsal time might seem self-defeating, but aspiring creative musicians will bring enlivened scope and passion to the large ensemble framework. Like all other aspects of the curriculum, modifications may be needed to place the development of the (re)emergent and broadened artistic profile front and center.

Curricular Upper Structure

The combination of breadth, integration, rigor, and creative exploration provided in the reformed core curriculum offer students a foundation that will be conducive to self-directed development. The upper structure of the curriculum, *i.e.*, typically the "upper division coursework," which may or may not coincide with particular years of study, based on this foundation could incorporate an array of options, including coursework previously deemed part of the core and new courses that cut across traditional boundaries. It is important to keep in mind that a curricular paradigm that expands options for students can also enliven and expand creative avenues for faculty. There are many possibilities:

- a technology-mediated class that unites contemporary trends and centuries-old practices
- a class exploring time, cognition, and consciousness
- a course in Dalcroze eurhythmics, Laban, modern dance, or creative movement, any of which provide the physical engagement of the body in response to music and invite movement that expresses or emanates from musical ideas
- a course exploring improvisation across Western and Eastern genres
- a course uniting meditation and movement
- a seminar in the neurological correlates of performance, participation, and listening
- a project-oriented course that connects students to community musicians or venues and facilitates music for diverse audiences, like children, seniors, or differently-abled populations

Within the proposed creative frame, it is expected that students will continue to develop their individual and ensemble performance skills and advance their work in domains such as musicology, music teacher education, music therapy, theory, and other conventional fields. It is also expected that many more integrative opportunities could arise, opportunities that combine diverse areas of interest within and beyond music, which would be consistent with musical developments outside the academy. Students live in an age of advancing technology, instantaneous global information, awareness of growing demographic diversity, and an unending array of musical expressions. They seek connections and relationships in their studies that will enhance and enrich their contributions. Music students sometimes seek double majors or other opportunities to combine music with other fields of study. Mechanisms should be developed to assure that the greatest possible learning will accrue from students' chosen trajectories.

New Degree Program and Unit

TFUMM recognizes and supports the autonomy of institutions relative to their own contexts, profiles, and inclinations to change. While TFUMM has taken a broad and radical approach to transforming the undergraduate music major curriculum, a variety of change strategies could be employed within the spirit of these recommendations. Some programs may have a few faculty interested in piloting certain aspects of the recommendations; others may open full-faculty dialogues about change and its implications. The most important element of change is a philosophical commitment to serving 21st-century musicians, the art of music, our communities, and our society. This commitment requires a rigorous music education that focuses on creativity and relevance in the world beyond the academy.

> *The most important element of change is a philosophical commitment to serving 21st-century musicians, the art of music, our communities, and our society.*

An approach that may be viable in some schools or departments involves establishing a degree track that embodies the TFUMM vision as a pilot program. The degree track could be overseen by a new unit—a department, area, or division—that involves existing faculty whose work aligns with the TFUMM vision. This cross-disciplinary approach conforms with a movement in higher education generally that seeks to diversify and integrate faculty units and collaborative efforts, moving beyond the isolationist identification of faculty only with others in their own disciplines and moving toward faculty organizing around more holistic themes, such as creativity.

The value of creating a specified degree track is that it can shift the overarching identity for students and faculty involved in that track. A new degree track could provide a cohort of students and faculty with the overarching identity of a contemporary improviser–composer–performer. The creation of a new faculty unit could help promote an identity shift among faculty, similar to what is being promoted among students. TFUMM argues, however, that the improviser–composer–performer identity should not be limited only to students who elect the new degree track, but should be available to all students. Students from any major should be able to identify as a contemporary improviser–composer–performer. In fact, such a shift in identity could be as crucial for students planning to teach as it is for students focused on performance. It is possible that the faculty unit piloting a new degree focused specifically on creativity could also offer student-designed minors or other mechanisms to assure the availability of this identity to all students.

A new degree track and unit (perhaps called Contemporary Creative Musicianship) would appeal to a variety of constituencies and could have positive recruiting ramifications for institutions committed to paradigmatic change and leadership in the field. Those attracted might include string players who want to combine standard repertory with contemporary creative explorations for string quartets, including improvisation and arrangements and compositions by group members. Other constituencies might include jazz students seeking the broad horizons embraced in the jazz world; music technology and popular music students who play a handful of instruments and traverse multiple stylistic boundaries; or students who identify as "world music" practitioners. In the proposed curriculum, students would benefit from a reformed core curriculum that integrates musicianship and musicology classes; expands approaches to private instruction; enables them to chart their own pathways through wide-ranging options; and centers the ensemble program on small creative music ensembles, where students compose most of the music and have space for improvisation.

Teacher Certification Option

A teacher certification option in the contemporary improviser–composer–performer vein could be placed within the proposed degree track or incorporated as a dimension of a more traditional music teacher curriculum. A contemporary improviser–composer–performer emphasis in a teaching certificate would expose aspiring music teachers to a new paradigm for public school music, which could include conventional large ensembles (which currently prevail in public school music programs), but it need not be limited to that approach. Under the proposed certificate program, aspiring teachers would gain performance skills drawn from a diversity of local and global cultures—from blues to bluegrass, from gospel choir to *kulintang*, from *samulnori* to *son jarocho*. With strong creative grounding, these teachers would be able to invent new musical expressions based on a diversity of elemental features and nuances.

TFUMM imagines the proposed foundational shift would occur through a reformed curriculum and by infusing such knowledge and skills throughout existing methods courses, so that students would not be burdened with a fifth year of study. The proposed music teaching program is imagined as streamlined, relevant, highly integrated, and resonant with the overarching paradigm shift in the music major program at large. It could resolve longstanding questions about the increasing number of course requirements and their relevance to musicianship and pedagogical excellence. Rather than responding to certification mandates by designing new courses, new requirements could be woven into current courses. Cultivating high levels of ability in improvisation, composition, and performance will directly and powerfully enhance music pedagogy.

The TFUMM vision also lays groundwork for new levels of pedagogical expertise by restoring the creative foundations of artistic development to musical education. When musical artistry is reconceived from the conventional interpretive performance model to the improviser–composer–performer model, the false dichotomy between musical and pedagogical expertise is resolved: one cannot have the second without the first.

Change in the education of music teachers should thus be a high priority, given the dichotomy between professional assertions that the arts are basic and the small percentage of students who actually participate in high school ensemble programs. Out-of-school participation rates in music suggest that large numbers of students are engaged in self-initiated and informal music performance and study. However, in-school participation rates have remained the same for many years and indicate a need for music learning experiences that reach larger numbers of students, particularly in secondary schools. TFUMM believes that expanding the profile of 21st-century musicians and music teachers as advocated here will have direct bearing on student involvement in school music programs.

Any curriculum innovation affecting teacher certification programs will face challenges in the form of state and school of education standards and requirements. TFUMM recommends that advocates pursue sustained conversations with school of education colleagues and state certification officials. In these conversations, it will be important to make the provision for faculty units to have creative latitude in delineating the curricular needs of students. The proposed paradigm allows music education faculty to make significant strides toward a more relevant and efficient curricular framework, enabling needed diversification and allowing school music programs to enhance the holistic development of all students.

Music and Human Learning

TFUMM believes that the current paradigm for university-level music study (focused as it is on European classical music and interpretive performance), significantly underestimates the value of music to human life—intellectually, emotionally, and socially. On the contrary, TFUMM finds indicators coming from a variety of academic disciplines and venues that show a burgeoning interest in music cognition, neuromusical processing, and the impact of music on human health and well-being. The impressive literature that offers an understanding of music and human life and learning should inform not only students' experience and development, but also the reform discourse advocated here. Faculty forums, retreats, study groups, expert-led workshops, and other mechanisms could be used to enlarge faculty members' understanding in these arenas.

New Curriculum Oversight Protocol

The proposed curriculum change suggests a need for change in curriculum approval processes. TFUMM endorses a greater degree of field-specific responsibility for determining the curriculum of concentrations within the music major, in areas such as theory, history, performance, or creative studies. TFUMM proposes that centralized curriculum committees should deal primarily with structural and organizational issues and entrust course content and distribution issues to faculty with expertise in the given domains. Curriculum committees should, of course, review change proposals with an eye to the validity of justifications, an emphasis on students' learning, and the relevance to students' readiness for careers and leadership. Curriculum committees could also look at school-wide issues such as overlap in courses, competing requirements, number of program hours, credit policies, etc. However, once guiding principles have been established, faculty in the domain should be charged with responsible implementation of the curricula.

Summary of Institutional-level Initiatives

To summarize, TFUMM proposes a three-pronged protocol for practical initiatives at the institutional level: sustain a high level of critical discourse; invoke option-rich strategies for change that allow students greater choice in their curricular pathways; and initiate institution-driven innovations in the form of new coursework, degree programs, and curricular oversight protocols. Ideally, aspects of the three prongs will work in concert. However, schools and departments are encouraged to focus in whatever areas they are inclined, and to pursue creative alternatives that fit their unique circumstances. Most important is that the self-organizing, creativity-driven development that TFUMM advocates on the *student* level is also manifested on the *institutional* level, which will ensure that even the most modest steps toward change move toward foundational overhaul.

PATHWAYS TO CHANGE II: NATIONAL/INTERNATIONAL

When the institutional changes mentioned above occur in tandem with national and international changes, the prospects for foundational overhaul of music curriculum become more viable. To leverage the pioneering efforts of an initial wave of leading institutions toward a broader transformation, a series of national and international change strategies will be needed. These strategies will in turn enhance and empower local efforts. Following are three suggestions for national/international actions: a change consortium, change conferences, and new accreditation protocols.

Change Consortium

A wide range of organizations devote themselves to music study. Many of these organizations have issued appeals for change in varying degrees, and some have implemented changes that resonate with TFUMM recommendations. However, no larger organization is, as yet, predicated on change. TFUMM believes a new organization is needed, one whose entire focus is the transformation of university-level musical study. This organization (which need not be conceived as a CMS or TFUMM project) could work on multiple levels. This high-level, change-oriented group might take the following actions:

- Form a national/international network of faculty and students committed to change in the field
- Identify ten or more initial sites for implementation of the new model
- Engage progressive public school music teachers in the change discussion
- Engage progressive school principals and superintendents in the conversation to enliven receptivity to new models of school music engagement, learning, teaching, or inquiry
- Engage deans, provosts, chancellors, and presidents in the conversation, particularly under the auspices of diversity, which most of them already champion
- Convene think tanks with representatives of varied constituencies
- Form a consulting team to visit sites and assist with implementation
- Provide summer workshops for colleagues who wish to gain skill in facilitating the new model

All these actions could help initiate and support widespread, lasting, paradigmatic change within university-based music education.

Change Conferences

A series of national and international gatherings could serve as high-impact events to support the proposed shift in values and curricular content. A conference title such as "Breaking the Logjam: Paradigmatic Change in a Field at Risk" would begin to set expectations for outcomes from such conferences.

New Accreditation Protocols: NASM

Systemic change in the field of music will never transpire without corresponding change in accreditation criteria. Those who support the proposed paradigm shift must work with the National Association of Schools of Music (NASM) to ensure that institutions so inclined are incentivized to break free from the conventional mold.

III. CONCLUSION: A CALL FOR LEADERSHIP

An extraordinary opportunity awaits individuals and institutions committed to transforming music study into a force for creativity, diversity, integration, and transformation; a force that can benefit a world in urgent need. Though the rationale for this kind of reform might be obvious in light of the global nature of today's musical and societal landscapes, TFUMM makes the case that European classical music has much to gain from such reform. Key to TFUMM's proposed vision is restoring the creative template that prevailed in the European tradition through the mid-nineteenth century, and which has profound ramifications for multi- and transcultural navigation in the 21st century.

TFUMM also argues that the proposed transformation of music study offers potential to shape a new generation of artists-visionaries who may then transmit their broad and transformative wisdom to society and positively impact many of the most pressing issues of our times: ecological crises, poverty, famine, disease, violence against women, child abuse, ideological and extremist tensions, the threat and manifestation of war and violence. The time has come for a world that is also brimming with beauty, ingenuity, connection, and peaceful interchange through the transformative power of music, which potentially connects all cultures. The field of music study has the capacity to contribute significantly to global transformation, provided it invokes its own internal, foundational rebuilding around principles that are adequate to this task.

TFUMM has identified what it believes are the most essential features of music and human creative experience, has provided an analysis of the prevailing model's constraints, and has identified a far-reaching vision for the future of music study.

TFUMM advocates a shift from additive adjustments toward a creativity-driven, diversity-rich, and integrative curricular model that can enliven strong, self-organizing capacities in students and institutions. TFUMM also suggests a multi-tiered change protocol that surpasses in scope anything that has come before it. Thus TFUMM hopes to alter the tide of reform discourse in the field. Our hope is to break the logjam of pseudo-change that has pervaded the curricular reform movement and the broader field.

The time has come for a world that is brimming with beauty, ingenuity, connection, and peaceful interchange through the transformative power of the musical river that connects all the world's cultures.

All who are willing to step outside their comfort zones, critically examine the prevailing model, and entertain and celebrate new visions of the possible are invited to join with us in this critically significant project.

SUMMARY OF RECOMMENDATIONS FOR CHANGE

- Music schools and departments should sustain a high level of critical discourse about the purposes and potentials of music study. Discussion should be informed by far-reaching questions, corresponding literature, and a commitment to critical evaluation of assumptions and practices within the conventional model. *Creativity, diversity*, and *integration* may provide uniquely powerful lenses to focus and deepen discussion about more meaningful musical education.

TFUMM further recommends that music schools and departments consider the following:

- Bottom-up, self-organizing strategies for change that provide students with expanded options for navigating their artistic pathways. These bottom-up strategies might also allow faculty greater latitude to determine the curricular needs of their student constituencies, with the goal of the aspiring, contemporary, improviser–composer–performer in mind.

- Top-down strategies (implemented in conjunction with bottom-up provisions) that involve careful course and curricular design informed by the needs of the contemporary improviser–composer–performer in a global society. TFUMM urges that top-down processes be driven by an openness to new ways of thinking about the music core curriculum and by a receptivity to less conventionally recognized studies such as improvisation, composition, movement, rhythm, or mind-body practice.

- New possibilities regarding applied instrumental or vocal study geared toward the skill set of a 21st-century improviser–composer–performer. Possibilities might include more improvisation in lessons, more small-group instruction, or other avenues of achieving even greater skill development than in strictly private-lesson contexts.

- New possibilities in large-ensemble instruction and format oriented toward the needs of a 21st-century improviser–composer–performer and toward the potential for students' emergent artistic identity to open new programming possibilities and bring new levels of vitality, meaning, and understanding to the standard large-ensemble repertory.

- New conceptions of the 21st-century public school music teacher informed by the contemporary improviser–performer–composer model and encompassing opportunities for diversity and integration within the certification program.

- Implementation of pilot degree programs that embody the new principles as a preliminary pathway toward institutional reform.

- Joint initiatives with national and international groups or programs in the quest for broad and progressive change in the culture of music study. Broad initiatives would then enhance localized initiatives.

5

NAVIGATING THE MANIFESTO AND THE WAVES OF PARADIGMATIC CHANGE

Creativity, Diversity, and Integration Reconceived

Edward W. Sarath

As a long-time change activist in music studies, it was my great honor to be part of The College Music Society Task Force on the Undergraduate Music Major and serve as lead author of its Manifesto. Never in my wildest imagination did I envision the document would catalyze the kind of conversation that began to take hold soon after it appeared and which continues to this day. I am thrilled to team up with Patricia Sheehan Campbell and David Myers in this book to take the conversation and consideration of resultant practical strategies to new levels.

I hope to contribute in this chapter and the next through reflections on key issues and controversies encountered in the formulation of the report and after its release. As one might expect, highly contrasting perspectives on important areas are not only inevitable in a project of this nature, they are essential to the depth and substance of any statement that might result. In this chapter I approach this inquiry using multiple readings of creativity, diversity, and integration—the three pillars of the Manifesto—as a primary lens. Inasmuch as these themes are nothing new in over 50 years of change deliberations, a clear understanding of how their foundational positioning in the Manifesto differs from prior advocacy is key to the emergence of a new change platform.

Central to my perspective are distinctions between what I call "lower-order" and "higher-order" change visioning, and that if the full ramifications of the Manifesto are to be harnessed in the paradigmatic change strategies it advocates, a higher order reading of the document must guide reform deliberations. The creativity pillar, for example, entails more than improvisation and composition as add-ons to the existing model, a lower-order interpretation, but rather a wholesale shift in musical identity—within individuals and across the culture of the field—to that of the "contemporary improviser–composer–performer" that is at the heart of the higher order vision. This identity shift in turn generates new possibilities in the diversity realm, which the Manifesto argues needs to move from the lower-order multicultural thinking that has pervaded change conversations to a higher order transcultural perspective. I even go so far as to suggest in the next chapter that the multicultural paradigm may exacerbate the very ethnocentrism that it seeks to counter; only through the creativity-based, transcultural framework outlined in the Manifesto and probed more deeply here will significant diversity strides be achieved. Direct parallels come into view with the integration pillar, which when situated within a creativity-based framework is apprehended from a transcultural standpoint. Here, in contrast to piecemeal efforts at connections between the conventional curricular pillars of performance, theory, and history, a deeper organic synthesis is identified that involves a far broader scope of components which is uniquely accessed and integrated through the creativity turn.

In short, the three pillars from a higher order perspective are understood not as a horizontal inventory of areas that warrant more curricular prominence, but rather a vertical account of the key facets of a music studies paradigm that is grounded in the creative foundations of human art making. As I argue, the deeper the vertical penetration to these roots, the more diverse—and more integrative—the overlying curricular and cultural expanse. Bringing the commentary back once again to the issue of change, in order to invoke and sustain this higher order reading of the Manifesto, new levels of critical interrogation are needed into the assumptions that underlie it and its lower-order competitors. Correlations are directly evident with David Myers's appropriation in Chapter 3 of Agyris and Schön's single-loop and double-loop critical inquiry, which roughly correspond respectively with my lower-order and higher-order models. This chapter takes the next step in providing specific examples of both single-loop/lower-order and double-loop/higher-order visioning.

Inasmuch as some of what follows may admittedly be contentious for even the most fervent change advocates, I believe two points bear emphasis regarding the manner in which I derive and frame my ideas. First, while my observations about prevailing patterns are at times anecdotal, drawing upon my personal experiences as creative artist, pedagogue, curriculum innovator, scholar in multiple disciplines, and change agent, I believe this range of background represents a formidable platform from which to formulate and share insights. Given the absence of literature that might be cited on many of these issues, identification and critical interrogation of dominant patterns needs to start somewhere, at which point personal experience represents an inevitable backdrop. Moreover, while my perspectives on any given issue might be readily questioned as the result of bias, I believe the overarching coherence these perspectives exhibit when taken as a whole lends support to the viability of my vision, with my distinctions between lower-order and higher-order change conversations a primary example.

However, to make a second point, my primary intention is to exemplify a level of critical interrogation that I believe has been lacking in reform circles rather than to impose upon readers a particular interpretation of the Manifesto. It is thus important that the views in these two chapters are taken as my own and not necessarily as representative of the task force. To be sure, I weigh in with a degree of conviction and issue challenges to fellow reformers that may at times appear confrontational. Whether colleagues embrace or reject my ideas, however, I hope they share my view that, without deep penetration to the conceptual bedrock that underlies reform deliberations, ornamental change will continue to masquerade as the fundamental overhaul needed and called for in the Manifesto. I believe the time has come for an entirely new conversation and I invite the reform community to consider what follows as among the perspectives that might be part of that conversation.

Creativity: From Additive Approaches to Creative Identity Shift

How is creativity defined from the higher-order change vantage point represented in the Manifesto? How does this differ from lower-order conceptions? How do the different conceptions shore up with creativity research? What are the curricular ramifications of the different viewpoints on this fundamental topic?

The principle of systematic approaches to improvisation and composition provides a fruitful point of departure for replying to these questions. If I were to choose the most important passage in the Manifesto, it would be the following:

> A systematic program of improvisation study may unite multiple improvisatory languages, including style-specific (for example, jazz, Hindustani, or European classical) and stylistically open approaches. Such study would provide for creative exploration and analysis and reflection on a wide range of modal-tonal-post-tonal pitch systems and rhythmic practices. At the same time, studies could embrace training in aural performance, movement processes, history, culture, aesthetics, cognition, and mind-body integration. The development of technical skill and knowledge required for expert improvisatory development has ramifications for both conventional interpretive performance and contemporary musical explorations. Systematic composition studies that intertwine European-tradition concert music practices with songwriting approaches from popular music and small and large ensemble jazz composition strategies expand the creative process spectrum in ways that are relevant to both traditional and contemporary music.
> *(p. 58)*

Important features of higher order change visioning come quickly into view and distinguish the Manifesto as a unique voice in reform deliberations, with subsequent elaboration revealing further aspects that are less immediately evident yet equally significant. First and foremost is an expansive, inclusive, and nuanced view of creativity that regards improvising and composing as foundational processes that support creativity within all aspects of musical inquiry and engagement.

I elaborate on distinctions between what I call primary (improvisatory and compositional), secondary (interpretive performance), and ancillary (analytical inquiry) creative processes elsewhere and will not take space here to comment further, suffice to emphasize the unique capacities for improvisation and composition to promote creativity throughout the overall spectrum. Here, lingering stereotypes that an emphasis on creativity runs the risk of compromising scope, and rigor within that scope, are powerfully dispelled. The systematic improvisation/composition principle underscores the potential for the opposite to hold, where not only an expanded spectrum of knowledge areas, but strong unification within that spectrum, makes possible new levels of rigor and achievement. This exemplifies Howard Gardner's (1993, p. 182) assertion that process-rich learning models enable distinguishing between the "sophomoric 'multiple-choice-cum-isolated fact' mentality" that conflates "superficial conformity" with "genuine rigor" points toward higher order and more nuanced understanding of key curricular principles. If anything, the conventional notions of rigor, which are more aptly comparable to *rigor mortis*, are what ought to be suspect.

The idea of nested synergies, though only mentioned in passing in the Manifesto, is readily inferred in the previous passage and refers to how any given area within the systematic creativity model interacts dynamically with all other components and the whole to enhance assimilation and meaning. This further underscores the higher level achievement that is possible in a creativity-driven framework.

Note as well how, in this context, conventional areas such as theory and history can encompass broader constituent knowledge areas, and new realms such as cognition, aesthetics, and musical embodiment/mind-body practices organically extend from the improvisation–composition foundations. Whereas lower-order change discourse wrestles with the problem of fragmentation by urging connections between the so-called silos, which are typically construed in terms of the conventional core disciplines of performance, theory, and history; higher order discourse—predicated on the creative identity shift—recognizes and generates entirely new kinds of integration.

In the diversity realm, clearly evident in the earlier passage are both process-mediated and culture-mediated diversity pathways, providing a basis for far broader global connections. Most important in terms of optimal reading of the Manifesto is that in a single stroke, the centering of systematic creative development at the heart of artistic development enables entirely new levels of fulfillment and progress within the second and third pillars—diversity and integration. In short, I believe the conception of creativity begins to illuminate how the view of this pillar in the Manifesto differs from that found in much prior change visioning. What, then, do I mean by a shift from creativity as an add-on to the invoking of a creative identity?

Here I am talking about the difference between two kinds of musical orientations. In the first interpretive performance is primary to music students' daily activity and sense of musical self, even if improvising and composing are part of that activity. In the second, improvising and composing are central to students' daily activity and artistic self-awareness, with interpretive performance—as exemplified in Contemporary Improviser Composer Performer (CICP) identity—among the areas, such as pedagogy and scholarship, that may be also incorporated. When CICPs envision their personal futures—areas for further exploration and discovery—as well as the phenomenon of music and its place in human society and development, they do so through the lens of music as primarily a creative phenomenon and secondarily an interpretive phenomenon. As the Manifesto emphasizes, the conventional music studies model, even with its ostensible grounding in the European classical tradition, represents a stark deviation from the creative roots of that very tradition, in which up until roughly two centuries ago most practitioners were active as improvisers, composers, and performers. I thus refer to the conventional model as "neoEurocentric" in order to distinguish it from its creativity-rich European origins. Instead of seeking foundational rebuilding atop these creative roots, lower-order change visioning—not grounded in the creative identity shift—tends to approach creativity through additive means.

Key indicators of the additive framework are the use of improvisation and composition as pedagogical aids, as might be found in teacher education methods coursework, or some musicianship coursework. While these applications are of value, it is essential not to conflate them with the *creative identity* through which musicians reflect on their work and the musical world and beyond through the lens of their continuously evolving improvisatory and compositional voices, which are direct conduits for infusing influences from the broader spheres. Short of the creative identity shift, musicians—no matter how much improvising and composing they might do atop their interpretive performance orientation—may still be prone to ethnocentric biases as they peer out on the broader landscape through that lens. By contrast, entirely new models of diversity, integration, critical thinking, self-sufficiency, pedagogical insight and expertise, advocacy, and entrepreneurship are among the important outgrowths that extend from the creative identity shift, which may be thought of as the individual manifestation of a wholesale shift in the culture of music studies.

A more complete look at creativity through the kind of higher-order lens described earlier brings into focus an array of principles that have impacted change visioning and lays groundwork for new curricular strategies. Through access to and enlivenment of the interior dimensions of creative experience via a creative identity, important kinds of exterior development occur that are not likely otherwise.

Fathoming Creative Interiors for Optimal Exterior Growth

In addition to expanded frameworks for creativity, diversity, and integration, a number of key facets and outgrowths of the creative musical identity may be noted that underscore distinctions between additive and foundational approaches and thus the conception unique to the Manifesto. These include the "self-transcending" principle that reveals how styles and disciplines penetrate beyond their localized boundaries to foster broader connections, evolution of the individual voice, self-organizing or self-driven development, and expanded critical thinking capacities.

Self-Transcending Principle

Key to the "self-transcending" principle is that the central pulse of the musical world lies not in the discrete, language-bound genre and disciplinary categories that dominate academic (and much commercial) thinking, but rather in the underlying dimensions of the creative process that give rise to these categories in the first place. This exemplifies Susanne Langer's (1948, p. 206) insights as to the capacities for music to take awareness "beyond the pale of discursive thinking" to new levels of "emotional and organic experience." Creativity enables access to dimensions of musical experience in which boundaries dissolve between theory, history, and performance—to cite the conventional curricular pillars—and areas typically excluded or marginalized, such as aesthetics, cognition, culture, and consciousness/spirituality.

Creativity is thus analogous to deep sea diving in which access to underlying, unified experience at the ocean's depth enables entirely new understanding of the endless series of seemingly discrete waves—which correlate with musical genres and disciplines—that flow at its surface. A new impetus arises for musical engagement and study: Whereas conventional models tend to approach styles, traditions, and disciplines as self-confining domains, the purpose of engagement in any given domain is to render it a self-transcending gateway to the whole. The degree of competency in a given domain is thus measured not only by localized skill development but by the capacity to which the domain penetrates beyond its own boundaries to connect with the broader musical world and beyond. This self-transcending, unified goal does *not* suggest compromised rigor or engagement in any given localized part; as glimpsed earlier in the context of systematic creativity, it is just the opposite.

Were degree programs and curricula to be based in the experience of improvising and composing as musicians contact deep and unified dimensions of musical reality, they would look radically different from that which has prevailed for a century or more. Hands-on, creative engagement would underpin analysis; contemporary practices would serve as entryways into the past; overarching, integrative principles would precede tradition-specific detail; separate coursework in history and theory would come only after significant grounding in integrative, creativity-based coursework that yielded entryways into analytical terrain; and a broader yet more integrative range of study would be possible. Moreover, the very notions of theory and history would give way to headings that would accommodate a much broader range of inquiry, which would include cognition, aesthetics, and consciousness spirituality, that is endemic to artistic development. If headway in this direction is to be made, reform visioning needs to similarly ground itself in the creative foundations that are unique to higher-order visioning.

Individual, Creative Voice

Next is the evolution of the individual, creative voice, which—because it is informed by influences of aspiring improvisers' and composers' inner (cognitive, emotional, spiritual) and outer (sociocultural, economic, political, geographical) worlds—reveals creative development as a path for not only personal artistic expression but overall self-realization. Over time, access to deeper dimensions of creative awareness promotes the evolution of highly personalized modes of creative expression, which in turn serves as a powerful lens for understanding not only one's musical and personal self, but the role of music as a reflection of the world in which it exists. Central here is the crystallization of style features in musicians' improvisatory and compositional work. As these style features are informed by a wide range of interior and exterior influences, improvising and composing become more than a hobby, but in fact are central vehicles for artistic and personal growth. How does this transformation occur? The impact of musical influences on the personal voice is direct and obvious, understandable in terms of simple input-output mechanisms: Aspiring improvisers–composers hear, play, and dream about a range of music and this shapes their creative expressions and personal styles.

The impact of extramusical influences requires a broader explanatory mechanism, one that shows how experiences outside of the domain (music) are, as it were, metabolized into musical structures. The art historian Walter Abell (1961) posits a model that invokes aspects of Jungian thought to broach this terrain; elsewhere (Sarath, 2013) I situate his model within a broader scheme based on principles of an emergent consciousness-based worldview called Integral Theory. Because the individual creative voice is a direct reflection of students' interior and exterior worlds—their inner emotional, cognitive, spiritual realities; their outer sociocultural, geographical, economic realities—musicianship development in general, and development of improvising and composing in particular, take on entirely new significance. What might have been viewed as a means for enjoyment and perhaps social engagement opens up to a rich pathway for self-realization and transformative human development. What bears emphasis is the essential role self-transcending creative experience plays in this process of "musical individuation"; penetration to deep strata of musical awareness, where foundational musical elements (and extramusical influences) are perceived/sensed in fluid and interconnected forms, promotes the metabolizing of these phenomena in personal style structures (Sarath, 2013). In the context of diversity, the emergence of personal style structures in creativity-based individuation is key to understanding the mechanics of collective style evolution, and how music is a reflection of culture—thus shedding light on Patricia Campbell's insights on the latter point in Chapter 2. This analysis underscores the foundational role of creativity in the evolution of diversity awareness as construed from a transcultural perspective; one cannot begin to understand or appreciate the role of music as a direct reflection of another culture unless one understands how music is a direct reflection of not only one's own culture, but one's own self

Reflection and Self-Sufficient/Student-Driven Development

With the previous section as groundwork for further aspects of curricular change rooted in the creative identity shift, there emerges an expanded platform for reflection, and for the closely related realm of self-driven development. Reflection entails the moments apart from direct creative engagement in which students ruminate on the meaning of specific creative episodes as well as the overarching voice and also fathom areas to be pursued for further growth. This is not to ignore Schön's (1983) important notion of reflection in action, but to highlight the importance in the present context of retrospective reflection, what Schön called "reflection *on* action."

While reflection certainly occurs to some degree in the conventional, interpretive performance-based musicianship framework, and when creativity is added to that model, reflective capacities take a paradigmatic leap forward when the creative identity shift is invoked. Similarly, there is greater enlivenment of self-driven development faculties, which I analyze in terms of "self-motivational" and "self-navigational" aspects (Sarath, 2013). Self-motivation entails an interior impetus for investing the time and energy toward necessary skill development, which as the Manifesto argues entails far more than that which is sought in conventional models. Self-navigational capacities entail abilities to fathom new areas of exploration independently. Because virtually every facet of experience may inform creative expression and development, the potential range of self-motivational and self-navigational pursuits is infinite. The deeper the self-transcending access to underlying strata of creative awareness, the more expansive and lively the platform for reflection and thus enlivenment of self-driven faculties.

Higher-Order Critical Inquiry

The creative identity shift also gives rise to yet another attribute, involving new levels of critical inquiry. Self-transcending penetration to deeper levels of musical awareness enables practitioners to step beyond language-bound conditioned assumptions about the musical world and how it is accessed. Access to strata of perception in which creative impulses are experienced, albeit on deep intuitive levels—prior to their differentiation into melodic, rhythmic, harmonic, timbral, and other features—gives rise to capacities for critical interrogation of overlying disciplines that are simply not likely without creative foundations. From this standpoint, an exclusive interpretive performance identity is ill-equipped to critically examine the practices that define its learning models. As these practices become reified through language, without creative mechanisms that enable transcendence of language, conventional terminology uncritically perpetuates conventional practice. Lower-order change conversations, not informed by self-transcending creativity, are arguably as prone to this limitation as conventional models.

An important attribute of higher-order, creativity-based critical inquiry is the capacity to step back and interrogate one's musical identity as a worldview that is based in its own set of assumptions and principles that might be considered in contrast with other worldviews and their underlying premises. Here is where the creative identity shift is thus an essential aspect to the development of a genuine diversity awareness—until this shift takes hold, the musician will inevitably view the musical world through the lens of the prevailing neoEurocentric model, or some derivative such as one in which some improvising and composing are added rather than central. Recall Patricia Campbell's emphasis in Chapter 2 on how different cultural values yield different forms of expression that can be elusive to practitioners from other backgrounds. As she explained, conceptions of tone, timbre, and formal architecture that are central to musical meaning in one tradition might be dismissed as less mature from a European classical standpoint. I have argued extensively on a parallel point when comparing an improvised music aesthetics with a composed music aesthetics (Sarath, 2013); individuals steeped in the second may be challenged to see substance in the first. Even with the addition of significant experiences in improvisation and composition, if the overarching identity remains rooted in interpretive performance of European repertory as the central mode of engagement, practitioners will continue to view the overarching landscape through that lens. The shift to a creative identity provides a considerably more adequate lens, one that is not only more receptive to the global panorama, but in fact may yield enhanced capacities to engage with, embrace, and understand the European tradition. Here a perhaps ironic axiom comes into focus: When European classical music is approached as a world music, which can only happen when the means for approach are the fundamental creative processes of improvisation and composition, entirely new levels of excellence, understanding, and vitality will be possible in that tradition.

In sum: When creativity is absent, or viewed as add-on, domains are prone to self-confining conception, where they are experienced as isolated and fragmented. Musical development is confined to more or less an assembly line affair, involving engagement with the various areas as intact, self-contained entities. When the creative identity shift called for in the Manifesto is invoked, the overlying musical landscape is perceived in a radically different way due to deeper interior grounding. Disciplines and genres are not understood as discrete entities in a fundamentally fractured musical universe but rather as richly interconnected facets of an overarching musical wholeness. Creativity therefore needs to be understood not as one among a litany of items to be added to an overflowing shopping cart—but rather as a core facet of human art making that, having been astonishingly absent in music studies, needs to be positioned as the central pillar atop which a new paradigm is built.

A central axiom sums up the nature and magnitude of these comparisons between additive and foundational views of creativity and the importance of a shift in identity from interpreter (albeit who may sometimes create) to creative artist: The purpose of including improvising and composing in the curriculum is NOT, in contrast with many prevailing reform views, to enhance musicianship skills or other conventional areas associated with either interpretive-based or even creativity-based paradigms. *Rather, the purpose of musicianship studies (and the need for a vastly expanded approach to such) is to inform improvising and compositional development.* In other words, the time has come to move beyond embellishing the conventional, interpretive-based pedagogical and aesthetic center in the field and to restore the creative foundations of human art making as the guiding vision for musical development.

And with this creativity turn come entirely new conceptions of diversity that further distinguish the Manifesto from its precursors. The multicultural platform that predominates the diversity conversation correlates with the additive approach to creativity; when creativity is foundational, a transcultural vision guides these all-important efforts.

Diversity: From Multicultural Encounter to Transcultural Synthesis

The importance of expanding the cultural horizons of music studies has long been among the prominent themes in change deliberations, with an intensive commitment to this area among the primary galvanizing forces among the CMS task force. The Manifesto does not mince words on this account when it deems "the culturally narrow horizons of music study as nothing short of a social justice crisis" (p. 60). However, as with creativity, multitiered conceptions of diversity are possible, and it is important to differentiate the diversity vision advanced in the Manifesto with prevailing notions. Moreover, the fulfillment of diversity aspirations is directly tied to creativity, and readers will note how the various themes addressed earlier pertaining to higher-order conceptions of creativity—self-transcending principle, development of the individual voice, self-sufficiency, and critical thinking—directly inform the higher-order, transcultural diversity model and strategies. As the following analysis reveals, the multicultural platform, due to its limited creative foundations, may even work against diversity aims, the realization of which I argue is dependent upon the aforementioned principles.

In distinguishing between multicultural and transcultural paradigms, a point that the Manifesto broaches only briefly, I draw upon personal observations as practicing musical artist, pedagogue, and scholar. Through my navigation of diverse musical traditions in my own improvising and composing and collaboration with many artists engaged in similar pursuits, I have spent much time in reflection and dialogue about the challenges, opportunities, and complexities inherent in the nexus of traditions that is characteristic of our times. In identifying a number of parameters by which multicultural and transcultural paradigms may be differentiated from one another, I do not suggest that the work of any given pedagogue or institution falls clearly into one model or the other. Surely there are instances where the lines are blurred. However, I believe that the distinctions I outline nonetheless obtain amid large sections of pedagogy and research, and are notably coherent with other parameters that I correlate with lower- and higher-order change visions, and therefore these differentiations may be highly instructive for taking diversity discourse and practical application to new levels. I also recognize that different conceptions of both multicultural and transcultural models exist and thus offer my own definitions in order to avoid confusion with others, and also to retain consistency with the broader analysis. In my articulation of a number of concerns with the multicultural position in my endorsement of the transcultural, I hope that my analysis stimulates responses of equal conviction and serves to elevate the critical integrity of dialogue on this important topic.

Basic Commonalities and Distinctions Between Models

To begin with identification of where the models unite: Both multicultural and transcultural perspectives are predicated on the need for music studies, as with all of education, to align itself with the ethnically diverse nature of contemporary society. Both models rightly seek to counter the monocultural, and arguably ethnocentric, horizons of the conventional, neoEurocentric paradigm. Both models seek to situate musical traditions within the broader sociocultural contexts in which they originate and evolve and illuminate how musical values are shaped directly by cultural values, thus underscoring the limitations of viewing one tradition through the lens of another.

The models differ in many significant ways, however, in terms of how they construe and approach musical diversity. Table 5.1 illustrates roughly a dozen lines of distinction. Contrasting views of the place of creativity and creative development in musical development are key. Typically occurring in ethnomusicology lecture classes, teacher education methods coursework, and perhaps world music ensembles, multicultural pedagogy pays minimal attention to the musical identity of the student (i.e., improviser–composer, interpretive performer, music educator), the means of engagement (i.e., lecture format, hands-on application, creative synthesis) with the traditions, and how these factors might impact the kind of diversity awareness that might result. Transcultural pedagogy, in sharp contrast, is predicated on the establishment of an individual creative voice and identity

TABLE 5.1 Multicultural and Transcultural Diversity Frameworks

Multicultural	Transcultural
Ambivalent about role of creativity in musical identity or assimilation of knowledge.	Establish of a creative identity—CICP—central.
Additive model: Diversity awareness the result of contact with some threshold of traditions.	Non-additive/organic: The locus for evolution of a diversity awareness lies not in how many traditions are studied but depth of connection.
Linear: Tradition-specific study precedes creative application.	Nonlinear: Creative application/exploration and tradition-specific study work in tandem from the earliest moments of study. Periods of focus in either realm are possible.
Compartmentalized view of musical landscape: Central thrust of musical practice and understanding begins and ends with engagement with traditions in discrete, intact forms.	Syncretic view of musical landscape: Central pulse lies in interstices between traditions that are access through creative engagement. This creative grounding then enlivens receptivity to tradition-specific study, when then informs this creativity, with the cycle continuing throughout a lifetime.
Self-confining impetus: Traditions not as gateways to the world but as entities unto themselves.	Self-transcending impetus: Traditions as tributaries that flow into the global ocean via creativity.
Teacher-centered/institution centered: Predicated on expert instructors disseminating knowledge to students.	Student-centered: Predicated on establishing self-driven capacities that guide diverse navigation throughout a lifetime.
Absence of exemplars—real-world global navigators who came up through multicultural training.	Plentitude of exemplars: Real-world global navigators who came up through transcultural training.
Hindered by post-modern leveling, thus ambivalent about key cultural contours for diverse navigation.	Predicated on robust musical topographies, and identification of key cultural contours for diverse navigation.
Ambivalent on place of African American music in a diversity-rich curriculum.	African American music as central for global navigation.
Ambivalent on the need for self-cultural grounding.	Predicated on self-cultural grounding as key to broader understanding of musical world.
Nebulous about aims beyond generalized aspirations of diversity awareness.	Four specific and wide-ranging aims: individual creative voice, collaborative skills, understanding, and pedagogy.
Inconsistent with the work of educational visionaries that multiculturalists otherwise espouse (in the context of overall educational reform).	Consistent with work of educational visionaries.

as the basis for meaningful engagement with the musical world and optimal appreciation for and understanding of its treasures. As seen in the earlier analysis of higher-order creativity, students who identify as Contemporary Improvisers Composers Performers will be able to establish degrees of intimacy, skill development, and self-driven and critical faculties to global navigation that are difficult to achieve when creativity is an add-on, let alone absent, in their identity. Later in this chapter, I identify both a transcultural continuum that spans a wide range of engagement and immersion in diverse cultures and an infusion of diverse influences into the creative voice to illustrate this point. I also delineate four key aims of the transcultural paradigm that are consistent with these ideas. Harkening back to the earlier assertion that the three pillars of the Manifesto are centered in creativity, the degree of diversity awareness achieved is directly predicated on the degree of creative grounding and evolution of the personal artistic voice. This is central to the transcultural diversity paradigm that is briefly mentioned in the Manifesto and now requires further elucidation if the principles of the report are to be fully realized.

The multicultural model may be characterized as additive, linear, and institution centered or teacher centered, whereas the transcultural approach is nonlinear, nonadditive and organic, and student centered. By additive and linear, I mean an approach whereby the central impetus is the study of diverse traditions, one by one, under the implicit assumption that contact with some baseline number of traditions will eventuate in sufficient diversity awareness. The multicultural worldview is of a musical landscape comprised of discrete stylistic or cultural compartments, with resultant musical understanding achieved through engagement with as many compartments as possible in intact forms. Rarely identified, however, are any such thresholds of contact or relevant skills and aptitudes, nor are questions addressed of—given that one could never cover all the music around the globe—how to fit everything in, a central challenge confronting all music studies and educational reform. Multicultural pedagogy is also linear in its view of creative application, if occurring at all, as something that happens after study of given tradition.

By institution or teacher centered, I refer to learning models predicated on an expert practitioner or scholar imparting knowledge to students.

The transcultural is nonadditive, organic, nonlinear, and student driven in its shift of impetus from diversity skills and aptitudes resulting from some aggregate of traditions studied, to depth and personalized nature of creativity-driven engagement. Instead of a focus on imparting knowledge about various musical traditions, the focus is on enlivening self-driven faculties that will guide diverse navigation over the course of a lifetime. Recall the self-motivational and self-navigational facets of the prior examination of higher-order creativity. This offers a response to challenge of scope and how to cover all that is deemed important that confronts all educational domains. It is important to not infer in this student-driven model the notion that instructor expertise and other institutional resources are unimportant; they are enormously important. What shifts is how these are accessed. As connections with the overarching musical world unfold organically from the establishment of a creative identity, an interior receptivity to further growth is enlivened in which the expertise of instructors and other institutional resources may be optimally harnessed.

The transcultural worldview is not of a compartmentalized musical landscape but one of vast interconnectedness, in which the purpose of engagement in any given region is to render it—via creativity—a self-transcending gateway to the broader whole.

These distinctions are underscored by a look at a conspicuous lapse in the multicultural framework—the absence of exemplars.

Absence of Exemplars in the Multicultural Account

This has to do with the absence in multicultural advocacy of exemplars—real-world creative artists whose music traverses diverse cultural horizons. Even a cursory look at the developmental trajectories of leading artists who have traversed diverse cultural horizons reveals pathways far more consistent with the transcultural model than the multicultural. A short list includes Vijay Ayer, Jane Ira Bloom, Steve Coleman, Bela Fleck, Ronan Guilfoyle, Jamey Haddad, George Lewis, Bobby McFerrin, Edgar Myers, Esperanza Spaulding, and John Zorn, with several in this group having been named MacArthur fellows due to the boundary crossing that is inherent in their work.

What I call a "transcultural continuum" illuminates this point and the broader and inclusive nature of the transcultural approach. On one end of the continuum is perhaps the most common kind of appropriation, where artists encounter a new tradition and immediately begin to incorporate influences in their creative expression. I am thinking of Coltrane's incorporation of influences from Indian music, or Debussy's from Javanese gamelan; neither of these involved suspension of these artists' creative activity while they undertook intentional study of the respective sources of inspiration. Rather creative application was spontaneous and immediate, with results that were nothing short of genuine, powerful, and profoundly influential in the field. Moreover, this kind of engagement establishes within the artist an interior relationship with the diversity of the outer musical world that is the basis for significant insights, passion, and further development and immersion as appropriate to the needs of a given individual at a given time. At which point we approach the opposite end of the transcultural continuum, where artists such as percussionists Dan Weiss and Jamey Haddad, bassist Ronan Guilfoyle, flautist John Wubbenhorst, and guitarist John McLaughlin engaged in extensive study of non-Western traditions. Weiss and Wubbenhorst have even achieved skill levels whereby they concertize professionally in classical Indian (Hindustani) formats, while always breaking new ground with their innovative work of a highly syncretic nature. What cannot be overstated is that key to all points on the transcultural continuum is the establishment of a creative identity that is the basis for an intimate and highly personalized relationship with a given tradition, which in turn provides the basis for a new relationship with the overall musical landscape.

Dispelling commonly encountered stereotypes that often surround creativity-based pedagogy, the transcultural therefore promotes levels of depth and breadth that are unlikely through multicultural approaches. The task of the institution is to establish learning environments in which both this creative exploration is endemic to the culture, and in which resources are provided for rigorous, tradition-specific study that may include coursework similar to that which occupy the center of the multicultural approach. However, as the individual voice evolves, and students are able to optimally partake of the expertise of instructors, an entirely new relationship is possible with even the most conventional kinds of multicultural pedagogy. Ultimately I believe even more ideal is the design of new kinds of coursework that harness transpersonal principles even in the rigorous, tradition-specific study. Additional, important principles with strong pedagogical ramifications that are either implicit or may be inferred in the previous analysis shed further light on this point, in so doing underscoring multicultural/transcultural distinctions.

The first has to do with the identification of important cultural landmarks that are key to diverse navigation. Multiculturalism remains ambivalent when it comes to two kinds of such landmarks. One has to do with traditions within the overall landscape in which features inhere that are highly conducive to forging broader connections. Another has to do with the importance of the music of one's own culture serving as a gateway to the broader expanse. For Americans, black music is where both issues unite. If there is any credence in Christopher Small's and others' assertions of the prominence of African American music in not only American but global practice, then it follows that this point would factor significantly in diversity pedagogy. But the multicultural predilection for what Bennett Reimer (2003) has critiqued as "postmodern leveling" precludes recognition of this important cultural landmark. Here, the view prevails that no tradition is more important than another, and all efforts need to be made to not just replace one hegemony—that of the neoEurocentric—with another, in this case that of black music. The fact that, as one might reasonably infer, it is as essential for American students in largely black inner city environments, or of any backgrounds, to know about music in Nepal as it is to for them to know the musical expressions that have originated in their own culture connects this perspective with self-cultural ambivalence. From a transcultural vantage point, which always grounds its vision in the work of real-world global navigators, musicians enter the overarching landscape through creativity-driven engagement in music of their own culture, and also through engagement with key cultural avenues in the broader musical world. African American music thus looms large in the transcultural paradigm as both a key gateway for all musicians interested in forging diverse connections and as a self-cultural locus for Americans.

Pedagogical Ramifications

A look at the pedagogical ramifications of the two approaches strongly supports the transcultural. As I go into this, it is helpful to keep in mind a further principle—that creative artists tend to enter the broader landscape (beyond their primary cultural pathways) not through contact with other cultures in intact, tradition-specific forms, but rather through hybrid entryways that are the result of collisions between cultures. Modal jazz, to provide a first example, is the result—at least in part—of the nexus of the jazz mainstream and Eastern and Mideastern traditions. What better prerequisite, therefore, for study of *alap* and drone in Hindustani music than having students create in the style and spirit of Coltrane's appropriation of these elements? The same holds for African American–based rhythmic grounding and delving into rhythmic practices of other cultures. What better means for venturing into African drumming traditions and others around the world than for students to have grounding—as improvisers and composers—in the various rhythmic time feels of their own time and place that originated in those traditions?

Another principle that factors prominently here has to do with musical embodiment. While, as Patricia Campbell has argued forcefully, embodiment is essential to all forms of musical expression, rhythmic literacy of the kind at hand dramatically exemplifies this point. Grounding in African American rhythmic practices is as much a new (for interpretive performers) mode of physical engagement as it is conceptual, technical, and expressive. I work extensively with classical performers in the areas of transidiomatic and also jazz-based improvising, and I can attest directly to the widespread incapacity for most musicians of this background to not only keep a steady beat when improvising in a rhythmic time feel format, but play with rhythmic authenticity—by which I mean grounding in the facets of the particular rhythmic language (swing, even-eighth note, etc.) To be fair, this kind of grounding requires immersion in the recorded legacy of rhythmic time feel–based music and a commitment to practice and study that is as extensive as the need for excellence in conventional performance arenas. On the other hand, if we are to advocate the cultivation of a genuine diversity awareness and skill set, does not this kind of rhythmic training represent an enormously foundational area—one that must absolutely be core in any emergent curriculum? Moreover, harkening back to Campbell's strong endorsement of *ngoma*—within which embodiment is essential—in music studies reform, would not this kind of development be central to any such aspirations?

In my view, these considerations further illuminate the shortcomings in not only the linear, additive, and teacher-centered aspects, but also in many other aspects of the multicultural paradigm. While, as the Manifesto argues, the multicultural model may at best yield a kind of "distanced fascination" with the broader musical world, it is incapable of engendering the breadth and depth of connections—technical, analytical, aural, physical, emotional, spiritual—that are developmental characteristics of creative artists and the transcultural framework.

Multiculturalism also runs counter to the thinking of the educational visionaries to whom music studies reformers, including multiculturalists themselves, tend to pay homage, underscoring my concern of internal inconsistency in the framework. I am thinking here of visionaries such as Whitehead, Dewey, Maslow, Bruner, Greene, and Gardner, within the thinking of all of whom movement towards student-centered growth is central. Gardner's endorsement, moreover, of "process-rich learning environments" that aim toward enlivening student-driven development correlates particularly strongly with the creativity-driven transcultural model.

Contrasting Aims

A final realm of distinctions comes into view through the lens of four primary aims of the transcultural paradigm. The first entails, as stated earlier, an infusion of influences in the personal, creative voice. This is the basis not only for enriched, expressive capacities but for deeper connections with the various traditions that inform this voice. The second entails capacities to collaborate with musicians of diverse backgrounds, which is where as intimated—and further elaborated in the next chapter—a grounding in black music, and jazz in particular, is invaluable. The point is not that artists with this grounding are automatically equipped for collaborations with musicians from all backgrounds, but that when identifying common territory in which musicians from diverse cultures who are so interested might unite, African American foundations offer uniquely robust tools. The third entails development of a deeper understanding of the aesthetic, cognitive, and transpersonal dimensions of culturally varied practices and value systems. The transcultural platform not only extends the earlier-mentioned multicultural aspirations for students to learn "social meanings, functions, and values" to expanded terrain but also provides tools to achieve this. Such knowledge and experiences can directly inform scholarship, as well as pedagogy, which is a fourth transcultural aim. Multicultural literature tends to be both more narrow, and nebulous, when it comes to articulation of aims beyond general exposure to diverse musical cultures. And when more specificity is attempted, as in the earlier passage, identification of principles as to how such goals will be realized tends to raise questions such as those I have framed in the earlier analysis.

In sum, the multicultural framework is predicated on "teaching about" diverse musical traditions, whereas the transcultural is rooted in "enlivenment within" students of self-driven diversity capacities that will guide their development throughout a lifetime. Therefore, while at first glance, the differences may appear to be more semantic than ontological in nature, I believe that when situated within the contexts of lower- and higher-order change discourse, their enormity is illuminated. I would even go so far as to argue that the paradigmatic gulf that separates multicultural and transcultural positions as I define them here exceeds that which separates the multicultural from the conventional, monocultural/ethnocentric paradigm it (multiculturalism) rightly seeks to counter. For this reason, I view the multicultural as more of a reaction to the monocultural than a paradigmatic alternative, and thus prone to untold conditioned assumptions that—consistent with single-loop, lower-order change discourse—have largely eluded critical examination. Until this point is recognized, multicultural efforts will continue to exacerbate—rather than counter—the diversity crisis in music studies.

Integration: From Surface Linkages to Creativity-Driven Synthesis

Concerns about the fragmented nature of the curriculum are nothing new, and in fact may be one of the prominent areas in which reformers and conventionalists agree. What has eluded lower-order change discourse is both the neoEurocentric paradigm as the origins of fragmentation, and the extent to which piecemeal attempts to rectify the problem, through piecemeal connections between the three conventional pillars—performance, theory, and history—actually exacerbate it. Just as multicultural, lower-order approaches to diversity may fuel ethnocentrism, lower-order attempts at integration may similarly fuel the very fragmentation that is rightly recognized as problematic. How could this be? Here, a sequence of developments comes into view that exemplifies the heightened critical inquiry faculties unique to the higher-order creativity platform.

The analysis begins with the performance-creation split, and the fact that performance—the first conventional pillar—is a disconnected component of a prior, creativity-based synthesis (improvisation–composition–performance). The division of labor that began to take hold roughly two centuries ago—as a result of which composition became the task of a distinct minority, improvisation essentially disappeared, and interpretive and reinterpretive performance emerged as the sole function of the majority—represents a major departure from the broader and integrated nature of earlier practice. As the very idea of being a musician became synonymous with the practitioner who plays works created by others, interpretive performance was firmly established as the central disciplinary pillar in the field. Theory and history would eventually be added as two additional pillars that, while not encompassing as many credit hours as performance, would be regarded as important components of the musicianship core. If the foundational positioning of performance—as a component that split off from a prior, creativity-rich framework—is not problematic enough, the further positioning of theory and history atop this already disconnected component would only exacerbate the problem. Not only would creativity, despite its essential place in the arts and human nature, be forever marginalized, but fragmentation would be encoded as an intrinsic facet of the system.

When, to continue the analysis, efforts to rectify fragmentation by connecting the conventional pillars instead of rebuilding the model atop the creative identity, the fragmentation became reified. Why? The core creative means for integration is still kept at the margins of the system. "[E]xhortations [in reform circles] that music performed in ensembles should be studied in theory and history classes" represent, as the Manifesto stipulates, not only "partial strategies," but "might actually perpetuate the problem of fragmentation by reinforcing a limited terrain within which integration is sought" (p. 61). Within a change culture in which the Contemporary Improviser Composer Identity is central, the conventional curricular pillars would be more readily recognized as deviations from an integrative, creativity-based core, and thus addressed accordingly. It is not that there is no place for performance, theory, and history within a creativity-based framework, and as the Manifesto states, even greater mastery in these areas may occur in such a framework. However, when disconnected from a creative identity and corresponding engagement, performance, theory, and history are not equipped to uphold a musical foundation that lays claim toward artistic development for the 21st century. The fact that reformers have been oblivious to the origins of the fragmentation in the first place is a primary example of the compromised critical inquiry, or what David Myers, following Argyris and Schön, would call single-loop learning, characteristic of lower-order discourse. Among the ramifications of this analysis is the urgent need for the voice of the contemporary creative artist to be more fully represented in change deliberations if higher-order visioning is to guide the field forward.

Summary

If it appears that I have devoted an inordinate amount of attention to the creativity pillar, with diversity occupying half its space, and the integration pillar section spanning just a few paragraphs, it is due to a broader conceptualization of creativity than has typically informed reform conversations. Even the first version of the National Arts Standards/Music, which designates improvisation and composition among its nine core standards, falls short in achieving the creativity-based, vertical alignment that, in fact, could be seen as an organizing principle for seven other standards. Similar observations may be made regarding the Comprehensive Musicianship Project, Manhattanville MusicCurriculum Project, and other otherwise important change initiatives that are mentioned in the opening chapter. One sees in these frameworks little if any mention of the importance of a shift in identity from interpreter to creator, fathoming the interior dimensions of the creative process, acknowledgement of the scope and integration inherent in systematic approaches to improvisation and composition, or new platforms for reflection and self-driven development. The expanded perspective on creativity advanced in the CMS Manifesto represents a distinctly new viewpoint on this essential topic. When creativity is understood through the higher-order lens of the Manifesto, diversity and integration are recognized as inherent in this essential facet of human artistic expression. It is thus imperative, in order to harness the full impact of the Manifesto, to place this principle front and center and distinguish it from prior change discourse. Whereas additive approaches to creativity, multicultural approaches to diversity, and piecemeal linkages between the conventional pillars of performance, theory, and history, comprise a lower-order reform matrix, the positioning of creativity as foundational gives rise to new, higher-order model. Here transcultural conceptions within the diversity realm and transdisciplinary conceptions—encompassing not only a broader range but also heightened synthesis along that scope—within the realm of musical disciplines are possible atop the reconceived creativity core. The fact that, as the earlier analysis has shown, multiple paradigms are identifiable within each of these reform themes, underscore the heightened critical inquiry characteristic of creativity-based, higher-order visioning, as well as limited critical capacities in lower-order change discourse—not to mention conventional perspectives.

References

Abell, Walter. 1961. Toward a Unified Field of Aesthetics. In Morris Phillipson (Ed.), *Aesthetics Today* (pp. 432–465). New York: Meridian.
Gardner, Howard. 1993. *Multiple Intelligences: The Theory in Practice*. New York: Basic Books.
Langer, Susanne. 1948. *Philosophy in a New Key: A Study in the Symbolism of Reason, Rite, and Art*. New York: Mentor.
Reimer, Bennett. 2003. *A Philosophy of Music Education: Advancing the Vision*. Chicago: University of Chicago Press.
Sarath, Edward W. 2013. *Improvisation, Creativity and Consciousness*. Albany: SUNY Press.
Schön, Donald. 1983. *Reflective Practitioner: How Professionals Think in Action*. New York: Basic Books.

6
BLACK MUSIC MATTERS
Jazz as Transcultural Gateway

Edward W. Sarath

In this chapter I directly extend the analysis of the last in exploring a topic around which lower-order discourse clearly needs to give way to higher-order visioning. I am talking about the prominence of what Christopher Small terms African American "musicking" in not only American but global music practice, and the elusive nature of this key principle in reform deliberations, despite their ostensibly strong commitment to diversity. By African American musicking, I refer to a set of practices that are characteristic of black musical traditions as they have taken hold in the United States and the African diaspora, and I use jazz as a primary lens through which to view the impact of this important wave in 20th- and 21st-century musical oceans.

Why jazz? Jazz exemplifies a number of principles that are central to the vision of the Manifesto and the present discussion. Jazz embodies the higher order readings of each of the three pillars introduced in the previous chapter. From the standpoint of creativity, jazz is the primary site for the return of the Contemporary Improviser Composer Performer and the systematic and self-transcending approaches to creativity discussed earlier. These robust creative foundations support entirely new dimensions within the diversity realm, where, as I have argued, a movement from multicultural to transcultural approaches is needed. Jazz epitomizes the transcultural principle through its capacities to connect with European classical music and wide-ranging traditions around the world. In relation to the integration pillar, jazz organically brings together not only an unprecedented creative process spectrum but also conventional core domains such as theory and history along with important areas such as aesthetics, cognition, embodiment, and consciousness/spirituality that are typically marginalized or absent in conventional curricular models (core or beyond).

In advocating for jazz in this way, I do not—nor does the Manifesto—seek to replace one hegemony with another. Instead, I argue for jazz as a uniquely powerful example of the opposite—a fertile gateway to further horizons. I draw upon not only my personal experience as creative musical artist who has been long involved in this kind of navigation, and researcher who has written about it, but also the insights from a wide range of literature on the topic. In addition to Small's (1994, 1996) work, important sources includes Lewis's (1996, 2008) notion of Afrological and Eurological musical paradigms, Pressing's (2002) "Black Atlantic Rhythm," Banfield's (2010) case for black music as a "game changer" in contemporary practice, Floyd's (1995) argument for the emergence of a black music identity in America at least as far back as the 18th century, Jones's (1963) closely related recognition of the survival of "Africanisms" despite unusually harsh circumstances of slavery, and also important contributions on this topic from Monson (1996), Ramsey (2003), and Hester (2009).

In making this case, I believe it is also instructive to call attention to resistance to this idea that I have encountered both within the CMS task force in its deliberations and after the release of its Manifesto. To encapsulate the central concern expressed by some colleagues: In reform efforts that are predicated on embracing a multitude of musical lineages in the world, too much emphasis—the feedback has it—is being placed on one particular genre, jazz, which in turn runs counter to the diversity aims articulated. While there is some validity in this concern, I find it typically framed from the standpoint of what I introduced as lower-order discourse in the last chapter. Jazz's unmatched process scope, its robust rhythmic foundations and their pervasive impact across the globe, the idiom's rich pitch languages tended to go unrecognized, with instead a reaction of "jazz privileging" emerging as a kind of catch-all slogan. That some kind of African American musical grounding is commonly prevalent among many of the leading artists in the realm of global synthesis and syncretism was absent from these exchanges, or the fact that jazz, as recently reiterated by the US House of Representatives, 25 years after it passed HR 57 is a distinctly American cultural expression, a "national treasure" with strong global connections that warrants preservation.

I come away from these conversations not with the sense of being enriched by the juxtaposition of well-articulated, thoughtful, opposing viewpoints, but rather uneasiness—a feeling that perhaps there were other things going on that were fueling the jazz privileging reaction. In this chapter I examine the resistance to the idea of jazz playing a foundational role in music studies—resistance encountered even among colleagues who may hold an affinity for the genre and advocate its inclusion but not its centering—as resulting from deeply rooted and unexamined ethnocentric tendencies in the change community. I realize this is not a popular argument for some and perhaps many readers but, inasmuch as I believe the case to be made is a strong one, I cannot see any way around placing this issue front and center. However, more important than whether or not one agrees with my conclusions is that a more robust examination of the diversity pillar, and its inextricable link to the broader conception of creativity core to the Manifesto, will inevitably extend from these thoughts. There is a conversation yet to be had about diversity, and particularly black music, in our field and I hope that readers will therefore keep the prospects for a more complete inquiry into these all-important themes in today's musical and extramusical worlds in view as they contemplate what follows.

I begin with a look at the attributes jazz offers today's musicians in order to set the stage for a critical look at resistance to the foundational positioning of this genre. The point is not to dwell on limiting tendencies in prevailing reform conversations, but rather to penetrate more deeply into the conceptual bedrock that is needed for the paradigmatic change that the Manifesto advocates. As I emphasized in the previous chapter, conditioned tendencies that are deeply lodged in individual and collective thinking will only be rectified through a commitment to robust introspection and a kind of "musical psychotherapy" that rivals its personal counterpart. Though this work at times may reveal unpleasant patterns, it is a primary distinguishing feature of the kind of leadership required in the field. I hope the following analysis challenges and inspires readers to strive toward this leadership.

African American Music as a Key Curricular and Cultural Landmark

It is difficult to imagine an informed conversation on the need for musicians in a global society to develop skills for global navigation in which black music, which I will approach largely through the lens of jazz, does not appear early and often. Even a cursory look at the backgrounds of leading innovators, at least in the West, bears this out, only to be underscored by a concurrent look at the creative foundations, structural scope, and integration inherent in the jazz idiom. For example, Bobby McFerrin, Jane Ira Bloom, Steve Coleman, Vijay Ayer, and George Lewis are just a few artists that might be cited in this context. The following assessment by Christopher Small (1994, p. 4) would thus appear so self-evident as to scarcely warrant articulation:

> By any reasonable reckoning of the function of music in human life, the Afro-American tradition is the major music of the west in the 20th century, of far greater human significance than those remnants of the great European classical tradition that are to be heard today in the concert halls and opera houses of the industrial world, east and west.

Later I will cite another Small passage that sets the stage for an Afro-American/European classical nexus. At the moment, however, let us consider the fact that, despite Small's near iconic status in change circles as a forceful and eloquent advocate for a more culturally comprehensive music studies framework, this aspect of his thought has eluded reform discourse. As noted previously, it is not that reformers have argued against the inclusion of jazz or black music in the curriculum, but that recognition of the extent to which these sources warrant foundational positioning—and Small's stance on this could not be more clear—has been elusive. Reactions, moreover, against a perceived privileging of this importance musical wave underscore the need to look closely at the issue.

It is instructive in this regard to compare multicultural and transcultural readings of Small's viewpoint. Ambivalence and even aversion to the foundational positioning of black music are consistent with multicultural concerns about ascribing prominence to any particular region as a landmark to navigating the 21st-century musical landscape. Because the notion of process-rich, self-transcending gateways that may open up to wide-ranging regions is foreign, the sense prevails that it is more important than harnessing any such gateways is to ensure a politically correct egalitarianism in which all musics are regarded as equally important to all music students, regardless of their cultural origins. To reiterate a prior point through an example; it is more essential, according to a multicultural standpoint, for a black student in America to gain exposure to music from all corners of the globe than grounding in his/her own African American heritage. (Of course, the same could be said for white and other students in America, who share the same roots.) In generalizing about prominent tendencies, I do not of course mean to suggest exceptions do not exist. I believe an overall look at the cultural orientation of tertiary-level music studies, and much work at primary and secondary levels, supports my contention. Therefore, even if this particular heritage were not the treasure trove of global connections ascribed to it, nor exhibit the expanse Small indicates, the limitations of the multicultural vantage point are clearly evident. When the attributes of African American musicking come into view, the shortcomings of the multicultural framework as considered in the previous chapter are all the more evident. And when coupled with the lapse in capacities for a critical examination of language—and thus recognition of the potential for multitiered readings of the word "jazz"—the genre is viewed as but another of the infinite series of stylistic compartments, one that comes early on under the *J*s in the alphabet—the limitations of the multicultural platform are all the more underscored.

Two transcultural principles may be inferred in Small's words that are key to realizing the higher-order aspirations in the Manifesto. Of initial significance is the horizontal scope implicit in the assessment. Black music is important due to its sheer pervasiveness, not only in the West, but in all corners of the globe. Here Pressing's (2002) notion of "Black Atlantic Rhythm" is of singular significance. While certainly one can cite the existence of European classical symphony orchestras, chamber groups, and opera companies across much of the same planetary spectrum, the presence and influence of this music in today's world, harkening back to Small's assertion, pales in comparison to that of African American origins. Furthermore, when jazz is construed as "writ large," meaning encompassing not only mainstream practice but the infinite array of global offshoots, this first transcultural reading of Small's wisdom is illuminated.

But a second principle that may reasonably be inferred in Small's words, which is clearly supported by his broader work, has to do with the self-transcending properties inherent in creativity-rich, African American musicking—which, in fact, give rise to its horizontal expanse. Here we shift toward a process-based reading of the passage. It is not only that black music is pervasive from a strictly linear vantage point, it is that it also brings to the enterprise of global confluence powerful syncretic resources due to not only its creative foundations but also a rhythmic infrastructure that, due to features that have scarcely been analyzed, seems to be uniquely disposed to global synthesis. As noted in the Manifesto, jazz is the most complete embodiment of the contemporary improviser–composer–performer profile, which was seen to possess robust self-transcending capacities. The task now is to center this principle so it may serve as a platform for further connections and growth.

If the fostering of self-transcending creative musicianship represents a central artistic goal, then the same principle needs to guide the reform enterprise if it is to shift from lower order to higher order visioning. An enormous challenge in change deliberations is to recognize the limiting impact of conventional labels and terminology in the field; until this impact is critically interrogated, change efforts will be encumbered by neoEurocentric interpretations (of which as I have argued multiculturalism is a modification, not a paradigmatic alternative) of language that needs to be construed from a broader, and more artistically grounded, transpersonal perspective. Recall in the way of defining neoEurocentric my differentiation between it and the creativity-rich European classical tradition, in which the Contemporary Improviser Composer Performer identity that has made its return through jazz prevailed up through the early 19th century. Jazz means radically different things from neoEurocentric/multicultural and transcultural vantage points, the second of which recognizes the idiom in its process breadth and integrative scope.

A key requisite of curricular change, therefore, is to establish formats for dialogue and thinking in which colleagues step back from conventional, language-bound categories and pose questions that direct change agents toward new reconstructive, transcultural pathways. Recall the principle discussed in the previous chapter regarding the shift from thinking of music and music studies landscapes in terms of discrete genres and disciplines, and instead thinking of these in terms of process-structure regions. Whereas much reform discourse is rooted in the question—What genres and disciplines comprise a viable music studies curriculum? I propose the question—What are the processes and structures in which students need grounding? Even to ask—What do today's students need to know and be able to do? This is a question that is perfectly capable of eliciting a transcultural response in a critically robust change climate, and yet it still runs the risk of eliciting conventional assumptions about disciplines and genres. When thinking shifts to processes and structures, we are more able to transcend typical categories and rebuild from deeper, artistically grounded principles.

Improvisation immediately comes into view in response to the process question, particularly with transcultural engagement in mind, with composition not far behind. Performance skills that support the two foundational creative processes are also of importance. In terms of structural or content considerations, grounding in rhythmic and pitch languages that are key to transcultural creativity is paramount. More specifically; African and African American rhythmic foundations, consistent with Pressing's case for "Black Atlantic Rhythm," are seminal in what I propose as "21st century rhythmic literacy" (Sarath, 2013). From this foundation a broader scope of rhythmic studies is possible that draws from diverse sources in Africa and across the African diaspora—particularly in North America, South and Central America, and the Caribbean.

In the pitch realm, modal languages are arguably of greater significance than tonality, particularly when it comes to collaboration with musicians from traditions outside the West, although I believe a case could be made for a hybrid program of modal-tonal-transtonal studies that is ideally suited to the broader spectrum of transcultural pursuits. This would include studies of harmonic structure and function, following the progression of diatonic to nondiatonic practices as unique to the West, and architectural formal considerations, even if approaches to these areas might differ with transcultural aims in view. Here an important point bears emphasis: The claim is not in any way that musicians with jazz grounding (or any kind of style specific grounding) can automatically interact with musicians from any part of the globe regardless of participants' backgrounds. Rather, musicians each have to arrive at a kind of common ground and bring an intention to move past their respective horizons. However—and this is crucial—when one inventories the processes and structures that a given background offers for this kind of collaboration, I believe the pitch-rhythmic spectrum of jazz is unmatched. Strong arguments could also be made for the importance of inquiry into cultural, cognitive, aesthetic, and consciousness/spirituality realms.

Here, Karl Berger's work with such collaborations at the Creative Music Studies, founded in the 1970s, is instructive. Featuring artists/instructors such as Naná Vasconcelos from Brazil, Trilok Gurtu from India, Ismet Siral from Turkey, and Aïyb Dieng from Senegal, powerful and magical kinds of interactions would often result. "The idea" Berger states (Berendt, 1991, p. 213), "is not so much to combine styles but to look at the elements common to all the different forms of music," such as pitch and rhythmic languages, and allow the creative process to organically weave these together. As Sweet (1996) points out in his book on the project, meditation and other kinds of spiritual practice were also important aspects of this work, which has significantly informed my own application of these ideas and approaches (Sarath, 2013).

Having identified a basic inventory of skills (not meant as exhaustive here, but at least covering fundamental areas) through a process-structure lens, the next question reformers need to address is this—Are there areas in the present model that are particularly rich sources of these process-structure regions?

While no area can be expected to comprise the totality of what today's students need, it is clear that jazz, particularly when construed as writ large to encompass its many global offshoots, spans an unprecedented portion of any skill set that might be identified. This is particularly so given the disproportional emphasis that improvisation and composition need to receive in a creativity-driven approach to music studies. If the case for jazz is strong from a linear perspective, again relating to Small's assessment of the prevalence of African American musicking across today's musical ocean, an equally strong case might be made from a nonlinear standpoint, which would be rooted not in the knowledge areas that jazz directly encompasses, but those to which the idiom—due to its improvisatory/compositional core—opens up. The point is not to endorse jazz as a de facto destination, but rather as a self-transcending gateway to be expanded with other culturally rooted (and transculturally rooted) process-structures regions.

Here the principle of Occam's Razor invoked from the sciences comes to the fore. The basic idea could not be simpler—that of looking first to the most immediate sources for solutions to a problem prior to searching far and wide for answers. In terms of the daunting problem of diverse navigation in music, the question could not be more direct: Why not harness resources directly in one's midst prior to expeditions to distant lands? At which point, if lower-order, multicultural concerns about simply replacing one hegemony with another have not begun to dissipate, a second passage from Small (1994, p. 48) invites us to give shape to exactly what these jazz-driven openings might look like: "The meeting between African and European music has been one of the most fruitful exchanges in the entire history of music."

From a multicultural standpoint, the most that might be inferred in this statement is a flat juxtaposition of African-based (or African American–based) and European-based genres and thus an expansion of the already overpacked curriculum with no way of organizing it into a meaningful, coherent system. From a higher-order, transcultural framework, a much richer, creativity-based synthesis is possible that is far more directly rooted in contemporary, and arguably even traditional, musical practice, not to mention the way in which musical traditions have typically evolved. And it resolves the challenge of ever-widening scope. Here an organic interweaving takes place, the contours of which are shaped not by pedagogical, expediency, academic protocol, or politically correct egalitarianism, but rather the self-organizing exigencies of creative expression, exploration, and development. While this represents relatively uncharted terrain in music reform discourse, and a range of approaches is conceivable, I propose two overarching principles and then specific manifestations that, if not immediately bearing fruit, at least lay groundwork for productive further consideration.

Afrological Gateway Principle

First is that key to the Afro-Euro nexus will be positioning "the Afro" as a gateway to this union. Here the abbreviations "Afro" and "Euro" refer to what George Lewis (1996, 2008) terms Afrological and Eurological streams of musical practice, a differentiation that I find particularly useful in appreciating their important distinctions as well their potential for synthesis. Instead of a flat conjoining, or perhaps even, as I would imagine some might be inclined, a Euro-based foundation that is then augmented with Afro aspects; I believe Western musicians will venture into this melding most fully through an Afro lens. Why? It is because of its creativity-based foundations and its global span, which is particularly evident in so many syncretic forms. Here it is also important to emphasize that, once it is recognized that the neoEurocentric framework is a deviation from the creativity-based European core, the jazz-based contemporary improviser–composer–performer may be then recognized as the current and most complete manifestation of that core. The present—as noted in the previous chapter's discussion on how creating musicians apprehend historical, theoretical, and other material—is the entryway to the past. It thus naturally follows that creating musicians will immerse themselves in the creative languages of their times as a gateway for broader synthesis.

Second is that the Afro-Euro nexus provides a framework for broader global excursions and synthesis. In no way is this to suggest that the establishment of this framework needs to be a prerequisite for the broader explorations. Rather, these can take place from the outset as organic and spontaneous offshoots, depending on student interest and faculty and other resources available, but the core thrust should be establishing the Afro-Euro synapse so that it can inform further growth. There is something about these two particular currents in the musical ocean that are important to American musical culture in general, and particular that of the West, that when embraced can provide a basis for further global assimilation.

A look at practical manifestations of the African American/European nexus illuminates these points.

Practical Manifestations: Musicianship Studies and Private Lessons

To begin with musicianship coursework: I have designed, and taught for over 20 years, a musicianship class predicated on this principle (Sarath, 2010, 2013). Contemporary improvisation practices with modal, tonal, and free jazz at the core open up gateways to European-based species counterpoint, approached improvisationally and compositionally, and nonsyntactic improvisation. Jazz-based approaches to modal and tonal harmony, where all students (regardless of principal instrument) realize progressions at the keyboard, provide a gateway to a unit on Baroque-figured bass keyboard realization, which is approached as a precursor to 20th- and 21st-century jazz/pop keyboarding where contemporary chord symbols function in ways that figured bass lines were used in former times. Altered and extended jazz harmonies precede altered European harmonies (French-augmented sixth chords). The system is not confined to African American and European resources: Consistent with my earlier reasoning, units on Indian, Arab, and African rhythmic principles, cross-cultural aesthetics, and contemplative practices and inquiry are among a broader range of investigation.

Viewing the Afro-Euro nexus through the lens of improvisation and composition: Although African American-based improvising skills are key to transcultural navigation, for musicians coming from a strictly neoEurocentric, interpretive performance background, it is more productive to invite them to create from their current musical experience than introduce foreign language structures at the outset. Though this may appear as a contradiction to my earlier delineation of an Afro-based entryway, it is a pedagogically sound strategy given the need for students, particularly who are new to improvisation, to begin their creative journeys by drawing from their own internal reservoirs rather than being forced into a new musical universe. Again, the argument for grounding in African American music as transcultural gateway is not an argument for this musical region to also serve as exclusive destination—the goal is to provide tools that support infinite possible destinations. It might also be mentioned that the approach does not entail students improvising strictly in classical styles, but rather simply allowing them to draw upon that grounding. It is also important to emphasize an essential facet of African American improvisatory grounding, which is immersion in aural exposure through, for most students, recordings and as much live performance as possible. There is no other way to internalize the language structures; emotionally, physically, or spiritually. Accordingly, however, it is first necessary to lay interior grounding for this work by laying seeds for creative identity through the lens of one's personal background. Most important is that multiple entryways into improvisatory creativity may be identified, and a curriculum will make as many as possible available to students.

Composition from a transcultural perspective is a domain in which multiple entryways are also possible, and for which many students will find Afrological entryways highly conducive. Recall the three types of composition mentioned earlier—song form, small and large ensemble jazz, and European classical—that comprise a systematic approach. Songwriting is a huge facet of contemporary musical culture and offers students a rich entryway into composition. Small jazz composition, generally speaking, takes aspects of songwriting into more adventuresome harmonic, melodic, rhythmic areas, although notable exceptions are not hard to find that remind us to make such generalizations with great caution. Large jazz ensemble composition draws much more significantly from European classical resources in its orchestrational, contrapuntal, and formal architectural possibilities. A continuum thus emerges by which students who might not otherwise take this step may venture into European-based concert music composing. The point is not that the Euro-based is the goal, or inherently superior, and that songwriting, or small and large ensemble jazz, ought be regarded as merely stepping stones; nor that students who happen to traverse several or all of these possible domains will do so in strict linear sequence. Rather, by organizing these approaches, among others, into a coherent system of possibilities, students will find their own pathways from a richly informed slate of options.

What might a private lesson program look like that was oriented toward transcultural navigation rather than monocultural interpretive performance, and which drew from an Afro-Euro nexus? From a transcultural perspective, students need even higher degrees of virtuosity on a principal instrument than typically achieved, though of a different nature. Characteristic of the transcultural are high levels of technical proficiency, sound production, and expressivity, but instead of being oriented largely toward, and fostered through, European classical repertory, these will be oriented toward, and thus informed by, a wider variety of sources. The next paragraph gives just a tiny snapshot of a specific application in which jazz resources excel (and then can work in conjunction with European and other materials).

Anyone who harbors questions about the kind of virtuosity achieved among jazz musicians might try to play a transcription of an improvised solo of any of the jazz masters, or for that matter, even of an undergraduate jazz major. Or—as is common in development of jazz improvising skills, one might do the transcription oneself and report back upon completion. And because jazz performance skills are sought with improvisatory abilities in mind, an important and closely related strategy is aural transposition—the working out of passages by ear in all keys. Imagine what it might take to work out a piece such as Charlie Parker's *Donna Lee* by ear in all keys, up to speed, and what sorts of virtuosity might result from this kind of practice! Interesting possibilities arise here pertaining to the ramifications of technical foundations grounded in this kind of ear-hand integration for learning European repertory. The fact that this technique is attained in conjunction with improvisatory skill development suggests enormous gains may be had in terms of expressivity and interpretation. When it comes to broader transcultural navigation, another realm of ramifications becomes evident.

Compare, for example, the double-tonguing technique used by classical brass players, flautists, and saxophonists in rapid, non-slurred passages with the kind of articulation used by their jazz counterparts. Characteristic of the first is highly precise rhythmic definition, with a staccato expressive effect superseding the sense of lyrical flow and connectivity between notes (this is not to suggest such connectivity is absent, it is a secondary expressive effect). In the second, equally precise rhythmic definition coexists with a strong sense of connectivity and flow. While my terminology admittedly falls short of capturing the full distinctions between the kinds of articulation, the significance of even these crude differentiations comes into full view when one imagines them in a collaborative framework involving musicians from, or music informed by, drumming traditions from around the world—whether North India *tabla*, South Indian *mridangam*, Mideastern *dumbek*, African *djembe*, and Brazilian *pandeiro*. In other words, which kind of articulation, and thus dexterity, is more conducive to the broader frameworks? For anyone even moderately conversant with this kind of cross-cultural collaboration and practice, the first (European-based) highly precise rhythm is not even remotely conducive to such frameworks, while the second (African American based) highly precise rhythm tempered by connectivity and flow is profoundly conducive. A transcultural program of private instruction will thus recognize this important skill area and position it accordingly in the mastery of an instrument.

Is this to suggest that European-based articulation and resources for technical development need to fall by the wayside? Absolutely not, and it is conceivable that when situated within these jazz-based technical/aural/improvisatory foundations, new levels of proficiency may result. Moreover, engagement with European sources would inform this new model by providing grounding in some of the most extraordinary composed-notated repertory—with its rich orchestrations, harmonic complexity, and large-scale, formal architecture—the world has known. The possibilities are endless in terms of how this cross-fertilization might take place in principal instrument studies. What is important is that until reform advocates, let alone conventionalists, begin to transcend categories and navigate their ways across both the musical world and the various realms of music studies from a transcultural/transdisciplinary perspective, these kinds of possibilities will be undermined by knee-jerk reactions and stereotypical assumptions. The repositioning of knowledge and skill areas need not be construed as the wholesale removal of conventional approaches, and may result in new levels of conventional achievement. The private lesson that is so emblematic of conventional practice is a potential site for extraordinary progress providing colleagues can view it with new eyes.

A New Purpose for Private Instruction

In order to aid this shift, here I offer a statement that parallels my earlier remarks on improvisation and composition not as pedagogical aids to enhance musicianship studies, but rather musicianship studies as aids for improvisatory and compositional development. That is, *the purpose of instrumental studies is not, as conventionally construed, to develop skills to play standard repertory, or in other words, music created by others. Rather, the purpose of instrumental studies is to develop skills that facilitate one's own improvising and composing, a direct byproduct of which is the development of skills in playing standard (and other) repertory.*

Inherent in this shift of purpose is that most musicians will gravitate toward the pathway of the contemporary improviser–composer–performer, with a small minority gravitating toward interpretive performance specialists. While this represents a dramatic reversal of conventional career directions, it addresses several important issues. First, it places creative artistry at the center, and situates interpretive musicianship in that context. Second, more precisely, it places transcultural aural/creative/technical foundations at the center and situates monocultural performance skills in that context. Third, it provides a more realistic distribution of career pathways that is aligned with the professional realities on the musical world. The vast majority of students graduating in today's monocultural performance pathways has little hope for orchestral positions or solo careers: Why not render this avenue a self-driven choice rather than de facto, institution-driven trajectory? And while improvising and composing musicians will encounter their share of challenges in musical livelihoods, the creativity, breadth, and integration of their artistry will open up pathways otherwise not available.

Perhaps ironically, jazz-based musical foundations, from which connections to European and other sources are carefully fashioned, may have the capacity to uphold this transformative function in the very European classical world that shuns the idiom. However, as emphasized previously, if these possibilities are to be harnessed, new levels of change discourse and critical inquiry are needed that are rooted in new principles. If limitations in change advocates' capacities to transcend conventional categories, or multicultural conditioning, are formidable obstacles in themselves, it would be naïve to overlook lingering ethnocentric tendencies that have eluded critical attention. I saw this first hand in conversations leading to the formulation of the Manifesto as well as following its release. A matrix of patterns may be identified that support this contention.

To be sure, the earlier analysis turns upside down how some of the most cherished domains in our field are conceived—with the private lesson arguably at the top of the list. More important, in my view, than the particular details of what I propose—e.g., the exact proportions of Afrological, Eurological, or other sources, whether in musicianship coursework or lessons or ensembles—is that I have identified contours within the diversity realm. I have gone beyond the general, politically correct espousal of support for diversity, which rarely moves the past postmodern leveling discussed in the previous chapter, and sought to delineate key principles for actual musical navigation. This is what I find missing in objections to jazz privileging—a well-developed conception of diversity that reflects critical interrogation of this realm and how to operationalize a commitment to it. It is imperative that reformers identify a cultural topography beyond the multicultural hodgepodge; how can one forge pathways through the infinite expanse without key landmarks? I believe it is also imperative that the question of black music is placed front and center in diversity conversations if these conversations are to be considered as having even a modicum of integrity. Regardless of one's conclusions about the ultimate place of black music in the curriculum and culture of music studies, deliberations that fail to address this question will inevitably be undermined by lower-order assumptions and patterns that elude critical examination.

Improvisatory Interlude

At this point, I thought it might be instructive to share aspects of a conversation I have had with one of my coauthors, David Myers, who has a fairly extensive improvisation background as an organist in classical and church traditions. His questions stimulate further perspectives on the aforementioned points.

DM: You have emphasized the self-transcending properties of jazz. Are there/could there be other potential self-transcending gateways that would arise if we approached pedagogy differently? While you've persuaded me of the value of African American traditions, you've not convinced me that one couldn't achieve the same outcomes via other routes.

ES: As I have emphasized in the previous chapter, the purpose of engagement within all areas of music is to render them self-transcending gateways to the whole. The question then becomes how to achieve this. Improvisation and composition are central, particularly when established as part of one's musical identity. The next step is to identify domains in which improvising and composing are most fully represented, so they can work synergistically. Jazz comes to the fore, particularly when considering the improvised music offshoots that extend from the idiom, and the compositional achievements beyond basic song form (an art in itself) that draw from European classical influences and incorporate large scale formal architecture. Grounding in jazz would provide a creative infrastructure that helps musicians realize all areas of engagement as self-transcending gateways.

DM: What I want is to move freely between French Romantic and the blues, or to improvise in the style of Bach; can jazz help me do this?

ES: Jazz grounding will not circumvent rigorous study in any given genre, but rather will provide formidable foundational tools that are aligned with the present moment and also promote wide-ranging explorations. Your aspirations underscore two points discussed earlier. One is that we enter the timeline of history through creative engagement in the music of the present. Second is the nexus between Afrological and Eurological streams discussed previously. Jazz can be a key entryway to that nexus for 21st-century American musicians and many others around the world.

DM: I'm a good improviser (in the classical and church organ tradition) who can change keys easily without ever having had any jazz background. I can take a hymn-tune and completely reharmonize it and improvise on it between verses such that when I return to the tune itself, perhaps a half step or step higher than original, I can enhance congregational singing to a point that lifts the roof—and by indicating that the verse is to move to unison singing. It's not African American based but it's fully engaging—Where and how does this fit, if at all?

ES: It fits in wonderfully! But let's go back to our mission, which is to provide a framework that will approximate the needs of the majority of musicians to gain creative, diverse, and integrative grounding that enables 21st-century transcultural navigation. Your background is unique; most students—even keyboardists—do not come up through formats in which this kind of improvising thrives. But even so, in order to move toward fulfilling key transcultural goals such as evolution of a personal voice informed by globally diverse traditions, collaboration with musicians from these traditions, and development of corresponding pedagogical skills; musicians with backgrounds like yours would benefit considerably from jazz grounding. It would be difficult to imagine, however, a more powerful example of the Arological/Eurological nexus.

Interrogating Objections/Unearthing Ethnocentrisms

The first indicator that jazz and black music might represent an "ethnocentric blind spot" in reform circles was the resistance encountered in the task force itself, as well as after the release of the report, to the foundational positioning of these musical practices. Even as I attended carefully to their every mention, taking care to emphasize the self-transcending impetus that would provide students with powerful tools for broad navigation, the response of "jazz privileging" was still encountered. The fact that these realms of musicking only appeared sporadically—a few handfuls of times in an over 13,000-word document—underscores my point. I would add that in much of this mention, jazz was not endorsed per se but simply listed among a range of genres in order to underscore the sheer expanse of today's musical landscape. Again, this is not to deny the possibility that a self-confining approach to jazz, as one might reasonably characterize at least some of conventional jazz studies, might undermine the broader intention. But here I might argue that even a conservative approach to jazz still offers tools that, in existing under a single roof, could still considerably contribute to the musicianship needed in our time. However, no such conversation transpired; instead a knee-jerk reaction that one hegemony was being replaced by another shrouded any kind of productive exchange.

When I situate this pattern within a broader range of factors, I find my concerns substantiated. Here it is important to recognize that the vast majority of change advocates, who are naturally products of conventional music studies culture and training, are not jazz practitioners or contemporary improvisers–composers of any kind and that this may certainly contribute to the response. Combined with minimal critical interrogation of language in reform circles, it is inevitable that the conversation would be tainted by a lower-order reading of the term "jazz"—as a kind of music that, existing among the infinitude of stylistic compartments in the overarching landscape, comes early on under the *J*s in the alphabet. With the idea foreign in the reform community of important cultural topographies that might exist within this landscape that are key to its navigation, it would be inevitable that Small's and others' recognition of African American music in this capacity would remain elusive. Might, then, the problem be not so much ethnocentric aversion to certain musical forms but simply narrow musical horizons in the reform community?

While this partially holds, I believe there is reason to look further into the possibility of lingering ethnocentric tendencies. The fact that Small has been such a prominent figure in reform conversations, yet the African American musicking that has long been central to this thought has remained at the periphery of these conversations, is notably consistent with my concerns. These concerns are exacerbated when I reflect on personal observations from my extensive travels within and beyond music studies. Within the field, I have noticed over the years an almost palpable sense among some colleagues a sense of pride in their ignorance of jazz, as if somehow the fact that one's musical erudition remains "untainted" by understanding music outside of the European classical tradition is a sign of sophistication. While I do not encounter this in reform circles, it would be inevitable that at least of this attitude is inherited by reformers who have come up through this system. One need not denounce jazz and black music, and could even pay it lip service, as long it is still kept at a safe enough distance.

By contrast, I encounter the opposite in my extensive work in interdisciplinary circles. When I lecture and collaborate with colleagues in business, sciences, and the humanities, I am often deeply impressed by the conversance with jazz—and the broader musical world—displayed by practitioners in widely disparate fields. It is not that these colleagues have the kind of technical understanding one finds among specialists, but they have well-developed musical instincts and can grapple with higher-order issues. I find I can have conversations in medical schools and English departments about topics such as the establishment of a creative identity, jazz as a self-transcending pathway to global navigation, and the development of an individual voice that I am hard-pressed to have with colleagues in music. Moreover, while it is near impossible to have an informed dialogue among music colleagues—and even many reform advocates—about the parallels between African American music in music studies and the newly enlivened black-white race relations in society at large that have cropped up in recent years; I routinely have deeply insightful and meaningful conversations on this topic outside of music.

If the previous observations give some degree of substance to my concerns, I believe a further realm of inquiry significantly underscores my position. Here I am talking about the use of hegemonic, discriminatory language in the field and in reform circles that flies in the face of even the most modest diversity aspirations. While critical interrogation of language as a powerful agent for perpetuating limiting ethnocentric and racist stereotypes is a prominent aspect of diversity efforts in overall education and society, music studies and music studies reform has been immune to this fundamental recognition, thus leaving marginalizing terminology intact.

Hegemonic Language in Reform Circles

I have been increasingly struck in recent years at the frequent use of the heading "Art Music"—or some variation thereof (i.e., Western Art Music)—to refer to what is commonly known as the European classical tradition. In other words, as an alternative to the informal, and ostensibly less erudite heading "classical"—because technically it also refers to a particular period within the European heritage—some form of "Art Music" is favored. The problem is that, in stipulating that this particular musical tradition warrants characterization as art, the statement is made loud and clear that other traditions do not. As I queried several colleagues at the 2015 Conference for Diversity in Music Education: "So you are suggesting that the musical expressions of John Coltrane, Miles Davis, Bobby McFerrin, and Pat Metheny do not constitute art?" While of course, the reply is that this not what was intended, one cannot deny that it is the effect. Nor the pernicious nature of what is conveyed. Think about it: If one insists on the essential place of the arts in human experience, and then one uses language that clearly stipulates that only the music of a given culture—in this case, Europe—is worthy of being categorized as art; does one not, then, perpetuate both the most egregious denigration of the vast majority of the world's musical cultures? Might it not be unreasonable to infer in this terminology the denigration of the societies from which the artistic expressions not worthy of being considered art originate? Even if it is insisted that this use of the heading Art Music is not intended in this way, how can it be justified to our students, or our children? Whereas diversity conversations at large tend to devote considerable attention to language, diversity conversations in music are arguably oblivious to this important dimension.

I believe, furthermore, that a strong case may be made that the use of Art Music to refer exclusively to the European classical tradition is even more pernicious than the use of overtly derogatory racial, sexist, and homophobic slurs. Why? Because it takes the power of language a step further—moving from the overt harmful impact resulting from words that *are* spoken, to an even more harmful impact that results from words, due to how they are framed, that *are not*. Where the first, as distasteful as it is, operates within a specter of honesty and clarity of intention, the second operates in the shadows of deceitful discrimination and indoctrination. The term for this is "exnomination" (Lewis, 2008), with the common use of the heading Art Music a prime example, although others in music studies will be noted later.

To go into this more fully: Whereas overtly discriminatory language actually directs its destructive focus at the individual or group it wishes to belittle, exnomination deploys a more surreptitious maneuver. Rather than using overtly offensive language; neutral terminology—or even that which can be read as laudatory—is used that suggests, at least in theory, inclusion and progress, while in practice the opposite prevails. As a result, the message conveyed is that the reasons for the exclusion—namely the intrinsic unworthiness of that which is excluded—are so obvious, so self-evident, that they *need not even be stated*. Because this deceptively hegemonic use of terminology is not conducive to a critical reflection or response when it is uttered, exnomination exonerates speakers from the responsibility of the impact of their words. And in paradigm-blind circles, such as those that advance multicultural (versus transcultural) agendas, even the written word—which one would think would invite critical interrogation—eludes attention.

Other examples of exnomination include the common headings New Music, Contemporary Music, Early Music, and though not so current these days, Serious Music. As with Art Music, while all of these descriptors in principle might include a wide swath of music from across the globe, in practice they are typically reserved for European classical music and its offshoots. Listeners would have to look long and far to find contemporary or mainstream jazz, let alone hip hop, at an academic New Music concert, even if within these genres excluded might be music that is far more recent than the 20th-century European-based repertoire that is still often played at these concerts. In addition to the more blatant forms of exnomination noted earlier are those that are more subtle yet no less offensive given their use on a day-to-day basis. A term even as seemingly innocuous as "performance" is a good example. Colleagues who teach interpretive performance of European classical music are referred to as "performance faculty," when in fact there are many kinds of musical performance that are taught in and beyond music schools that are omitted from this categorization. It is presumed that a student getting a degree in violin performance is not learning to play in the style of violins in the Klezmer, or Turkish, or South Indian, or jazz styles—even if all of which are rich forms of violin performance.

The same principle holds for history, musicology, and theory, the study of which again is uncritically presumed to be centered in European roots. The term "ethnomusicology" is reserved for non-European traditions, with the heading Historical Musicology, a potently charged form of exnomination that includes not just one but two terms that uphold the effect, reinforcing its distance from the ostensibly unpalatable global embrace of ethno. The implication is that only the European tradition, despite the fact that most of what is studied, and the access to study within it, dates back only a few centuries, includes a history worth attention of musicologists.

I believe the time has come for the music studies reform community to take a strong stance on the issue of language. Every time hegemonic terminology is used, and our colleagues, students, and children hear it, the overarching ethnocentric indoctrination in our field is fortified—this at a time in human history when the need to combat this pathology has never been more urgent. The time has come for the music studies reform movement to not only embody the leadership exemplified decades ago in broader social justice movements—civil rights, women's rights, gay rights—and also in realms where the issue of terminology has arisen more recently.

What might be an alternative to the heading Art Music? Patricia Campbell and I have discussed this question at length. While I am somewhat amenable to her preference for the heading "concert music," I still believe the heading "European classical" is the most viable, even if not yet ideal. For one thing, the phrase is crystal clear—everyone, from the musicologist to the dentist to the middle school student, has enough of a sense of what it means for productive communication to take place. Concerns about confusion over whether the reference is toward the classical period or the heritage writ large are immediately resolved, if not by context, by word choice: Reference to the European classical tradition, or heritage, or lineage, denotes the centuries-long body of works and composers from Machaut to Copland, or however far back and forward one wishes to go in that continuum. The "classical *period*" within the European tradition, then, refers to the century roughly spanning the work of Haydn, Mozart, and Beethoven and their contemporaries. Colleagues concerned about appearing less sophisticated about this generic use of the word "classical" need only look at the Sunday *New York Times* music section, or the writings of Gunther Schuller, or more recently Robert Freeman's book *The Crisis of Classical Music in America*.

The fact that substantive dialogue about language and terminology, particularly with racial/ethnic implications in view, has been minimal in reform conversations confirms my deep concerns about the pervasive ethnocentrism in not only neoEurocentric practice but efforts to reform it. The broader vision of the Manifesto will not be realized until change visionaries place this point front and center and critically investigate it. I cannot see how anyone can lay claim to a commitment to diversity without taking this step.

As troubling as this recognition may be, it can also—once placed front and center—be liberating in that it allows us to move beyond hiding from the accusations of personalized shortcomings and realize that these tendencies, to one degree or another, are an inevitable aspect of growing up in any given culture. We all have these patterns—at which point we can move from whether or not individual X is racist to engagement with deep transformative work to replace these tendencies with a loving and celebratory embrace of persons of all backgrounds. But once again, this needs to be far more than the typical diversity gloss, where it is politically correct to profess an overarching affinity for all cultures and then ignore patterns of marginalization right at one's doorstep. For Americans (U.S.), the holocaust of slavery—and its many lingering ramifications—represents an enormously tragic yet pivotal gateway to enter into cultivating a genuine diversity awareness in our time and place. The same role could be ascribed to the history of Native Americans; these are aspects of our cultural identity that need to be dealt with if we are to truly integrate within a global society. Those who have taken this work seriously know how deeply imprinted the tendencies are, and that the work toward liberation from this conditioning is never finished: It is as lifelong as any program of addiction rehab, requiring ongoing vigilance about ingrained patterns in thinking, language, and behavior, not a task that can be completed by occasional attendance at academic seminars or weekend workshops.

Final Thoughts

If our field is to move forward, the change movement needs to adopt a more robust self-critical approach in order to identify and liberate from conspicuous patterns that preclude even moderate efforts at change. In this chapter and the last, I have emphasized the need for a deeper reading of creativity, inherent in which are deeper conceptions of diversity, integration, critical thinking, self-sufficiency, and a host of other key attributes for today's musicians, to underpin this shift. In arguing in this chapter that jazz and black music offer powerful resources for late 20th- and 21st-century musical navigation that have largely been overlooked to the detriment of the change project and what we can offer our students, I have placed front and center the possibility of lapses in diversity that directly extend from the broader creativity deficiency. If the principle of a creativity-based self-transcending gateway has been elusive in change conversations, when this shortcoming conspires with lingering ethnocentric biases that are triggered by arguments for the foundational positioning of black music, formidable psychological underpinnings for "jazz privileging" objections come into focus. Whether or not one accepts my conclusions on these points, I hope my analysis spurs further reflection on these points and underscores the need for deep introspection in order to ferret out conditioned tendencies that most change advocates have inherited from the neoEuroclassical model, which it is essential in this work to differentiate from the creativity-based European classical tradition.

In closing, I believe it is helpful to emphasize how jazz can help illuminate these tendencies and guide reform visioning from lower-order to higher-order platforms. When using the three pillars as a lens, it becomes clear that, in the realm of creativity, jazz exemplifies the role of improvisation and composition as more than an add-on to music studies, but as a foundational aspect of one's musical identity. Jazz exemplifies the principle of a self-transcending gateway, where an idiom or discipline is approached not as a self-confining destination, but as point of departure that opens up—through its creative foundations as well as other key facets (pitch-rhythmic languages)—to wide-ranging terrain.

In the realm of diversity, jazz's creative foundations make possible a shift from multicultural to transcultural engagement, where "teaching about" opens up to "enlivening interior connections to" diverse musical cultures via the infusion of wide-ranging influences in the emergent creative voice. The virtually impossible task of trying to cover all of the world's music in a given curriculum shifts from establishing patterns of connection and self-driven investigation deep in the creative wellsprings of the student.

In the realm of integration, jazz not only spans but integrates within a given stylistic range—the broad range of practice and inquiry inherent in systematic approaches to improvisation and composition, which as noted extend to a broad spectrum of creative, performative, theoretical, historical, cognitive, psychosomatic, aesthetic, and spiritual terrain.

The point, yet again, is not that jazz contains the whole picture of what today's musicians need, but that it represents a powerful platform—already in our midst—upon which an ever-wider range of important tools may be thoughtfully integrated in the foundational rebuilding process.

The deeper the reading of the musical ramifications of the Manifesto, the broader the range of extramusical ramifications that come into view, which is the focus of the next chapter.

References

Banfield, William C. 2010. *Cultural Codes: Makings of a Black Music Philosophy*. Lanham, MD: Scarecrow Press.
Berendt, Joachim-Ernst. 1991. *The World Is Sound: Nada Brahma*. Rochester, VT: Destiny.
Floyd, Samuel A. 1995. *The Power of Black Music: Interpreting Its History from Africa to the United States*. New York: Oxford University Press.
Hester, Karlton. 2009. *Bigotry and the Afrocentric "Jazz" Evolution*. San Diego: University Readers.
Jones, LeRoi. 1963. *Blues People: Negro Music in White America*. New York: Harper Collins/Perennial.
Lewis, George E. 1996. Improvised Music since 1950: Afrological and Eurological Perspectives. *Black Music Research* 16 (Spring), 91–119.
Lewis, George E. 2008. *A Power Stronger Than Itself: The AACM and American Experimental Music*. Chicago: University of Chicago Press.
Monson, Ingrid. 1996. *Saying Something: Jazz Improvisation and Interaction*. Chicago: University of Chicago Press.
Pressing, Jeff. 2002. Black Atlantic Rhythm: Its Computational and Transcultural Foundations. *Music Perception* 19:3, 285–310.
Ramsey, Guthrie. 2003. *Race Music: Black Cultures from Bebop to Hip Hop*. Berkeley: University of California Press.
Reimer, Bennett. 2003. *A Philosophy of Music Education: Advancing the Vision*. Chicago: University of Chicago Press.
Sarath, Edward W. 2010. *Music Theory Through Improvisation*. New York: Routledge.
Sarath, Edward W. 2013. *Improvisation, Creativity, and Consciousness*. Albany: SUNY.
Small, Christopher. 1994. *Music of the Common Tongue*. London: Calder Riverrun.
Small, Christopher. 1996. *Music, Society, Education*. Hanover, NH: Wesleyan University Press.
Sweet, Robert. 1996. *Music Universe, Music Mind*. Ann Arbor: Arborville.

# 7

WIDER RAMIFICATIONS OF THE MANIFESTO

David E. Myers

The model of musician education that took hold in the early 20th century in the United States—a model that reflects Western European assumptions and practices—was part of a cultural ecosystem that advanced the professionalism of classical music in American society. From the time of their beginnings in the late 19th century, American orchestras considered education to be an important mission. Increasing professionalization, however, led toward viewing education as ancillary to the primary goal of performance, emphasizing the work of highly talented musicians who were observed and listened to by sedate, well-attired, increasingly affluent audiences. Conner (2008) notes that today "We are accustomed—and conditioned—to treating the . . . concert hall . . . as a kind of sacred place where there is no touching and no talking" (p. 105).

A thorough discussion of the social and cultural dimensions of the growth of classical music in the U.S. and its European antecedents is beyond the scope of this chapter, though enlightened understanding of this intriguing history is valuable for every music faculty member and student. Conner (2008) explores the demise of an "active, participatory ethos that defined Western audiences for more than 2000 years. . . . [and] . . . . the emergence of the passive twentieth-century arts audience." (p. 109). Noting the development of controlled lighting that darkened the audience and spotlighted performers, Conner asserts that this change "transformed the . . . concert hall from a site of assembly—ripe for public discussion and collective action—to one of quiet reception" (p. 110). In addition, she references what Levine (1988) called sacralization of the arts—notions of "high" culture that led toward the expectation of worship-like demeanor among audiences and unquestioning acceptance of the authority of artists in performance. Such attitudes are at odds with perceptions of the arts as integral to the experience of being human, says Conner, arguing that people want the "interplay of ideas, experience, data, and feeling that makes up the arts experience" (p. 115).

In the case of music, these behavioral conventions and perspectives that diminished engagement between performers and audience left growing numbers of audience members literally "in the dark" with regard to classical music and its relevance to everyday life. Moreover, the invention of the phonograph, which provided opportunities to hear classical music in the comfort of homes and in classrooms, led to extolling listening as a primary means of music "engagement." School music participation consequently trended toward rising prominence of organized ensembles mimicking those of the professional world—choirs, bands, and orchestras—with little to no education for personal and small-group social music making, or for the spontaneous creation of music.

The promise of music-for-all listening classes embodied in marketing the phonograph ironically contributed to a prevailing culture of school music in which students who wished to participate beyond classical music appreciation classes had to begin structured, notation-based instrumental lessons by age nine or ten, or to pass voice auditions to sing in choirs. Teachers, encouraged in part by their collegiate music training, preferred to specialize in performance teaching and conducting, viewing music-for-all classes as less worthy of their expertise. Over time, a combination of student dissatisfaction with poorly taught classical music appreciation classes and teachers' lack of interest in teaching them resulted in an almost exclusive emphasis on large, conducted ensembles as the secondary music curriculum. This performance emphasis and specialization, fueled by interscholastic music competitions and the music industry, ultimately became the basis on which higher education programs educated aspiring music teachers for schools. Music-for-all became equivalent to "elementary school general music," and performance dominated secondary school programs.

Such a normative music and music education curricular culture derived *not* from the nature and structure of music and music experience in all times and places, but from a desire to perform and advance classical repertoire among talented students. These students, presumably, would then become music majors in college and, in turn, career performers and music teachers who would perpetuate the cultural status quo. One by one, schools and the music education professional establishment simply dropped a sense of commitment to the public good through secondary-school music classes for *all* students—classes that might build a continuum of music interest and expertise from amateur to professional, from monocultural to transcultural, and that would enrich communities on a broad and sustainable scale. John Philip Sousa wrote in 1906 that

> There are more pianos, violins, guitars, mandolins, and banjos among the working classes of America than in all the rest of the world. . . . [but] The tide of amateurism cannot but recede, until there will be left only the mechanical device and the professional executants. Then what of the national throat. . . . What of the national chest? Will it not shrink?
>
> *(Sousa, 1906/1993)*

Sousa's legitimate cause for worry is no more apparent than when one witnesses the failure of American sports audiences to engage in respectful, full-throated singing of the national anthem, replaced instead by watching commercial singers perform absurd and frequently out-of-tune embellishments that are an assault on feelings of national pride.

Following the lead of professionalization and specialization, conservatories and music schools adopted the staged performance model, emphasizing adulation of the talent and expertise of the professional performer and building concert halls and other performance spaces as part of their physical facilities. Naturally, the curriculum thus required that enormous amounts of time be devoted to preparing formal concerts and recitals, regardless of the proportionately small number of graduates who would ever earn their livings as performers. In these settings, even America's indigenous art form of jazz, which originated in social gathering places, became a "concert" event. And chamber music, with its assumption of intimate spaces and close-up audiences, became a concert hall experience, fortifying the claim that student musicians had to learn to "project" their sounds to fill large halls.

These observations are not intended to suggest that concert halls and performances therein are necessarily antithetical to shared participatory experiences among both performers and audience members, nor that active listening in concert settings is not a valid form of engagement. The issue, instead, is one of how, among a wide range of meaningful music experiences in a wide range of venues, the live and dynamic interactions of performers and audiences can achieve a sense of participation in co-constructed meaning. In the words of Christopher Small (1998), who views music as an action rather than an object: "To music is to take part, in any capacity, in a musical performance, whether by performing, by listening, by rehearsing or practicing, by providing material for performance (what is called composing), or by dancing" (p. 9). Adopting Small's premise as an animating source of assumption-testing, as described in Chapter 3, in what ways does, can, or should the undergraduate music major curriculum foster career musicians' knowledge and capacities as catalysts for music as participatory experience for all?

Within this performance-dominated thinking about the curriculum, even within "academic" music studies such as theory and musicology, one of the most apparent lapses is the failure to acknowledge that the careers of music graduates generally rely on some measure of teaching for ongoing income, and to view this reality as both a curricular and professional opportunity rather than a fallback to performance careers. Unless one is specifically a music education major preparing to teach in precollegiate public and private school settings, the curriculum incorporates little to no education in the teaching of music to others, whether in amateur or professional contexts, in private studios or classrooms, in formal or informal situations, in higher education or in communities. Moreover, low regard for music teacher education programs within music schools and departments is widespread, as evidenced by a colleague who once opined that music educators have a "strange mindset." And, as aforementioned, there is virtually no preparation in how to teach classes for *all* students at the secondary level. The consequences of this lack of pedagogical knowledge are evident in the large numbers of individuals of all ages and types, many of them music lovers, including undergraduate music majors, who conscientiously undertake music study only to be discouraged by teachers having little to no understanding of or appreciation for research-based principles of learning and teaching.

Harbingers of Inevitable Change

It's often been said that change is inevitable and that, in higher education, change often follows practice by at least a decade. Over the past decade and a half, assumptions associated with the curricular manifestations described previously have been turned on their heads by younger music graduates who, of their own volition, have been developing innovative career models. These enterprising musicians have assumed and presumed a much more circumspect view of how classical music performance may best attract, energize, and maintain audiences. Rejecting the once paramount goal of either performing in a full-time, or mostly full-time, orchestra or opera company, playing at the direction of others, having repertoire selected for them, and surviving financially by teaching and "gigging," today's performers have formed collectives out of which smaller ensembles model intentional integration of audience engagement, self-management, artistry, and education work. The integration of these professional dimensions provides more control of their careers and more professional satisfaction in terms of the connections they wish to nurture with audiences. Moreover, such integration serves as a reminder that the longstanding separation of curricular content and process is not reflective of the way music works in everyday life.

Performing and teaching are no longer necessarily separate aspects of professional trajectories, but are united in a composite self-view of the musician working in society. Echoing in some ways the realities of the Western European history of arts experience as social interaction, venues may include concert halls, but also black box theatres, coffee shops, bars, outdoor settings, and other gathering places where people may converse with the artists and each other, sip a beverage while listening, and dress in casual attire. Audience deportment is not limited to rigidly established conventions of when it is "proper" to applaud, but involves spontaneous displays of appreciation (and perhaps sometimes nonappreciation) that may include the kinds of responses typically heard today only in rock and jazz concerts, and in African American church services. Groups are developing loyal followings and there is a repartee between audience and performers that is palpable and genuine. Repertoire crosses the lines of traditional stylistic parameters, ranging from newly composed to historic works, often incorporating works derived from and influenced by diverse cultural influences.

Individual artists are breaking new ground as well, albeit not that differently from the way virtuosic performers interacted with audiences throughout history. One example is the cross-generational fascination with the punk-styled, singlet- and sequins-attired, classically trained organist Cameron Carpenter. Vivascene described a Sony release of Carpenter's this way: "Determined to turn classical norms upside down and inside out, this virtuosic, audacious, quixotic musician presents here a hand-picked selection of classical and popular repertoire, all performed with his trademark flair, verve and panache."[1] Whether these creative approaches to music performance, engagement, and career development represent a "movement" that will last remains to be seen; however, what is clear is that conventional 20th-century thinking about music, audiences, and society, as well as musicians' roles therein, is changing. These experiences increasingly demonstrate that it is not classical music that is off putting, but rather the conventions that have evolved around classical music that too often intimidate and discourage audiences.

Entrepreneurship Studies and Curricular Change

As entrepreneurship has become a buzzword in many fields, including higher music education, some have tended to relegate the term to an advocacy focus, offering business-oriented tactics designed to convince audiences to buy into what musicians are selling. This popular conceptualization of entrepreneurship is frequently extolled as the key to musicians' achieving livable wages by properly marketing and selling their products, whether it be through crowd-sourcing or other means. In other words, this form of entrepreneurship requires no innovation with regard to music itself, the work of musicians, or the social implications and dimensions of musicians' service to the public good.

Groups and artists such as those described earlier, however, are taking a different approach, thinking about the interests, needs, and responses of audiences and the responsibilities musicians have for understanding them. While cognizant of the business dimensions of their work, they emphasize, often charismatically, artistic value, creativity, engagement, and diversity as the bases of their operations. Gerald Klickstein, Director of the Music Entrepreneurship and Career Center at the Peabody Conservatory, notes,

> entrepreneurship grows from creativity, [thus]one of our primary educational missions should be to encourage creativity. . . . All too often, music students are so overburdened—say, by being obliged to perform in several ensembles each semester—that they're unable to pursue goals of individual interest. In effect, some students wind up serving the institutions where they study instead of the educational institutions serving the students' needs. As a result, many students learn more about conformity than independent thinking. Let's ensure that the college experience prepares students to flourish as self-directed musicians after they earn their degrees.[2]

In a 2013 address to music students at the University of Minnesota, Claire Chase, founder and artistic director of the International Contemporary Ensemble, offered the following perspectives on being a professional musician in the 21st century:

a. To perform is to teach, to teach is to perform
b. To learn is to be creatively engaged
c. Nurturing new audiences is a shared responsibility of all those claiming the profession of music
d. Artistry, engagement, and entrepreneurship are inseparable
e. The Twentieth Century was the century of specialization; the Twenty-first Century is the century of integration and collaboration

(Keynote Address, 2013)

Chase's perspectives and those of other creative contemporary musicians align with those of the brilliant Austrian economist, Josef Schumpeter, who argued for the duality of innovation and entrepreneurship. In this view, entrepreneurs are those who create change, the embodiment of both innovation *and* implementation of innovation (Śledzik, 2013, p. 91). In a column that bears Schumpeter's name, the *Economist* queried in a 2010 article titled *Declining by Degree* whether American universities may be going the way of its car companies (p. 74). More to the point, could American schools, departments, and colleges of music be in a potential decline from a failure to change?

The musicians described previously are building new career models that integrate, rather than segregate, functions such as artistry, engagement, and entrepreneurship, and that place a high priority on creativity, teaching, and collaboration. However, as the Manifesto asserts, despite the essential role of these functions, both historically and culturally, for musicians across classical, vernacular, and popular realms, higher music education largely maintains a curricular mindset that contradicts this reality. Undergraduates thus too often experience curricula based on the acquisition and demonstration of technical expertise in performing and studying music, delivered in a fractured environment of isolated and seemingly unrelated experiences in which it is assumed the student will make the necessary connections. By contrast, the Manifesto argues for knowledge and skill development nurtured in the context of a creativity-based, socioculturally responsible approach that explicitly derives its structure from the holistic experience of music outside academe, i.e., in the "real world." Technical here is not defined as performance *technique*, but rather refers to information and skill across the curriculum acquired absent contextual realities or purpose, as well as a lack of double-loop thinking among faculty relative to curricular needs of students in relation to their career development.

David Byrne (2013) points out that this lack of experiential context is not limited to higher education's views of music. It is promoted by other segments of the music ecosystem as well. "Most arts grants;" Byrne says, "focus on the work, rather than on the process that the work comes out of" (p. 296). Noting that music is an experience "more than it is a thing," Byrne echoes Lynne Conner in arguing that the evolution from "making" to "presenting" music has close analogies with selling and consuming. As noted earlier, even with the rise of contemporary interest in music entrepreneurship, higher education music curriculums tend to perpetuate this one-way presenter-to-consumer mentality. The approach of the Manifesto, however, is to base curricula on the experience of music, socially and societally contextualized, so that musicians may in turn be leaders for musical experience in their communities. Such an approach aligns with the views of cultural anthropologist Ellen Dissanayake (1995), who has posited that participatory arts experience, in dually engaging mind and body, supersedes taste and connoisseurship and may serve to counteract tensions, divisiveness, and alienation in society.

In short, unless entrepreneurship studies lead toward creators, innovators, and implementers of change in the ways professional musicians build careers in a context of societal well-being, they represent only the kinds of superficial change that have characterized the field historically. Given the complex and complicated challenges of the music ecosystem identified by Freeman (2014) and others, and both implicitly and explicitly addressed in the Manifesto's call for curricular change in higher education, purporting entrepreneurship as radical change in music studies will ultimately be perceived as much ado about nothing. Those who believe in the importance of entrepreneurship must, themselves, be entrepreneurial about defining its value and relationship to the musical needs of society, not just musicians, and in integrating it holistically into undergraduate preparation.

Curricular Implications of Musicians' Roles in Society

Today, there are healthy dialogues and creative curricular approaches emerging that resonate with some aspects of the Manifesto's recommendations.[3] However, these efforts are the exception rather than the rule, and are too often relegated to electives or to nondegree classes at the periphery of curriculums. Rarely are they manifest as core principles of musician education. Students are neither frequently taught to speak about music in ways that even truly interested individuals may understand, nor are they taught to write about music in enlightening and accessible ways that serve those who pay a considerable price to attend performances.

Because their educations are technically focused, students often fail to grasp the anthropologically/ethnomusicologically documented human affinity for music, thus performing with a kind of spectator-event demeanor rather than inviting audiences into a sense of participatory engagement with music. In too many instances, higher music education continues to hold itself aloof from the idea that the public at large deserves to benefit from the values of classical music and, more importantly, that musicians have an obligation to assure the engagement of diverse audiences with diverse musics and musicians. And among the arts, music is perhaps the most conservative in considering the ways music and musicians may play important and strategic leadership roles around issues such as social justice and cross-cultural understanding.

As part of its ongoing documentation of adult participation in the arts, the National Endowment for the Arts recently released a report entitled *When Going Gets Tough: Barriers and Motivations Affecting Arts Attendance* (2015). Based on a study designed to look more deeply into arts participation declines over the past two decades, the report notes that

> attending the arts presents individuals with opportunities both to define their own sense of identity, and to socialize and deepen bonds with others in their families and in their broader communities—whether they be communities of geography, communities of shared cultural heritage, or communities of common interests.
>
> (p. 1)

It offers a wealth of data and interpretations that could be useful to music faculty and graduates in considering curricular and professional issues, such as the high prevalence of "learning" as a motivating factor for attending arts events, particularly among lower-income populations. Among racial/ethnic minorities and first-generation immigrants, attending arts events is closely related to celebration of cultural heritage, and there is reluctance, even among those *interested* in attending, if they don't have someone to accompany them. Location is another reported barrier to attendance, including lack of time and transportation.

The relevance of this and a host of other studies and reports on arts engagement and participation rests with the call to seize the opportunities that await today's music graduates *if* they are prepared with attitudes of service to society, an understanding of the meaning and value the arts are self-reported to hold in people's lives, and the knowledge and skills to apply their artistic expertise across diverse sectors of society. Double-loop learning questions in this regard might ask whether musicians should be prepared to incorporate *learning* as an embedded quality of their careers. What do the data regarding people's interests in learning something new about the arts imply beyond musicians' traditional teaching roles in public schools, community music schools, private studios, and universities? What kinds of knowledge and skill will musicians need in the context of changing demographics that place them among diverse racial and economic audiences and constituents? Will they know how to engage children, adults, and older adults according to documented age-related change across the lifespan? As noted in Chapter 3, professional impact is a result of understanding problems in social context and applying one's knowledge and skill in relevant ways. Were music schools and departments to assume this crucial mission as part of the education of musicians, it might go far in ameliorating the perennial angst about a perceived lack of value and respect for music and the arts in American society, and it might convey a clear sense of value-added work by musicians that is worthy of being compensated at a living wage.

It bears repeating here that many "problems" facing the arts today are a function of impediments that can be remedied by creative artists themselves, traditional arts organizations, newly emerging arts enterprise, and the philanthropic-government funding complex. A recent report from the James Irvine Foundation (Reidy, 2014) notes the importance of taking art to the people rather than expecting people to come to the art, particularly given the reluctance of disadvantaged populations or individuals from some cultural traditions to enter the sacred and often intimidating space of concert halls. Knowledge, as it is often said, is power, and it is essential that music students engage in exploring and understanding the realities and opportunities for greater societal good associated with their career trajectories. The Manifesto suggests many critical questions that faculty and students may confront as part of the curricular process leading toward music careers. Moving these topics into the mainstream of higher music education and contemplating them in relation to performance, academic, and creative studies is increasingly essential amidst the technological, social, economic, and artistic dimensions of students' futures and livelihoods.

The Urgency of Diversity and Inclusion Initiatives

A survey of philanthropic and institutional websites quickly reveals that the issues of access, equity, diversity, and inclusion confronting society at large are very present in music and the arts generally. A 2015 *Wall Street Journal* article (February 6) reports on Mellon Foundation funding to the Orpheus Chamber Ensemble in hopes of diversifying its membership. The article cites Jesse Rosen, President of the League of American Orchestras, who notes that "The biggest part of addressing diversity of musicians on stage is growing the pipeline. . . . The number of minority musicians coming out of conservatory is extremely small."[4]

Beyond trying to incorporate ethnic diversity into professional ensembles, however, lies the opportunity for musicians to lead in programs and projects that honor diversity in society. The *Chicago Sun-Times* (January 7, 2016) reported on a project of the Lyric Opera of Chicago entitled "Chicago Sings." Spurred by funding from the Mellon Foundation and other sources, it will be a multiyear initiative designed to celebrate the diversity of vocal traditions in Chicago.[5]

In addition to the two programs described previously, there are many high-profile projects underway across the U.S. that indicate the priority and necessity of efforts to build bridges across diverse community sectors and to connect artists and arts organizations with local populations. These are clearly worthy efforts in their own way, but questions remain as to whether they are getting at the issues of access, diversity, and inclusion as embedded values in the lives and work of musicians.

The Manifesto advances diversity as one of its three pillars, operating in tandem with creativity and integration. The aforementioned need for the cultivation of artistic creativity would lay important groundwork for developing diversity as an embedded value in music curriculums and thus, among music students and graduates, by integrating diverse musics fully, knowledgeably, and respectfully into undergraduate music studies. In other words, in the field of music, efforts for equity and inclusion cannot be based solely on people's sharing their cultural heritage through music, or on providing space for diverse musical expressions alongside the primary focus of classical music. Neither can it be based on inculcating persons of color into the Western European classical tradition, valuable as that might be.

Diversity and inclusion, in Manifesto terms, mean that students of all colors graduate with an understanding of the ways in which the musics of the world are endemic within geographic and cultural contexts, but also universal in their sonic expressions of the shared humanity of a global society. As students come to understand both the sonic structures *and* the influential sociocultural contexts of music, they equip themselves to navigate successfully the growing demographic plurality in which they will live and work. Rather than add-on and targeted projects to enhance the perception of classical music organizations as community friendly, musicians educated according to the principles of the Manifesto will—as improvisers, composers, and performers—integrate peoples and musics in ways that dissolve artificial barriers across the musical spectrum.

From a curricular perspective, the mandate to educate such musicians means that higher education must view classical music as one among many. The value of classical music should not be diminished, but it must also be recognized that other heritages bring dimensions of engaged music understanding that the Western classical tradition does not. Students must experience, for example, the sense of musical completeness that arises in the integration of composing, improvising, and performing found in North Indian and Persian classical music, an integration that makes discrete use of the terms difficult to apply. And, as Ed Sarath has documented in Chapter 6 of this volume, they must understand the important and seminal role of African American music in the evolution of music internationally. The Manifesto endorses the curricular centrality of these complementary functions within a holistic perspective that equips musicians not only for confidence, independence, and aesthetic and technical competence, but also for extending their artistry and creativity toward engaging others in rich, socially and aesthetically fulfilling music experiences. As the Manifesto indicates: "A systematic program of improvisation may unite multiple improvisatory languages including style-specific . . . and stylistically open approaches" (p. 58).

Music Among the Disciplines and Professions in Higher Education

While manifest in different ways, the issues and concerns raised by the Manifesto coincide with wider discussions and reports occurring across other disciplines in higher education. In 2011, for example, the American Medical Association (AMA) began offering incentives for medical schools to transform curriculums in relation to 21st-century needs and interests, thus reconsidering the 100-year old pattern of physician education common across the country. The AMA called for changes that might address issues such as enhancing high levels of care through more integration of previously disparate facets of knowledge, educating physicians to be more attuned to cultural differences in diverse communities, building physicians' leadership and communication skills, and emphasizing more personalized diagnoses and treatments. At the University of Michigan, Erin McKean, a surgeon teaching a class on communication and leadership, notes that these are serious issues for students who will have to communicate life and death matters during their careers:

> I was not taught this in medical school myself, [. . . .] We haven't taught people how to be specific about working in teams, how to communicate with peers and colleagues and how to communicate to the general public about what's going on in health care and medicine.[6]

What Michigan and other schools are trying to do now is prepare future doctors for the inevitable changes they will face throughout a long career. Recognizing that no one can predict exactly what that system will be like in years to come, Dr. Raj Mangrulkar, Associate Dean for medical education, University of Michigan, states, "we need to give students the tools to be adaptable, to be resilient, to problem-solve—push through some things, accept some things, but change other things."[7]

In 2006, as referenced in Chapter 3, the Yale School of Management, under Dean Joel Podolny, undertook a complete overhaul of its Master of Business Administration (MBA) curriculum. The goals were to provide a more integrated program of studies that emphasized relevance among previously distinct bodies of knowledge and to encourage stronger relationships between business education and society's interests. Noting the importance of business school graduates' commitments to positive values for society, Podolny noted in 2009 that

> Business schools provide students with many technical skills, but they appear to do little, or nothing, to foster responsibility and accountability. . . . The traditional MBA curriculum has divided the challenges of management and leadership in a dysfunctional way. . . . Because of this distinction, students are convinced that nitty-gritty work can be done without consciously considering factors such as values and ethics.[8]

In his book on refiguring collegiate English studies, Berlin (2003) begins the book's introduction by stating "English studies is in crisis" (p. xi). Later, Berlin makes an observation particularly relevant to the issues of music curriculum raised by the Manifesto: "The notion of 'high' culture was constructed in the eighteenth and nineteenth centuries with the institutionalizing of certain ideologically interested notions of taste" (p. xviii). Following his extended historical overview and critique of the current state of rhetoric instruction in higher education, he cites a proposal for a course focused on students' daily experiences of culture in the broadest possible sense. Beginning with the experiences of the students, not unlike the Manifesto's emphasis on option-rich learning, Berlin notes:

> We start with the personal experience of the students, with emphasis on the position of this experience within its formative context. Our main concern is the relation of current signifying practices to the structuring of subjectivities—of race, class, sexual orientation, age, ethnic, and gender formations. . . . The effort is to make students aware of cultural codes, the competing discourses that influence their positioning as subjects of experience.
>
> *(p. 124)*

In relation to the Manifesto, it is impossible not to wonder how Berlin's observations and proposals for change in the teaching of rhetoric might apply to music students, and to the opportunity to begin the freshman year of music studies with reflective work on music experiences and tastes, their formulations, and their relationships to personalized learning goals and outcomes. As the first set of entries in an undergraduate portfolio, the questions could be revisited multiple times as students mature in their understanding and commitments.

Among the three authors of this volume, significant explorations of the impact of music studies on broader issues in our world may also be noted. In Ed Sarath's seminal appropriation of a consciousness-based worldview called Integral Theory to music, he draws connections between what he calls "improvisatory ecologies" that are inherent in the interactions between music improvisers and their social and physical surroundings and new ways of understanding and addressing today's environmental crises. Just as improvisers need not only to spontaneously adapt and create but also to reflect critically upon the interactive dynamics that govern their creativity, humanity also needs to engage in the same spontaneous creative adaptation, and critical examination thereof, in response to the ecological and other challenges of our times.

Today, there are many calls for creativity as an essential survival trait that crosses the boundaries of global and local problems in many arenas. While arts advocates perennially point to the arts as the genesis of transferable creativity, the truth is that arts pedagogy and practice are not necessarily creative unless creativity is intentionally built into them. In the case of improvisation, for example, the kind of transcendent awareness that may emerge as musicians create, listen, reflect, criticize, extend, develop, and collaborate while maintaining distinctive expression suggests that such collective consciousness may be harnessed to effect a harmonizing influence on society (Bache, 2008; Hagelin et al., 1999). As Byrne (2013) observes, "The way we are taught about music, and the way it's socially and economically positioned, affect whether it's integrated (or not) into our lives, and even what kind of music might come into existence in the future" (p. 268).

Musicians as Community Music Leaders

Over the past two decades, nearly every institution of higher education has developed experiential programs that engage students and faculty with their communities. Often structured via the additive approach discussed elsewhere in this volume, rationales for such programs rarely articulate or evidence value-added—for students and faculty, institutions, or the public—*that derives from within the nature of the academic disciplines themselves and the relevance of that nature to societal issues and concerns.* Who can argue, for example, with the value of helping people learn to complete tax forms, or providing health care assistance, or assisting racially diverse communities in communicating with more shared respect? These are all useful aims, and they undoubtedly raise the consciousness of students around social concerns while also providing important advantages to communities.

But when it comes to the arts, what kinds of added value result from music students' engagement with communities? There are relatively easy answers for career-focused internships that may acquaint students with the artistic and business operations of orchestras, opera companies, community music schools, and other institutions. The prime beneficiaries are the students, though institutions and their constituents may also realize some benefit from having extra hands available to assist with demands.

Some institutions list student teaching as an example of community engagement, but again, the primary beneficiaries here are the students who are on a professional track to become teachers. Some cite "service days," when students go into communities and clean up litter or help to build houses, or provide childcare activities. Others cite after-school tuition provided by students and faculty, which is often largely an extension of formal learning opportunities during after-school hours.

For schools and departments of music, considering community engagement as a viable facet of curricular work provides opportunities to ask double-loop style questions about the role and purpose of music in society and the ways in which they may be tied to professional preparation. Christopher Small (1998) asserts that "to take part in a music act is of central importance to our very humanness" and that "[i]t is only by understanding what people do as they take part in a musical act that we can hope to understand its nature and the function it fulfills in human life" (p. 8). Small's perspective urges faculty to consider the human importance of music by understanding how it functions in people's lives.

By definition, community engagement is meant to be a mutual process of listening, understanding, interacting, and sharing responsibility as well as value. Looking at community engagement this way requires a different approach from sending students out to lead singing in a center for elders, or playing music games in a preschool, or managing patients' clinical compliance by using music for positive behavioral reinforcement. These may all be worthy service goals for music students, but they cannot be construed as value-added community engagement from a truly musical perspective.

Community engagement for music students needs to entail a commitment to being change agents for a greater good *in and through* music creation and participation that provides expressively rich experiences consistent with the realities of musical experience across times and cultures. Potential planning for such experiences should first ask the question of *why* such work is important, particularly if it is to be credentialed in the undergraduate degree program. Other than being good citizens, why should music students travel to New Orleans and help rebuild houses after Hurricane Katrina? Do such experiences exploit opportunities to listen and to understand the musical cultures of those most desperately affected by Katrina? Will music students seek to understand how music ritual and tradition have been part of cultural sustenance and survival? And will they incorporate music experience into their engagement in ways that build relational value between themselves and those of different cultures? Will they consider the devastation that may occur in the artistic richness of these communities by rebuilding projects that potentially destroy their cohesiveness?

In working with domiciled older adults, will music students seek to understand, by researching and listening, the important connections between creativity, overall well-being, and cognitive functioning among older adults? Will they facilitate music engagement that derives out of the traditions, meaning, and experiences that music has provided over a lifetime? Will they assure that experiences are musically valuable in the sense of being sonically and expressively satisfying? Will they understand and evidence the importance of mind-body integration that may relate to the spiritual dimensions of life for those in later years?

Within the Manifesto model of the contemporary improviser–composer–performer, undergraduate students may realize the indelible and transcendent nature of music in real-world contexts that in turn informs their formal studies within the academy. They may become collaborative leaders in mutually worthy engagement that benefits constituents *musically* as a bottom line, and that builds their own understanding and awareness of how music works across cultures and societies. They may become change agents for integrating music and musicians fully into the everyday life of communities.

Conclusion: Educating Students to Shape Society

In a 2009 address to the National Association of Schools of Music, Henry Fogel, former CEO of the League of American Orchestras, ended his comments by asking several hundred heads of music schools and departments this question: "are we preparing [music] students to go forward in this world and help to shape the America of the 21st Century?" From the Manifesto perspective, this is, perhaps the crucial question that those who educate musicians must confront and contemplate. Whereas there are strong tendencies toward trying to advocate for the arts and artists' work, it may be that artists need to approach their work in the context of service and contributions to the greater public good. When music schools and departments graduate students whose knowledge, skills, and value commitments urge them toward full engagement with the roles they may play in societal well-being, it's entirely possible that society in turn will validate the importance of music and musicians as a crucial component of society's fabric.

Notes

1 Cameron Carpenter. 2014, March 5. If You Could Read My Mind. *Vivascene: The Music Magazine*. Retrieved from http://vivascene.com/cameron-carpenter-if-you-could-read-my-mind-album-preview/
2 Gerald Klickstein. 2009, October 26. Music Education and Entrepreneurship. Musicians-Way.com. Retrieved from http://musiciansway.com/blog/2009/10/music-education-and-entrepreneurship/
3 For this reason, the authors have elected not to cite or analyze specific programs that are emerging, respecting the individuality of these efforts. For relevant papers and examples of preliminary change, the reader is directed to programs and proceedings of the national conferences of the College Music Society and the National Association of Schools of Music in 2014 and 2015, as well as the Reflective Conservatoire Conference held at the Guildhall School of Music and Drama, London, UK, in March 2015 and numerous other discipline-specific American higher education meetings. It is important to note that the considerations of the Manifesto and this volume are international in scope.
4 Corinne Ramey. 2015, February 6. An Orchestra Grapples with Diversity. *The Wall Street Journal (online)*. Retrieved from http://www.wsj.com/articles/an-orchestra-grapples-with-diversity-1423255510
5 Hedy Weiss. 2016, January 7. Lyric Opera Project Designed to Set Chicago Singing. *Chicago Sun Times*. Retrieved from http://chicago.suntimes.com/entertainment//lyric-opera-project-designed-set-chicago-singing/
6 Julie Rovner. 2015, April 9. Michigan Medicine. Transforming. Creating. Leading. Medical Schools Reboot for 21st Century. *Kaiser Health News*. Retrieved from http://curriculum.med.umich.edu/updates/medical-schools-reboot-21st-century
7 Ibid. Retrieved from http://www.npr.org/blogs/health/2015/04/09/390440465/medical-schools-reboot-for-21st-century
8 Joel M. Podolny. 2009, March 30. Are Business Schools to Blame? *Harvard Business Review (online)*. Retrieved from https://hbr.org/2009/03/are-business-schools-to-blame.html

References

Bache, C. 2008. *The Living Classroom: Teaching and Collective Consciousness*. Albany: State University of New York Press.
Berlin, J.A. 2003. *Rhetorics, Poetics, and Cultures: Refiguring College English Studies*. West Lafayette: Parlor Press.
Byrne, D. 2013. *How Music Works*. San Francisco: McSweeney's.

Conner, L. 2008. In and Out of the Dark: A Theory about Audience Behavior from Sophocles to Spoken Word. In S. Tepper and B. Ivey (Eds.), *Engaging Art: The Next Treat Transformation of America's Cultural Life* (pp. 103–124). New York: Routledge.

Dissanayake, E. 1995. *Homo Aestheticus: Where Art Comes from and Why*. Seattle: University of Washington Press.

Fogel, H. 2009, November. Speech for the National Meeting of the National Association of Schools of Music, San Diego, CA.

Freeman, R. 2014. *The Crisis of Classical Music in America: Lessons from a Life in the Education of Musicians*. Lanham, MD: Rowman and Littlefield.

Hagelin, J., M. Rainforth, D. Orme-Johnson, K. Cavanaugh, C. Alexander, S. Shatkin, J. Davies, A. O'Hughes, and E. Ross, 1999. Effects of Group Practice of the Transcendental Meditation Program on Preventing Violent Crime in Washington, D.C.: Results of the National Demonstration Project, June–July 1993. *Social Indicators Research* 47:2, 153–201.

Keynote Address. 2013, September 26. Engagement and Entrepreneurship with Contemporary Music. Convocation Keynote Address at the University of Minnesota School of Music.

Levine, L. 1988. *Highbrow/Lowbrow: The Emergence of Cultural Hierarchy in America*. Cambridge: Harvard University Press.

National Endowment for the Arts. 2015. *When Going Gets Tough: Barriers and Motivations Affecting Arts Attendance*. Retrieved from National Endowment for the Arts website: https://www.arts.gov/sites/default/files/when-going-gets-tough-revised2.pdf

Reidy, B. 2014. *Why "Where"? Because "Who"*. San Francisco: James Irvine Foundation.

Schumpeter. 2010. "Declining by Degree" [Column]. *The Economist* 396:8698, 74.

Śledzik, K. 2013. Schumpeter's View on Innovation and Entrepreneurship. In S. Hittmar (Ed.), *Management Trends in Theory and Practice* (pp. 89–95). Retrieved from: https://www.academia.edu/5396861/SCHUMPETER_S_VIEW_ON_INNOVATION_AND_ENTREPRENEURSHIP

Small, C. 1998. *Musicking*. Hanover, NH: Wesleyan University Press of New England.

Sousa, J.P. 1906/1993. Machine Songs IV: The Menace of Mechanical Music. *Computer Music Journal* 17:1, 14–18. Originally published in *Appleton's Magazine, 8*, September 1906.

8
FROM WORDS TO ACTION

Practical Steps Toward Realization
of the Manifesto's Vision

*Edward W. Sarath, David E. Myers,
and Patricia Shehan Campbell*

Our highest priority early on in the CMS Task Force project was to catalyze a new conversation about change in music studies that could fill the needs of educated musicians in the 21st century. This conversation was expected to lay groundwork for subsequent action steps by which a vision of a reformed, revitalized undergraduate program could be realized locally on university campuses of various sizes, shapes, and missions. Long after its release in Autumn 2014, the sheer volume of attention the Manifesto continues to receive, including the enthusiastic embrace of colleagues across many music specializations to dialogue together and convert ideas to action, suggests that the first phase of this work has been a resounding success. Yet we believe significant work remains to be done in terms of fathoming the proposed vision in its fullest dimensions.

We hope that this book illuminates this point and helps fill in some of the gaps in order that steps toward practical application are optimally informed by the principles articulated in the report. We thus turn our attention in this closing chapter toward the implementation phase with dynamic interplay between the two realms—concept and action—always in view. Change, in other words, is not a strictly linear affair whereby one lays out theoretical groundwork in complete form prior to action steps, but rather a nonlinear endeavor in which both continue to evolve in interaction with each other. Thus, as the following commentary emphasizes, while the conceptual foundations of the vision still require elucidation that may best be determined by local factors in every campus context, change and proposals for change must happen in conjunction with practical considerations.

Some preliminary thoughts are in order that set the stage for what follows. First, as the three authors of this text, we realize that foundational change does not happen overnight, and many institutions will choose to proceed via small steps. However, as the Manifesto states, there is an enormous difference between incremental change made with either a blurry or perhaps even constrained vision in mind and that achieved with a wholesale transformation in view. The former will inevitably confine efforts to more of the "curricular tinkering" lamented in the report. The latter makes it possible for seemingly modest strides to trigger openings, perhaps unforeseen, for a more fundamental shift consistent with the proposed vision. Accordingly, we remain vigilant in differentiating between superficial and paradigmatic change. This paradigmatic change requires due diligence and underscores the need for further conversation in which deeper dimensions of the vision are illuminated.

Second, though we personally have worked through dimensions of change on varied fronts, including innovations within conventionally named courses, creation of new courses that provide spaces for the pillars to be revealed within the limitations of a term's work, creation of entirely new curricular models for small cross-sections of students, and establishment of campus-wide initiatives, we view our primary roles as catalysts for the kind of substantive reflection and dialogue that is characteristic of innovation. Reform of a full program of undergraduate music studies, moreover, is new territory for all of us. Requiring the collaborative input of colleagues of varied experiences and receptivity to change, it would be egregious on our part to pretend that we have all the answers in terms of orchestrating this transformation.

The following commentary falls into two basic parts—one that continues to elucidate the Manifesto's key conceptual principles, and a second that offers more specific guidance through the wide array of practical pathways identified in the Manifesto. While our approach remains not to be overly prescriptive and to invite colleagues and institutions to invoke their own creativity in terms of practical implementation, we respond in this volume to many requests for more focused recommendations—within which ample latitude for individual and institutional creativity is never far from view.

Deepening the Conversation in Schools and the Field at Large

As an initial step in expanding the dialogue, we recommend identification of important ways in which the vision of the Manifesto differs from, or extends, much of the previous reform thinking. The following principles or ideas are those that are not commonly broached, or are largely unique to the Manifesto. In addition, we include terrain that is not broached in the Manifesto itself but explored in these pages, thus rendering this chapter a kind of summary of key principles of the book. These can be seen as directly unfolding from expanded conceptions of the three pillars of the Manifesto—creativity, diversity, and integration. We believe that change deliberations that place these principles front and center will be capable of attaining and sustaining new levels of critical integrity and laying groundwork for the new kinds of change we propose.

Unique Contributions of the Manifesto and This Book

A new vision of creativity is key to the emergent platform of curricular transformation, where improvisation and composition are viewed as more than add-ons or pedagogical aids but core to a new kind of musical identity. Principles such as systematic approaches to improvisation and composition, and self-transcending, creativity-driven engagement are core to an expansive and inclusive definition of creativity. This definition reveals how grounding in the primary creative processes of improvisation and composition can enhance creativity and excellence throughout the entire spectrum of music practice and inquiry. From this platform extend importantly reconsidered conceptions of rigor, and the assertion that a creativity-based, fundamentally reconceived paradigm of music studies will enable not only unprecedented achievement in conventional terrain—largely occupied by European classical music—but will do so within a richly diverse, contemporary purview consistent with the realities of 21st-century global, technological, and demographic change. The creativity-centered vision we advocate, moreover, grounds its robust adaptive capacities in new, expressive, and aesthetic principles that exemplify the transformative potential that has long been ascribed to the arts. We do not endorse change for change's sake, but change as an intrinsic feature of human art making.

Diversity, then, represents another key reform topic that is conceived more expansively than in previous reform documents. In directly linking diversity with creativity, the Manifesto provides unique insights into limitations of the prevailing neoEurocentric orientation in the field. Here our differentiation between the neoEurocentric focus on interpretive performance and analytical studies and the creativity-based European classical tradition is significant in that it suggests patterns that have been inherited even in reform circles. We recommend that all music studies across cultures, eras, and styles—from American old-time to Trinidadian steel band, Turkish maqam, and Tunisian pop rai—incorporate integrated listening, movement, performance and participatory experiences. A single world music course, especially one that is largely an academic effort in listening, is only an initial step in the direction of diversity: It is additive only. It typically entails a drive-by tour of music cultures, with little attention to opportunities to live music-making experiences, or the development of deep cultural understanding, or an integrated creativity. The Manifesto emphasizes a higher-order diversity paradigm that promotes the understanding of music as a set of pan-human expressions that are individual, culturally collective, and often cross-cultural in nature. This view of music as a diversity of many-splendored possibilities needs to permeate every facet of study, including core academic courses, applied and ensemble lessons, program events across the curriculum, and most importantly, the overarching artistic identity that is the guiding force for individual and collective engagement and growth.

The creativity–diversity bond further yields a context to appreciate the often-overlooked core musicianship tools inherent in African American musical practice, particularly jazz, and in the characteristics of African diasporic practices at large. There is wide recognition by artist-musicians, scholars, and the music-consuming public at large of the global impact of black music. There is yet the need for even broader connections to be fathomed, and thus the Manifesto treads new ground in illuminating the self-transcending, boundary-crossing capacities inherent in these musical practices. In contrast to conventional views of curricular areas as self-confining destinations, the Manifesto highlights capacities inherent in creativity-driven engagement to penetrate beyond prevailing categories. In urging a shift from a content-oriented view of change to one in which process is central, jazz may be recognized as a primary site in which the Contemporary Improviser Composer Performer artistic identity—which was once central in the European classical lineage—makes its return. The point is not to privilege African American, nor African or other African-diasporic, practices, but to harness the capacities of these expressions to open up wide-ranging connections. Recall the principles of systematic approaches to improvising and composing, where multiple improvisatory and compositional languages are identified to work in tandem with each other, and with rigorous studies in performance, theory, aural skills, rhythmic training, movement, and a host of other areas, to yield a core musicianship framework that significantly exceeds what currently exists in not only scope but also integration within that scope. Jazz is one style within the spectrum of such practices that uniquely encompasses a wide range of creativity, diversity, and integration and thus warrants a prominent place in any curriculum that aspires toward these fundamental artistic aims. This is not to suggest that jazz contains the totality of skills and understanding today's musicians need; rather it is simply to recognize the genre as a uniquely rich core resource already in our midst that, when situated carefully and approached with self-transcending aims, offers a basis for unprecedented further growth.

When one steps back from conventional categories and marvels at the sheer expanse of genres that might be important to the development of student musicianship, what becomes evident is the potential for diverse musical practices to pervade the creativity-driven process of embracing these musical practices in the acts of composition and improvisation. From the music of local communities such as the Mexican American *son jarocho* movement, the network of bluegrass and old-time musicians, Cajun and Creole traditions, to African American gospel choirs, Chinese-origin orchestras and percussion ensembles, drum-and-dance ex-pat populations from Ghana and Guinea, and the widespread extent of Irish traditional music, the challenges and opportunities inherent in 21st-century musical navigation render obsolete the assembly line approach of conventional practice and even reform thinking. Of course, we include European classical music among the expanse of styles worldwide that merit thorough-going creative engagement. The Manifesto argues for skill development in ways that encompasses diversity and creativity, both, through an evolving Contemporary Improviser Composer Performer identity that welcomes in a wide span of Western and world styles for full-on engagement in all of the constituent areas constituent areas.

Our advocacy of this model thus represents a process-based, creativity turn in reform discourse that is always framed with broader navigational aspirations in mind. Chapter 5 goes into specific ways this creativity-based framework can enhance skill development in conventional formats such as the private lesson and musicianship studies. The Manifesto turns on their head concerns that a reformed model of music studies may compromise achievement in arguing for even higher levels of skill development.

Another contribution of the Manifesto involves issues of topical integration. A creativity-based approach reveals deeper, more personalized, and more expansive kinds of cognitive and musical synthesis than are possible in prevailing exhortations for connections between the conventional realms of performance, theory, and history. The creativity-based model situates these established, often siloed areas within a broader and considerably more unified framework, thus embodying the deep and genuine encounters with music and musicians of local and global communities that are essential to the work of 21st-century musicians.

Therefore; while creativity, diversity, and integration are nothing new in change discourse, the Manifesto offers expansive conceptions of these areas that sets its vision apart. Not only are the areas inextricably linked, but the idea that progress along all three fronts extends organically from broader conceptions of creativity represents an important stride forward in change deliberations and positions the study of music squarely within the realities of music as it exists, and has always existed, across cultures and societies.

This yields openings for further areas of consideration and potential application that cut across the Manifesto's three pillars. Cultivation of critical thinking is a clear example. Though a commonly cited goal of higher education, when viewed through the creativity-based lens that is central to the Manifesto it takes on new dimensions. As Ed Sarath examines in Chapter 5, self-transcending creative awareness through improvisation and composition provides a basis whereby students optimally step back from the musicianship endeavor and critically interrogate it along multiple fronts. The meaning of music studies for one's personal and artistic growth, the identification of normative and potentially limiting patterns in the prevailing paradigm, investigation of underlying assumptions, and delineation of areas for further exploration are critical capacities that, as argued, are enlivened through a creative identity. Critical vigilance becomes more than an attitude or intention, and more than a vague outcome without definition, but rooted in actual tools of music and societal engagement. The distinctions between neoEurocentric performance-centric and creativity-based understanding of both the European classical tradition and multiple traditions beyond that canon can now be internalized through direct experience, rendering critical thinking to be far more than an intellectual concept.

The analysis in Chapter 6 of hegemonic language and patterns of aversion to foundational positioning of black music (again as a meaningful exemplar of growing diversity into a program of study) provides important examples of an expanded critical scope that are unique to the conversation catalyzed by the Manifesto. This highlights the intersections among creativity, diversity, and critical thinking. The situating, moreover, of the black music conversation within the context of overarching dialogues about race, and particularly black–white race relations in the United States, represents another layer of the diversity conversation that has been conspicuously absent in the reform discourse on undergraduate music studies. Though the attention to the overarching race issue in this book is admittedly limited, we believe it is nonetheless significant in its underscoring the urgency surrounding the need for this conversation.

In the same self-transcending stroke that is central to heightened critical thinking faculties, capacities for self-sufficient development, independent music making and learning, lifelong inquiry, and attitudes of contributions *to* society rather than entitlement *from* society are enlivened in the form of self-motivational and self-navigational instincts. New dimensions within yet another common reform theme thus come into view through the lens of the Manifesto and the present commentary. From a career development perspective, the emphasis changes from "what do musicians need to succeed" to one of "what does society need from its musicians." This reframing creates the potential for musicians to think entrepreneurially—not in the business and marketing sense—but in the sense of creating added value that leads toward new awareness of the importance of musicians in society.

To this list of further contributions we can also include Patricia Campbell's account of *ngoma*, which as we saw in Chapter 2 involves the inextricable link between music, movement, drama, and ritual. This exemplifies the close linkage between the Manifesto's position on diversity and integration, and opens into a consideration of facets of music learning (and pedagogical process) that encompass elements of orality–aurality, vocalization, and the physical realization of music in eurhythmic movement. New kinds of questions come into focus on this topic: How is *ngoma* to be incorporated in a reconceived music studies framework? Can this happen through modification of existing coursework, or might it require entirely new formats? Might the shift advocated from creativity as an add-on to creativity as foundational be key to accommodating this principle? Might principles of *ngoma* as they appear in the wide world of African Bantu cultures be modified, reinterpreted, and recontextualized for use in classrooms and rehearsal halls of colleges, conservatories, and universities?

Entrepreneurship similarly takes on new dimensions when it comes to the emergent conversation triggered by the Manifesto. As David Myers suggests in the preceding chapter, today's musicians need to focus their marketing and self-promotional efforts on more than cultivating audiences for European classical music. Their efforts must emerge organically out of philosophical and cultural perspectives that incorporate understanding of the role of music in human life and learning, using both musical creativity and broader forms of creativity to engage people in meaningful music-making and development. In a techno-global society, musicians can no longer hope to succeed by advancing a spectator-sport mentality among audiences or, as noted in that same chapter, by maintaining psychological, aesthetic, and physical distance between performers and audiences. Technology, to name yet another pressing reform topic, similarly calls for more nuanced approaches and understanding that ground technological application in robust and deepened musicianship. Our position on technology is consistent with our position on all facets of musicianship: The establishment of creativity-based, CICP foundations will promote higher capacities for exploring, understanding, and critically examining the expressive and pedagogical capacities of technology amid the continuing line of technological developments that will undoubtedly continue to loom as prominent in 21st-century musical practice as life at large.

The Manifesto's Relevance to Music's Specialized Programs

The expanded conversation spawned by the Manifesto thus enables what are often reduced to, and thus readily dismissed as, change buzzwords to be understood and approached in substantive ways. As we begin to look toward practical strategies that may be inferred in the Manifesto and the preceding chapters in this book, a further topic warrants emphasis that is key to the paradigmatic change we advocate. This entails critical examination of the actual demographics of the reform conversation itself—which constituencies have prevailed, and which may be under-represented. In our many years of engagement in these conversations, we find striking tendencies and disparities that we believe need to be acknowledged and rectified.

Music Education, for example, the field responsible for the education of music majors for state-mandated certificates leading to K–12 teaching positions, has been at the forefront of reform conversations from early on, and it is thus endemic to the culture of Music Education for colleagues to be abreast of a wide range of literature that impacts the reform of music studies—not just in terms of preparing music teachers and pedagogical researchers but the field as a whole. This includes the legacy of overall educational philosophy—a short list of whose visionaries might include John Dewey, Carl Rogers, Maxine Greene, and Paulo Freire—as well as music studies pedagogical and reform research. There is a burgeoning literature emanating from "music educationists" on issues of music cognition, learning and development, diversity and inclusion, school and community flows, and curricular innovations and challenges. Indeed, those working in university-level programs in Music Education are to be lauded not only for having produced the largest volume of critical inquiry of their own discipline but of music studies as a whole. Understanding the nature of the music-learning process that proceeds naturally, and that is aided by pedagogical techniques and sequences, should be central to the concerns of all tertiary-level music faculty. Our experience has been that colleagues outside of Music Education tend not to be conversant with this literature, a pattern that we feel needs to change if the required conversation, and corresponding foundational reform, is to transpire. The lack of systematic inclusion of this content in the education of *all* musicians is perhaps one of the most visible lapses in the current undergraduate curriculum, given the prolific presence of teaching as a career component of nearly every musician's work.

At the same time, it is important to recognize that even within the field of Music Education, which historically has been more concerned with reform and evolution than any other specialization, has not tended to be practitioners of the more expansive musicianship they advocate. If a music studies course is to reorient itself around the Contemporary Improviser Composer Performer, the voice of this creative artist needs to be prominent in change conversations. The Manifesto's call is for colleagues from *all* areas of music studies to engage in reflection and action on the issues of its foundational pillars, beginning with the foundational role of creativity across the curriculum.

Although we have maintained that jazz has the potential to be the most apparent embodiment of a contemporary improviser–composer–performer model, it is important to remember that the Manifesto acknowledges that jazz studies has too often failed to derive authentically from the three essential pillars. Here we note that the creative and global thrust that has characterized much of the jazz tradition is not reflected near to the extent possible and necessary in prevailing university jazz programs. Thus the marginalization of this quintessentially American art form must be recognized as a two-way affair, where lingering ethnocentric patterns from within conventional and even reform circles work in tandem with compromised visioning within the jazz constituency itself. If jazz is to deliver the creativity-rich, self-transcending, diverse and integrative musicianship it is capable of delivering to the change enterprise, the field needs to adopt new levels of critical interrogation and corresponding practice within its own horizons. That said, the underrepresentation of jazz at the curricular reform table has rendered change conversations flawed and incomplete.

Again, the point is not to endorse jazz as a self-confining destination—an approach that dominates in many schools and departments of music—but a self-transcending gateway, a principle that is of particular relevance when it comes to navigating the culturally diverse horizons of the musical world. Inasmuch as the ideas of self-confining and self-transcending engagement are among the key contributions the Manifesto and this book make to reform discourse, jazz may emerge as an important realm of study to not only the resultant musical and pedagogical vision, but also to the *process* of visioning. Here is where critical examination of language and terminology become paramount. Does the word "jazz" refer to a closed and finite genre, one among the thousands of genres that exist in the world, or it is understood as a uniquely fertile, self-transcending genre when it comes to fathoming broader connections? Clearly, it is the latter perspective that is endorsed by the Manifesto.

The field of ethnomusicology would certainly seem central to achieving diversity within the musical content of the undergraduate music major program. Yet while ethnomusicology is predicated on the embrace and study of music in cultural and social contexts, it should not be assumed that the answers to curricular reform, particularly relative to diversity, lie solely within the realm and responsibility of ethnomusicologists to achieve for the entirety of the music program. As articulated in the Manifesto, the efforts of those in both academic and performance fields are essential for adopting and acting upon ways of delivering diversity in accordance with the development of an understanding of music for its multiple sonorities, structures, meanings, and functions as well as contributing to the evolution of the individual musically creative voice. In addition, therefore, to ethnomusicology's supply of the stories (and cultural meanings and values) behind the music, students in the undergraduate music major program are well-served by ethnomusicology and world music performance opportunities that inform and enhance their development as keen and culturally sensitive listeners, performers, improvisers and composers. Performance and creative–expressive experiences, therefore, should not be construed as add-ons in the quest for cultural understanding, but as the full embodiment of music as experienced within one's self and across cultures, potentially forming a basis for cross-cultural empathy through lived experience. Consistent with the Manifesto's integration pillar, whether the music is from Korea or Kenya, or whether it is jazz or from Japan or Germany, the interaction of faculty from diverse specializations is critical to the design and delivery of curriculums that live out diversity at its deepest levels. Indeed, full transformation of the undergraduate curriculum might, in its most radical manifestations, transcend the specialized tracks and divisions of a school or department of music and instead arise from curricular organizations that revolve around inherently *musical* topics, questions, and issues to which individuals of all subspecialties may contribute. Such organizational areas might include studies of music in various social and cultural contexts, the art and science of music transmission, cognition, and pedagogy; spirituality; theoretical and historical studies of music; and so forth.

Composition is another field that has much to offer to the reform of the undergraduate music major program. While composition in the academy evolved as a largely European-based endeavor, the integrative ways in which composers think, and their fascination for sonorities and structures across a spectrum of Western and world styles, can contribute in important ways to the musical development of students. Yet here again new levels of critical inquiry into inherited patterns in the education and training of composers needs to transpire if the discipline is to align itself with the expanded horizons articulated in the Manifesto. The systematic approach to composition studies mentioned in Chapter 5, where European concert music, small and large ensemble jazz composition, song writing and other sources inform development, points to not only an expanded compositional palette but also one with a newly defined aesthetic center that is more oriented toward the contemporary confluence. The sounds and processes of music of the African diaspora, the European classical heritage, and the larger gamut of music in the world call for a new conceptual basis rooted in new cultural, cognitive, and transformative principles that, in turn, call for new expressive formats that are informed.

While there will always be a place for fully notated works, regardless of the extent to which they incorporate diversely cultural influences, there is also a need for compositional formats that leave room for improvisatory expression and interaction of performers in order to more fully reflect the emergent nexus. Even if many composers engage in some sort of improvising as part of their creative process, this is not to be conflated with the experience, aesthetic perspective, and pedagogical approaches of the artist who self-identifies as contemporary improviser, and thus reflects on music and life, from the vantage point of improvising musician. In other words, improvisation needs to be construed as more than pedagogical aid or compositional strategy, but as a wave of musical expression unto itself that requires its own conceptual and pedagogical systems. The emergence in the late 20th century of a clearly discernible domain of improvised music underscores this point. Therefore, important awareness raising may be in order even within creativity ranks if the contemporary improviser–composer–performer identity is to guide music studies.

With an initial consortium of most logical participants in place, as noted from the fields of composition, ethnomusicology, jazz and improvisation studies, music education, and technology, contributions from all the specialized realms of music could only expand the reform voice. Though at first glance, performance may be an area that appears less disposed toward the change we advocate, a quick look at the strings world and its increasing embrace of "alternative styles"—in which improvisation and diverse traditions are prevalent—reveals a promising rebuttal of this stereotype. Moreover, attainment of the highest possible levels of performance abilities is an important part of the contemporary improviser–composer–performer model. Percussion is a performance area that has long exhibited affinities for the global musical horizons articulated in the Manifesto's vision; this perspective can be celebrated and inspire other performance faculty to see benefits in this direction for their own students.

Above all, reform conversations need to welcome the participation of all voices from the outset, with the proviso that colleagues involved in the conversation commit to the new level of critical interrogation that is being advanced. We urge that faculty entering the reform conversation speak not as protectors of their turf, that is, representatives—either official or inherited—of their respective fields but as thoughtful teaching musicians responsible for the education of their undergraduate music majors. Change advocates of every hue have important things to offer the dialogue of reforming 21st-century, tertiary-level music major programs of study. A faculty of music comprising multiple areas of expertise can imagine together the shaping of music study in relevant ways that resonate with the needs and interests of contemporary society. To this end, identifying and encouraging key leaders and constituencies and encouraging intentional and conscious interaction among them is key. Emanating from these enhanced dialogues, trajectories for external action will come into view.

Pivotal Change Pathways

The Manifesto is not only distinctive within reform literature in terms of its identification of practical strategies, but also by way of the sheer number of approaches it has identified for achieving a more relevant education for students aspiring to professional lives as musicians in the 21st century. The task for those convinced of the need for change is to find and define effective pathways through this wide slate of options that will fit the needs of their campus context. In a sense, the challenges of navigating the spectrum of change strategies in the Manifesto directly parallel the ordeal of navigating the varied musical practices found globally and living locally in our communities: Central to the task is moving from a kind of flat inventory of change strategies and revised content and process to a richly contoured curricular perspective in which key areas emerge as gateways for significant progress.

For example, the Manifesto mentions the interplay of top-down (institution-driven) and bottom-up (student-driven, option-rich) change approaches, the idea of a decentralized curriculum that enables localized areas (e.g. music education, applied performance, theory) more freedom to delineate pathways for their student constituencies, and the establishment of pilot programs as possible avenues for reform. These are described in a fair amount of detail in the report (Chapter 4) and require further elaboration here, suffice it to mention that they can be pursued independently or in relationship with one another.

Of particular interest to us is a strategy that unites these approaches—involving the creation of a new division within a music unit that is conceived directly around the premises of the Manifesto. In a sense, this could be envisioned as the creation of an entirely new school of music within an existing school, or a specialized track or program within a school, developed even as the larger set of program changes play out in modified form. Consistent with this direction is the foundational reconception of areas that—even within reform conversations—tend to be assumed as the bedrock of any field. Recall distinctions made earlier between the conventional 19th-century curricular pillars (performance, theory, and history) and the Manifesto's change pillars (creativity, diversity, and integration). The creation of a new division affords an opportunity to critically examine these assumptions and the prevailing terminology and engage in the foundational overhaul process from a clean slate. Important to any conversation predicated on this approach would be receptivity to not only new curricular, pedagogical, and aesthetic principles, but the quest to establish an entirely new culture of music studies.

Consistent with the earlier emphasis on including all voices in the change conversation, the new division could be populated by colleagues from any or all existing areas of study. Inherent in this kind of confluence of expertise would be the opportunity to transcend conventional categories and unearth new forms of knowledge and practice. So, even as faculty press forward with change efforts in their core and upper-level courses, in their classrooms, studios, and rehearsal halls, this division would be launched from its foundation without need for dismantling or reassembling from what had come before.

Faculty Hiring and Development: An Essential Interplay

The question of who will teach newly considered content in new ways is essential. Clearly, an institution that begins to move toward the ideals of the Manifesto must consider faculty appointments that embody the artistic terrain delineated. A second strategy—faculty development—will also be needed. Understandably, faculty educated within the normative assumptions outlined in Chapter 7 will find many aspects of the Manifesto's recommendations indicative of a need to reconsider the content and process of their teaching. While one would logically expect that faculty retooling in response to a changing world would be an endemic condition within any population of colleagues in the arts, the highly specialized and technical nature of music studies in the reinterpretive context of performance and academic study has not necessarily instilled attitudes of constantly updated learning, as has to be the case in the corporate world if bottom lines are to be met. Creating occasions—symposia, workshops, and seminars—for addressing context-specific possibilities by which faculty can come to grips with creativity, diversity, and integration as applied to their work is imperative, and building those avenues of learning into faculty incentive and reward systems may well be essential if significant change is to occur.

We believe the interplay of the two approaches—hiring and ongoing professional development—is essential and could yield exciting results. The importance of new faculty appointments, which might even begin with a single new line, is underscored by a principle that obtains in conventional practice and we believe is as relevant to the new vision. We see that an essential first hire for achieving creative, artistic goals may well be (for those faculties absent this expertise) that of a practicing creative artist who serves as exemplar for students. (Such an individual could represent a Manifesto-style approach to a currently normative discipline or perhaps a newly emerging musician of the type described in Chapter 7, where embodying artistry, teaching, scholarship, engagement, and creativity offers a 21st-century model of a faculty profile.) In this context, the capacities for the contemporary improviser–composer–performer to create and teach entirely new core musicianship coursework around this process scope, which would naturally invite integration of diverse traditions, bear particular emphasis. Just as it is presumed that an aspiring violin performance major will study with a first-rate professional violinist, it is equally essentially for aspiring contemporary improvisers–composers–performers to learn in the presence of corresponding professional practitioners. Here we emphasize this not solely from the standpoint of technical prowess, but from a creative and aesthetic vision. The practicing creative artist teaches not only through direction instruction but by exemplifying and thus transmitting artistic and further human values. In addition to the obvious need for adequate representation of faculty Contemporary Improvisers Composers Performers, hiring of artist–musicians of such practices as African American gospel music, Mexican mariachi, Cajun or creolized traditions, or Bluegrass, would contribute to the threading of diverse musical expressions and experiences *within* its core courses as well as to providing specialized courses, seminars, and ensembles. While we fully realize the challenges inherent in creating even a single new faculty line, or in altering the profile of one that is vacated, we believe that even a single such line that is connected with a new program or degree track would be sufficient to generate significant movement toward the reform delineated in the Manifesto and that support for this line could be found with a thoughtfully framed proposal.

Aligning the Manifesto Vision with Existing Reform Themes

As we have emphasized in previous chapters, the vision of the Manifesto is closely connected with prominent reform themes on most college and university campuses. Common examples include creativity, diversity, integrative learning, critical thinking, student-driven education, service learning, and sustainability. Emergent areas in higher education such as contemplative studies and consciousness studies may also be noted as highly promising sites where a reformed music studies paradigm might make important contributions and gains. Among these possibilities, we believe diversity may be among the most fruitful in terms of eliciting support from the higher administration for the aforementioned reform initiatives that relate to the Manifesto. Here an important if ironic observation might be offered that is key to exploring such possibilities—that while music is a realm of human endeavor that is arguably unmatched in its exemplification of diversity, music studies in higher education have conventionally lagged far behind diversity efforts on most campuses. By now, the inherently ethnocentric nature of the prevailing focus on European classical music—which we are always quick to point out is a deviation from the creativity-rich European classical tradition—requires little elaboration. Here it also important to point out that diversity is being conceived broadly in recent years to include not only the all-important aspect of cultural, racial, ethnic demographics, but diverse ways of experiencing and learning, at which point issues such as creativity and all its related connections—including the aforementioned consciousness dimension—can be reasonably placed under the diversity umbrella. As we have emphasized, creativity is ultimately fundamental to the realization of diversity aspirations most broadly conceived as it provides an interior basis for cultivation of a diversity-rich awareness.

It is with diversity in mind that the Manifesto mentions the enlistment of higher administrators to aid in the change process. Though it did not take long for this contentious recommendation to elicit a strong reaction from some contingents, we view it as entirely reasonable and have in fact seen several instances where music schools or departments are feeling some pressure from the upper administration to invoke change, either due to declining enrollments or recognition of the uniquely strong inertia that besets our field.

We also strongly recommend that institutions that wish to strive for this kind of leadership identify themselves and join ranks with a coalition of other institutions. This is among our next phases of activity and we believe such a consortium brings with it many advantages. It allows institutions to share ideas and it empowers participants by emerging as the beginnings of a movement. We believe this will help bring attention and support to individual units on their campus, as well as potentially elicit support nationally.

A Voice for the Vision

The Manifesto represents a provocative and distinctive voice in reform discourse in music studies. This book illuminates and extends the vision of that document. In issuing challenges to both conventionalists and reformers alike, we hope our commitment to current and coming generations of music students is never far from view. Our intention is to inspire colleagues to look as much at their own assumptions and patterns as the model they seek to reform (or preserve). In addition we urge thorough interrogation and assumption testing of any possible alternatives they might propose. Recognition of this intention is perhaps most fully articulated in the following feedback we received from a participant in one of our many presentations on this work around the globe:

> The CMS Task Force Manifesto, perhaps unlike any of its predecessors in reform literature, asks us to probe deeply our most cherished assumptions about our field. This is not always easy and can even be painful at times, but this is what is needed if our field is to move forward. The Manifesto is a courageous and visionary work and asks us the same of us—to dig deep into our own reservoirs of vision and courage. This is not about us—it is about our students.

INDEX

Abell, Walter 92
accreditation protocols 82
administrators 38, 43
adult participation 133
African music / African diasporic music 19, 23, 145
African American music: creativity–diversity bond 145; as key curricular and cultural landmark 108–13; prominence in global practice 100; rhythmic grounding 101; as transcultural gateway 15, 16, 100, 114; in transcultural models 102
Afro-Euro nexus 113–15
Afrological gateway principle 113
alap 23
American Medical Association (AMA) 135–6
American Musicological Society 13
analytical inquiry 89
Argyris, Chris 16, 39, 44, 104
Articulation 115–16
Art Music 121–4
assessment (and evaluation) 43
assumptions testing 39–40
audience deportment 129–30
Ayer, Vijay 99

Banfield, William C. 107
Beethoven, Ludwig van 123
Berendt, Joachim-Ernst 111
Berger, Karl 111

Berlin, J.A. 136–7
"Black Atlantic Rhythm" (Pressing) 107, 109, 111
Blacking, John 19
Bloom, Jane Ira 99
bols 28
Bruner, Jerome 102
Bulgarian vocal–choral style 19
Byrne, David 131–2, 137–8

Campbell, Patricia Shehan 10, 37, 54, 86, 93, 94, 101, 147
career models 131
Carpenter, Cameron 129
Cartesian theory 28
chamber music 128
changdan 22
change: assumptions testing and substantive change 39–40; balances for 42; call for curricular transformation in report 33–6; curricular change 131–2; as curricular "tinkering" 40; employment of research-based theories and principles to foster 39; harbingers of inevitable 129–30; models of 34–44; motivating 38–9; non-linear endeavour 142; pivotal change pathways 152–3; resistance to 37–9; risks 35; strategic perspective 42–3; toward double-loop learning as a change strategy 40–3; tracking and evaluating impact of 43
change consortium 82

Chase, Claire 131
Chattah, Juan 10
"Chicago Sings" 134
Chinese *luogu* percussion ensemble 27
cipher notation 27
classical music 19, 21, 32, 36–7, 44, 126–7, 135
Coleman, Steve 99
collective musical experience 29
College Music Society, The (CMS) 11, 14
Coltrane, John 99, 101, 121
community engagement 25, 138–9
comparative musical study 19–20
composition 58–60, 88–9, 94, 114–15, 146, 150–1
Comprehensive Musicianship (CM) 8–9, 57, 104
concert halls 126, 128
conductors 27–8
Conner, Lynne 132
Contemporary Improviser Composer Performer (CICP) identity 90, 98, 104, 110, 145–6, 148, 149
Contemporary Music 122
Contemporary Music Project (CMP) 7, 9, 57
conventional curricular pillars 87, 91, 104, 152
Copland, Aaron 123
core proficiency assessment protocol 75
core standards 104
"Creative Approaches to the Undergraduate Curriculum" (Report of NASM) 57
Creative Instructional Residency Initiatives (CIRIs) 39
creative musical identity: evolution of individual creative voice 92–3; facets and outgrowths of 90–1; higher-order critical inquiry 93–5; reflection 93; self-sufficient/student-driven development 93; self-transcending principle 91–2, 110
Creative Music Studies 111
creativity: additive role of 14–15; as essential survival trait 137; foundational role of 14–15, 16, 86–7, 94–5; higher-order change visioning 88–90, 93–5, 98; as pillar for reform 58–60, 134, 144, 154–5; use of recitals as projects incorporating 43
creativity–diversity bond 145
The Crisis of Classical Music in America (Freeman) 36, 123

critical thinking 93–5, 146–7
cross-divisional dialogue 38–9
culminating capstone projects 43
Cultural Diversity in Music Education 13
curricular change 131–2, 143
curricular upper structure 77–95
curriculum oversight protocol 81

dance (movement) 27, 28
Davis, Miles 121
Debussy, Claude 99
Declining by Degree (Schumpeter) 131
degree program/unit 78–9
departmental determination of requirements 68
Dewey, John 102, 148
dhrupad 22, 27
Dieng, Aïyb 111
digital literacy 5
Dissanayake, Ellen 132
diversity: additive measures and 32; comparative musical study and 19–20; creativity–diversity bond 145; foundational role of 16, 86–7; from higher order change discourse 88–90; higher-order change visioning 95–6; initiatives 134–5; jazz and 124; lower-order change visioning 95–6; from multicultural encounter to transcultural synthesis 95–103; multicultural models 96–9; of musical features 21–4; as pillar for reform 60–1, 134–5, 144, 154–5; transcultural models 96–9; use of recitals as projects incorporating 43; of vocal traditions in Chicago 134
dizi 21
djembe 116
Donna Lee (Parker) 115
double-loop learning model 16, 31, 40–3, 87
double-tonguing technique 115
drumming: cultures 27, language 27, syllables 27–8, traditions 116
dumbek 116

Early Music 122
Eastman School of Music 36–7
educational reform 5–6
embodiment 23, 101
English studies 136–7
Ensembles 76–7, 104, 114–15, 127
entrepreneurship studies 130–2, 147
ethnomusicology 122, 150; ethnomusicologists 9, 23, 24, 26, 150

Index

eurhythmics 27
European classical composition 114, 115
European classical music 23, 26, 123
Exemplars 99–100
Exnomination 121–4
extramusical influences 92

faculty-cluster discussions 38–9
faculty development 153–4
faculty hiring 153–4
Fairchild Semiconductor 4
Fleck, Bela 99
Floyd, Samuel A. 107
Fogel, Henry 139
Ford Foundation 7
fragmentation 61–2
Freeman, Robert 36, 123, 132
Freire, Paulo 148
FSG Social Impact Advisors 36

gagaku 21, 27
gamelan 19, 21, 25
Gardner, Howard 89, 102
gesampkuntswerke 29
gestures 27–8
Greene, Maxine 148
group musicking 24–5
Guilfoyle, Ronan 99
Gurtu, Trilok 111
gyil 21

Haddad, Jamey 99
Harvard University 5
Haydn, Joseph 123
hegemonic language 121–4, 147
Hester, Karlton 107
Higgins, Lee 10
higher education reform 5–6
higher music education: call for curricular transformation in report 34–6; core deficiencies in conventional model of music study 58–62; crisis of classical music 36–7; current model of 36; ethnocentric orientation of 60–1
higher-order change visioning 16, 86, 88–90, 93–6, 102–4
Hindustani music of North India 23, 27, 101
Historical Musicology 122
history 87, 91, 104, 152
Holmes Group 6
human genome mapping 4

improvisation 58–60, 88–9, 94, 111, 114, 146
inclusion initiatives 134–5
individual creative voice 92–3
institutional level change activities 64–81
institution-driven (top-down) strategies: approaches for top-down reform of core musicianship 75–7; curricular upper structure 77–95; ensembles 76–7; music and human learning 80–1; new core skills and understandings 70–3; new curriculum oversight protocol 81; new degree program/unit 78–9; private lessons 75; teacher certification option 79–80; types of 69–81; use as gateway for significant progress 152
instrumental music 20
Integral Theory 92, 137
integration: creativity-based approach 146; foundational role of 16, 86–7; from higher order change discourse 88–90; higher-order change visioning 103–4; jazz and 124–5; performance-creation split 103–4; as pillar for reform 61–2, 134; from surface linkages to creativity-driven synthesis 103–4; use of recitals as projects incorporating 43; use of smaller ensembles 129
International Contemporary Ensemble 131
interpretive performance: as central disciplinary pillar 54, 64–6, 103–4; creativity and 50, 59–60, 89–90; discriminatory language 122; higher-order critical inquiry 94; is lone mode of engagement 61; jazz 25; private instruction 70; reconceived 80; reflection 93

James Irvine Foundation 134
jazz: African American music as a key curricular and cultural landmark 108–13; as "concert" event 128; creativity–diversity bond 145; diversity and 124; as gateway of self-transcending principle 124; integration and 124–5; mainstream 101; marginalization of 149; modal jazz 101; objections/ethnocentrisms 119–20; performance skills 115; as primary site for return of CICP 106; sense of community 25; as transcultural gateway 106–25, 149; in transcultural models 102
jazz privileging 107, 117, 119
Johns Hopkins University 5
Jones, LeRoi 107
Julliard Repertory Project 7

kabuki 27
kathak 28
kendhang 27
Kerr, Clark 5
khyal 27
Klickstein, Gerald 130
koto 27
Kramer, Mark 36

Langer, Susanne 91
large ensemble jazz composition 114–15
leadership 38, 42–3, 83, 108, 155
leadership programs 37
League of American Orchestras 134
learning 26–8
Levine, Victoria Lindsay 10
Lewin, Kurt 35, 39
Lewis, George 99, 107, 113
local communities 31
lower-order change visioning 40, 86, 88, 95–6, 102, 103
Lyric Opera of Chicago 134

Machaut, Guillaume de 123
mahori 27
Malm, William P. 18
Mangrulkar, Raj 136
Manhattanville Music Curriculum Program (MMCP) 8, 57, 104
Manifesto *see Transforming Music Study from Its Foundations: A Manifesto for Progressive Change in the Undergraduate Preparation of Music Majors* (Report of TFUMM)
Mapana, Kedmon 28
marginalized communities 32
Maslow, Abraham 102
McFerrin, Bobby 99, 121
McKean, Erin 136
McLaughlin, John 99
medical reform 4–5
Mellon Foundation 134
Metheny, Pat 121
Midwest Band Clinic 13
Minnesota Opera 39
modal jazz 101
modal languages 111
modal-tonal-transtonal studies 111
monocultural interpretive performance 115
Monson, Ingrid 107
Mountain Lake Symposium 13
mousike 29
Mozart, Wolfgang A. 123
mridangam 27, 116

multicultural communities 60–1
multiculturalism 9, 100
multicultural models: absence of exemplars 99–100; African American music as a key curricular and cultural landmark 109–13; characteristics of 98; commonalities and distinctions between transcultural model and 96–9; contrasting aims of 102–3; pedagogical ramifications 101–2; place of creativity and creative development in musical development 96–8
music: as an activity 24–5; among disciplines and professions in higher education 135–8; as behavior 24–6; comparative musical study and 19–20; and dance 28; forms 23; in global array 20–4; higher education in the ecosystem of institutionalized music 36–8; and human learning 80–1; learning 26–8; *ngoma* 28–31; oral–aural transmission 26–7; oral transmission 26–7; as pan-human phenomenon 20, 26; pedagogical practices 26–8; time in cross-cultural perspective, 21–2; treatments of pitch across musical cultures 22–3; words for 20
musical performance 25–6
music curriculum: alternative 8; reform 6–10
Music Education 148–9
Music Entrepreneurship and Career Center 130
music-for-all listening classes 127
music history studies 74–5
musicians: as community music leaders 138–9; innovative career models 129, 131, 153; perspectives on being a professional musician 131; roles in society 132–5
musicianship studies 113–16
musicking 24–5, 109, 119–20
music teacher education programs 128–9
Myers, David E. 10, 31, 86, 104, 118, 147
Myers, Edgar 99

national and international change strategies 81–2
national anthem 128
National Arts Standards/Music 104
National Association of Schools of Music (NASM) viii, 13, 57, 82, 139
National Core Arts (Music) Standards 8, 57
National Endowment for the Arts 134

neoEurocentric model 90, 113
nested synergies 89
Nettl, Bruno 58
new conversations strategy 65–7
new core skills and understandings 70–3
New England Conservatory (NEC) 36–7
New Music 122
ngoma 16, 28–31, 37, 101, 147
No Child Left Behind Act 6
"non-traditional" ensembles 23
"non-Western" traditions 32, 99
notation 27

Occam's Razor 112
options 67–8
oral–aural transmission 26–7
Orpheus Chamber Ensemble 134
Oxford University 5

Palisca, Claude 7
pandeiro 116
Parker, Charlie 115
participatory musicking 28–9
Peabody Conservatory 130
pedagogical practices 26
performance 76–7, 87, 103–4, 116–17, 122, 126–8, 151, 152
performance-creation split 103–4, 115
performance studies 61–2
pianists 25
pilot projects 16, 39, 42
pi phat 27
pitch 22–3, 111
pivotal change pathways 152–3
Podolny, Joel 36, 136
Porter, Michael 36
"postmodern leveling" 100
Pressing, Jeff 107, 109, 111
private lessons: new purpose for 116–17; oriented toward transcultural navigation 113–16; in top-down core curriculum reform 75; in transcultural model 115
process-rich learning models 89, 102
public education 5

qin 27

Race to the Top initiative 6
raga 23
Ramsey, Guthrie 107
The Reflective Conservatoire 13
reform: in companies and corporations 5; in education 5–6; fields of 4–6; hegemonic language 121–4; medical reform 4–5; in music teaching and learning 6–10; nature of 3–4; of teaching profession 6
Reimer, Bennett 100
resistance 37–9
rhythmic definition 115–16
Rice, Timothy 10
Rogers, Carl 148
Rosen, Jesse 134
Rudge, David 10–11

saapup 29
samba 19
Sarath, Edward W. 10, 12, 146
Schön, Donald 16, 39, 44, 93, 104
school music participation 127
The School Music Program 8
Schuller, Gunther 123
Schumpeter, Josef 131
self-organizing (bottom-up) mechanisms strategy: departmental determination of requirements 68; options 67–8; streamlining 68; student proposed pathways 69; types of 67–9; use as gateway for significant progress 152
self-transcending principle 91–2, 93–5, 110
Serious Music 122
single-loop learning 39–40, 87, 103
Siral, Ismet 111
Small, Christopher 24, 100, 106, 120
small ensemble jazz composition 114
sociomusical behaviors 25, 29
social interaction 129
Society for Ethnomusicology (SEM) 13
Society for Music Teacher Education 13
Society for Music Theory (SMT) 13
solmization systems 27
son jarocho 145
sonata form 23
song form composition 114
Sousa, John Philip 127–8
Spaulding, Esperanza 99
staged performance model 128
standard metrics 43
Stanford University 5
strategies: institution-driven (top-down) strategies 69–81, 152; national and international change strategies 81–2; new conversations strategy 65–7; to reform current curricular practice 16; self-organizing (bottom-up) mechanisms strategy 67–9, 152; wide-ranging practical strategies 63–82
student learning assessments 43

student proposed pathways 69
style features 92–3
substantive change 39–40
Sweet, Robert 111
Symposium 11, 12
Symposium on Multicultural Approaches to Music Education 9

tabla 27, 116
tablature 27
Tanglewood Symposium 7–8, 57
Task Force on the Undergraduate Music Major (TFUMM): areas of accord within 16; areas of disagreement within 15; call for curricular transformation in report 34–6; chronicle of work of 10–13; *Transforming Music Study from Its Foundations: A Manifesto for Progressive Change in the Undergraduate Preparation of Music Majors* 45–85
teacher certification option 79–80
technology 5, 148
Thailand 27
theoretical studies 61–2
theory 74, 87, 91, 104, 152
three-part change theory 35
tihai 23
timbre 94
time 21–2
tone 94
transcultural continuum 15, 99–100
transcultural models: African American music as a key curricular and cultural landmark 109–13; characteristics of 98–9; commonalities and distinctions between multicultural model and 96–9; contrasting aims of 102–3; pedagogical ramifications 101–2; place of creativity and creative development in musical development 96–8
Transforming Music Study from Its Foundations: A Manifesto for Progressive Change in the Undergraduate Preparation of Music Majors (Report of TFUMM): alignment with existing reform themes in higher education 154–5; call for leadership 83; change conferences 82; change consortium 82; chronicle of 10–13; context of 2–3, 51–2; creativity 58–60; diversity 60–1; executive summary 49–52; institutional level change activities 64–81; institution-driven (top-down) strategies 69–81; integration 61–2; in motion 14–17;

national and international change strategies 81–2; need for 57–8; new accreditation protocols 82; new conversations strategy 65–7; outline of 34–6, 54–6; practical steps toward realization of vision 142–54; preamble 52; as provocative and distinctive voice in reform discourse 155; reaction to 13–14; self-organizing (bottom-up) mechanisms strategy 67–9; summary of recommendations for change 84–5; three core pillars for reform 58–62; wide-ranging practical strategies 63–82
"transition" step 35
"21st century rhythmic literacy" 111

"unfreeze" step 35
unit leaders 42–3
University of Cambridge 5
University of Chicago 5
University of Dar es Salaam 28
University of Michigan 5, 136
University of Minnesota 131
University of Minnesota Creative Studies and Media Division 42
University of Minnesota School of Music 38–9
University of Washington Center for Digital Arts and Experimental Media (DXARTS) 42

vocalization 20, 27

Wagogo culture 29–30
Weiss, Dan 99
Western staff notation 27
When Going Gets Tough: Barriers and Motivations Affecting Arts Attendance (Report of NEA) 134
Whitehead, Alfred North 35, 102
Whitman, Walt 23
Wingspread Conference on Music in General Studies 9, 57
Woodcock, Tony xii
Wooden, John 35
written and aural theory integration 74
written notation 27
Wubbenhorst, John 99

Yale School of Management 36, 136
Yale Seminar 7, 57
Young Composers Project 7, 8–9, 57

Zorn, John 99

# Taylor & Francis eBooks

Helping you to choose the right eBooks for your Library

Add Routledge titles to your library's digital collection today. Taylor and Francis ebooks contains over 50,000 titles in the Humanities, Social Sciences, Behavioural Sciences, Built Environment and Law.

Choose from a range of subject packages or create your own!

Benefits for you
- Free MARC records
- COUNTER-compliant usage statistics
- Flexible purchase and pricing options
- All titles DRM-free.

Benefits for your user
- Off-site, anytime access via Athens or referring URL
- Print or copy pages or chapters
- Full content search
- Bookmark, highlight and annotate text
- Access to thousands of pages of quality research at the click of a button.

 Free Trials Available
We offer free trials to qualifying academic, corporate and government customers.

eCollections – Choose from over 30 subject eCollections, including:

Archaeology	Language Learning
Architecture	Law
Asian Studies	Literature
Business & Management	Media & Communication
Classical Studies	Middle East Studies
Construction	Music
Creative & Media Arts	Philosophy
Criminology & Criminal Justice	Planning
Economics	Politics
Education	Psychology & Mental Health
Energy	Religion
Engineering	Security
English Language & Linguistics	Social Work
Environment & Sustainability	Sociology
Geography	Sport
Health Studies	Theatre & Performance
History	Tourism, Hospitality & Events

For more information, pricing enquiries or to order a free trial, please contact your local sales team: **www.tandfebooks.com/page/sales**

 The home of Routledge books

www.tandfebooks.com